Recasting Autobiography

Reading
WOMEN
Writing

a series edited by
Shari Benstock and Celeste Schenck

Reading Women Writing is dedicated to furthering international feminist debate. The series publishes books on all aspects of feminist theory and textual practice. *Reading Women Writing* especially welcomes books that address cultures, histories, and experience beyond first-world academic boundaries. A complete list of titles in the series appears at the end of the book.

Recasting Autobiography

WOMEN'S COUNTERFICTIONS IN
CONTEMPORARY GERMAN
LITERATURE AND FILM

Barbara Kosta

Cornell University Press

ITHACA AND LONDON

First published 1994 by Cornell University Press.

Printed in the United States of America

⊗ The paper in this book meets the minimum requirements of the American National Standard for Information Sciences— Permanence of Paper for Printed Library Materials, ANSI Z39.48–1984.

Library of Congress Cataloging-in-Publication Data

Kosta, Barbara.
  Recasting autobiography : women's counterfictions in contemporary German literature and film / Barbara Kosta.
    p.   cm. — (Reading women writing)
  Includes bibliographical references and index.
  ISBN 0–8014–2889–0 (alk. paper). — ISBN 0–8014–8203–8 (pbk. : alk. paper)
    1. German prose literature—20th century—History and criticism.
    2. German prose literature—Women authors—History and criticism.
    3. Autobiography—Women authors.   4. Women motion picture producers and directors—Germany.   5. Women in motion pictures.   6. Women— Germany—Biography.   I. Title.   II. Series.
PT735.K68   1994
830.9'9287—dc20   93–42072
[B]

To my parents,
Konstantin and Barbara

Contents

Acknowledgments

I began writing this book in what used to be West Berlin, where the past was, and is, a visible part of daily life. It was the appropriate location to embark on a project that deals with the continuity of the past in the present, with German history and memory. The autobiographers considered in this book explore what Christa Wolf calls "patterns of childhood," the psychic mapping anchored in personal experience and historical specificity. For contemporary German women, both writers and filmmakers, who undertake this exploration, identity is the intersection of multiple determinants, some more audible than others. The most prominent factors that influenced the construction of identity in these memoirs are the buried vestiges of Germany's fascist past and the traditional assumptions that gave form to gendered subjectivities. These works reflect a process of rethinking and reconceptualizing the self, and, consequently, of autobiographical representation. These personal histories represent border crossings, because they challenge the demarcations traditionally set between fiction and autobiography, between past and present and between the private sphere and the public sphere. Personal histories also function as counterfictions, because they resist the dominant narrative of official memory and attempt to plot new conceptual spaces.

As with any work that has been a long time in the making, many people have influenced this book. My years as a graduate student in the Department of German at the University of California, Berkeley, provided me with many rich opportunities for research. Above all, I am profoundly grateful to Anton Kaes at Berkeley. It is difficult to express my appreciation for his enthusiasm, friendship, and advice, all of which have been invaluable in my writing. He is a constant source of inspiration, and his seminars paved the way for my own research and intellectual development. I also owe particular thanks to Helga Kraft at the University of Florida, who has been an intellectual and emotional support throughout my career. In many ways, this book is rooted in our long discussions on mother-daughter relationships back in the late 1970s, when that topic first entered feminist discourse. With the generous support of the German Academic Exchange Service, I was able to take my project to Berlin, where I met women authors and filmmakers with whom I discussed my work. My special thanks to Jutta Brückner, who shared her time and her films with me. I also want to express my appreciation to Hutch Brown, whose superb editing skills as well as friendship got me through the final phases. I am also thankful to Teresa Jesionowski and Ken Plax for their excellent editorial suggestions.

So many friends, colleagues, and students have contributed, directly or indirectly, to this book that it is impossible to thank them all by name. Let me mention those who read portions of the manuscript and offered criticism and encouragement and those who shared their work with me. I particularly thank Salean Maiwald, Richard McCormick, Leslie Pahl, and Hermann Rebel. Johanna Ridderbeekx was very kind in arranging a lecture at the Free University in Berlin, where I first presented a chapter of the book. My gratitude also goes to the faculty of the Department of German at Berkeley, especially Hinrich Seeba and Friedric Tubach, for their support throughout my graduate studies. Thanks go to the faculty in the Department of German of the University of Arizona, to Annette Kolodny for making the rare commodity of time available, and to the Women's Studies Advisory Council for providing me with a summer stipend to complete my manuscript. I am also deeply grateful to Bernhard Kendler of Cornell University Press for continuing support.

I should also like to express my gratitude to women scholars whose research on autobiography has not only fueled my own interests but also confirmed the necessity of exploring personal histories. My processes of memory and positionality have been challenged through this project. Most important, I came to realize how profoundly the memories and lingering effects of World War II had laid the foundation for my own development.

I especially thank my family and friends who were always there. They truly deserve much more than I can say here.

An earlier version of part of Chapter 5, "Jutta Brückner's *Years of Hunger*," appears in *Gender and German Cinema: Feminist Interventions*, edited by Sandra Frieden, Richard McCormick, and Vibeke Peterson (Providence, 1993). It is reprinted with the permission of Berg Publishers Inc. Wherever possible, I relied on available English translations; otherwise I provided my own. The films I discuss, *Germany, Pale Mother* and *Years of Hunger*, are available in subtitled versions through U.S. distributors. The illustrations appear with the permission of the Stiftung Deutsche Kinemathek in Berlin.

BARBARA KOSTA

Tucson, Arizona

Recasting Autobiography

Introduction:
Autobiography Reconsidered

> Then it seems to me that his calm comes from my ego being too familiar, too unimportant for him, as if he had rejected me as waste, a superfluous something-made-human, as if I were merely the dispensable product of his rib, but at the same time an unavoidable dark tale accompanying and hoping to supplement his own bright story, a tale which he, however, detaches and delimits.
>
> Ingeborg Bachmann, *Malina*

The 1970s in Germany saw an unprecedented surge of autobiographical expression. At first glance, this literary and filmic happening may arouse little suspicion because autobiography as both a genre and a classical narrative form has deep roots in Western tradition. Yet many factors cause one to assess the wealth of self-narration that emerged during a time marked by postwar repression of memory and by personal reflection. The sheer abundance of these texts, the number of works authored by women, and what seems to be the paradoxical appearance of these autobiographical explorations at a time when philosophers and critics alike were challenging the concepts of the self, self-representation, and notions of authorship—all call for a reconceptualization of autobiographical expression. Ironically, just as women and other disenfranchised groups begin to claim the status of author, the author is stripped of function and authority. This book is about the relationships among autobiography, women writing and filming, and German history. It is about recasting the autobiographical project— about finding new forms for autobiographical expression, supplying the text with new roles and characters, and uncovering repressed knowledges hitherto excluded from cultural consciousness. It means the casting of autobiography with lives that have seldom had the chance to participate publicly in self-reflection, as well as the broadening of the autobiographical project to include voices once excluded from the production of film and literature. The dramatis personae are the women themselves as they see and assign meaning to their lives, and as they define their relationships to the subject position and to authority.

Significantly, the process of mourning figures prominently in contemporary autobiographies by German women. In staging their lives, the authors and filmmakers discussed here work through the traumas of loss and participate in narrative emplotment in order to gain self-understanding. They also challenge what Alexander and Margarete Mitscherlich have diagnosed as the "inability to mourn" so often cited as part of the German postwar experience. Christa Wolf's novel *Kindheitsmuster* (*Patterns of Childhood*), Ruth Rehmann's novel *Der Mann auf der Kanzel: Fragen an einen Vater* (The man in the pulpit), Helma Sanders-Brahms's film *Deutschland, bleiche Mutter* (*Germany, Pale Mother*) and Jutta Brückner's film *Hungerjahre, in einem reichen Land* (*Years of Hunger*) represent the variety of autobiographical expression that has emerged in women's writing and filming since the 1970s.

Yet, is it tenable to recast autobiography when one could argue that to write an autobiography at a time when notions of the subject and authorship are placed in question is to imply the rescue of a genre that partakes of traditional illusions of a unified subject? To participate in autobiographical writing may intimate an overindulgence in "self"-deception, because producing a unified self (the subject of traditional autobiography—a linear, progressive development of an enlightened subject) has become an anachronism. The production of an autobiographical narrative appears as an even more obscure undertaking when one considers the epistemological shift to contemporary notions of the decentered self that has redefined the relationship between author and text. Before taking a closer look at the autobiographies themselves, I want to outline the debate surrounding the status of the author in order to help locate women's writing and filmmaking within a larger conceptual context and to understand the recasting of the autobiographical processes that dominate women's works during the 1970s and early 1980s in Germany.

Roland Barthes's "Death of the Author," proclaimed in 1968, serves as a theoretical landmark in transforming the relationship between reader, text, and writer.[1] The author's signature, as we have known it, is no longer privileged and paternal, belonging to someone who "owns" the text, whose intention is primary and who controls and assigns meaning as the unifying agent outside the text. Rather, the author appears only as a "guest" in the text, to use Roland Barthes's word. With the author no longer identified as originator, the text lives in relation to a larger network of inter-texts. The dispossession of the author as the sole creator of meaning transfers the production of meaning to the reader. Through this displacement, the text remains open to a number of possible inter-pretations.

With the author's traditional role diminished, it would seem that autobiography, insistent on referentiality, necessarily would be laid to rest. Yet, despite recommendations for its retirement, and even the outright proclamation of its death, autobiography has prolif-erated in German literature and film since the 1970s, especially in works by women.[2] Its persistence as a preferred narrative form whose status has actually risen indicates, as critics have exhaustively pointed out, that the status of autobiography has changed. No longer the bastion of the "self-made man," au-tobiographical writing, to a certain extent, and autobiography crit-icism, to a greater extent, have evolved with the changing view of the self and of authorship. A shift from an interest in displays of individualism as objective testimonies of historical processes to an interest in subjective interpretations of life has lent autobio-graphical writing, filming, and reading a new emphasis. The new focus has centered on subjective stagings of personal histories so that the borders once drawn between life and text, fact and fantasy, documentary and fiction have increasingly blurred. Self-representation thus is placed in the realm of self-invention.

The destabilization of monolithic notions of self and author, au-thoritative originator and proprietor of the text, has allowed for the inclusion of heterogeneous voices. Using poststructuralism as

[1] Roland Barthes, "The Death of the Author," in *Image-Music-Text*, trans. Stephen Heath (New York: Hill and Wang, 1977), 142–48.

[2] Michael Sprinker, "Fictions of the Self: The End of Autobiography," in *Auto-biography: Essays Theoretical and Critical*, ed. James Olney (Princeton: Princeton University Press, 1980), 321–42.

a springboard but proceeding beyond its repression of any writing identity, feminist critics perceive a positive development resulting from theories of the author's death. "It is, after all, the Author," as Nancy Miller notes, "canonized, anthologized, and institutionalized, who excludes the less-known works of women and minority writers from the canon, and who by his authority justifies the exclusion."[3] As a result, literary practices such as autobiography have been released from patriarchal plots to include heterogeneous forms of self-definition and their readings.

Yet the occupation of the now-vacant author position by no means suggests a revival of a position of exterior linguistic control and intentionality. Instead, that occupation calls for a redefinition of the role of author and a relocation of the authorial voice, contrary to the poststructuralist conceptualization of the author's disappearance, epitomized in Michel Foucault's often quoted query of 1969: "What difference does it make who is speaking?"[4] It makes a great difference, because to dismiss the author entirely not only undermines the struggle for presence and for a history and future for which many socially and politically marginalized writers have fought, but also implicitly imparts traditional notions of authorship and textuality, prescriptively male and Western, to all subjectivities. We need only remember the discussions surrounding the difficulty women had in writing "I" in the early phases of contemporary feminism. The necessity of recognizing who is speaking thus belongs to a larger political agenda.

Feminist critics have responded variously to the dilemma of female authorship in the context of ideas about the dispossession of the author. In a discussion outlining a number of feminist positions, Cheryl Walker convincingly retains a version of the author which echoes my own understanding. Moving away from the idea that the author is a unifying agent behind the text and from the critical perspective that expels the author altogether, Walker, borrowing from Cora Kaplan, asserts that "authors are subjectivities whom we may consider as contradictory, fluctuating presences in the text,

---

[3]Nancy Miller, "Changing the Subject," in *Feminist Studies/ Critical Studies*, ed. Teresa de Lauretis (Bloomington: Indiana University Press, 1986), 104.

[4]Michel Foucault, "What Is an Author?" in *Textual Strategies: Perspectives in Post-Structuralist Criticism*, ed. Josué V. Harari (Ithaca: Cornell University Press, 1979), 141.

which she [Kaplan] calls significantly a 'site.' "[5] The proper name of the author *functions* as one of "an infinite number of presences, or traces, in a given text."[6] By adopting Foucault's notion of the "author-function" as a structuring principle, which Walker also favors, the reader can distinguish texts from one another, as well as situate them within a field of discourses to establish their dependencies vis-à-vis different power structures and cultural formations. Walker proposes that the emphasis on the author-function, "also in terms of a politics of recognition," provides an analytical means of affirming the differences implied by the author's proper name or signature without erasing or denying writing subjectivities.[7]

By maintaining a signature, important extratextual references such as race, class, gender, ethnicity, and the cultural and historical background of the author are preserved as significant markers. The author, consequently, is read as one possible site of meaning, as a point of departure and not as the focus of absolute meaning or conclusion. With the opening of the textual barriers imposed by the "author," in the classical sense marked as male by both Foucault and Barthes, the reader also becomes active in the processes of production and interpretation. The author appears as a voice among many.[8]

The simultaneous death and resuscitation of the author, and consequently of autobiography, lead one to speculate polemically about autobiography's renewed function and the causes for its

[5]Cheryl Walker, "Feminist Literary Criticism and the Author," *Critical Inquiry* 16 (1990): 568.

[6]Ibid., 569.

[7]Ibid., 553.

[8]See *De/Colonizing the Subject: The Politics of Gender in Women's Autobiography*, ed. Sidonie Smith and Julia Watson (Minneapolis: University of Minnesota Press, 1992). In their introduction to a collection of essays on women's autobiographies, Smith and Watson argue that a new form of colonization takes place in theories that "erase the subject's heterogeneity" (xiv). Many theories have promoted a reductive approach that essentializes identity, such as earlier feminist writings that present "woman" as colonized and therefore limit women's experiences to the primacy of gender considerations. *De/Colonizing the Subject* focuses on works by "minority women" in a colonial and postcolonial setting, yet it theorizes an approach to reading autobiography which I explore. It advocates the grounding of interpretation in locales and temporalities which I see as possible only if one retains the notion of the "author-function."

revival in Germany since the 1970s. Is the resuscitated preoccupation with the self the result of a postmodern disorientation? Are authors attempting to draw borders in order to locate themselves within a culture that brings about fragmentation and the continued disappearance of historical consciousness? Does the loss of the self call for its reactive recovery? Is today's autobiographical inquiry motivated by working through the past in order to gain a vision for the future? Are these searches turning out to be powerful critiques of social practices and of the "metanarratives" that imprint culture and self-understanding? Do these autobiographical practices provide a creative space and allow for political intervention? These questions can be answered in the affirmative. They all suggest reasons for the autobiographical renaissance of the 1970s and 1980s.

In Germany, the politicization of the personal, an effect of the women's movement and an aftereffect of the 1968 student movement, provided an impetus for the sudden circulation of self-exploratory narratives.[9] Most of these narratives were written or filmed in response to a growing need to challenge established epistemologies, either ideologically propelled versions of history and the repressed German past or sedimented notions of gender. Women authors and filmmakers felt compelled to assess their lives anew and to explore personal and national identity in the face of new opportunities. The rupture that occurred during the 1960s also opened up inquiries into the self, not as essential or universal (meaning male), but as embedded within historical, cultural, and psychosocial contexts. Jacques Lacan's psychoanalytical writings on the paramount role of intersubjective processes in the constitution of the subject and Jacques Derrida's philosophical deconstruction of origins and of the traditional subject contributed to the reconceptualization of the contemporary subject, as well as to the recomposition of the autobiographical project. Yet in practice, this profile was already changing because more women were entering film and the literary arena, and interest in questions of subjectivity and female authorship was growing. Through female authorship and the challenge it posed to prescriptive notions of female sub-

---

[9]The lack of autobiographical writing during the 1950s reflects the difficulty many Germans experienced in writing about a past that was preferably left repressed.

jectivity, contemporary understanding of the subject was already becoming more complex and marked by difference.

Women today participate in the complex projects of self-representation, of writing, and filming, and of coming to grips with their own subjectivity. In Germany, contemporary women writers and filmmakers enter the wilderness of selfhood from a variety of angles because of the specificity of German history. In early experiential literature (Verständigungsliteratur)—as well as in the novels *Patterns of Childhood* by Christa Wolf and *Der Mann auf der Kanzel* by Ruth Rehmann, and in the films *Germany, Pale Mother* by Helma Sanders-Brahms and *Years of Hunger* by Jutta Brückner, all discussed in the following chapters—divergent selves are explored as textual surfaces upon which the sociohistorical context has left its traces. From the analysis of these personal histories two major themes emerge: the repression and devaluation of female sexuality and voice, on the one hand, and the confrontation with Germany's fascist past, on the other. The majority of these autobiographies are the consequence of crisis and inquiry, rather than catalogues of public achievements found in traditionally "authored" autobiographies.[10] They are written or filmed at a relatively early age; most of the autobiographers were between the ages of thirty and forty-five at the time of publication or filming. In a process of historical and personal transition, these German writers and filmmakers reexamine their own positions within the discourses that shape personal and national identity.

The many texts entitled "Verständigungstexte"—which make up an experiential, confessional, feminist literature predominantly

---

[10]Autobiographical expression has not been confined to the literary text. Many women have turned to the visual arts, and more often to film, to explicate their lives. Yet, historically in the visual arts as in literature, few women have been able to claim their place, which means that they confront problems similar to those of language and self-portraiture in literature. Here too, women have been the object of the look, a subject placed upon divans as a spectacle whose contours and textures have been left to male perception and enunciation. In her autobiographical search for female role models throughout art history, the artist Gisela Breitling claims that women have seldom been allowed to develop their own language or explore their own images on canvas or on the screen. See Gisela Breitling, *Die Spuren des Schiffs in den Wellen: Eine autobiographische Suche nach den Frauen in der Kunstgeschichte* (Frankfurt am Main: Fischer, 1986). See also Salean Angelika Maiwald, *Der fehlende Akt in der Kunst von Frauen: Psychoanalytische Betrachtungen eines Tabus* (New York: Lang, 1993).

written during the 1970s—were the first signs of women's large-scale entry into the literary market in West Germany. In these works women thematize gendered identity and explore new forms of expression to assert themselves against the cultural mandates that prescribe female identity. In this experiential literature, an act of mourning accompanies descriptions of loss, mutilation, and wounding of the female subject. Through the creation of a public forum for mourning (an integral aspect of the feminist agenda at the time), many writers staged possibilities for recovery that were marked by newness, uncertainty, and a predictable naïveté.[11]

Another surge of autobiographical texts focuses on family confrontations in which daughters, for the first time, take their parents to task. The many representations of the mother-daughter relationship and the predominance of literature labeled "Väterliteratur" (literature of the fathers) reveal a need on the part of these authors to come to terms with the sociohistorical inheritance of the politics of the Third Reich.[12] Interestingly, these texts appear, as did the claims of the death of the author, at a time of the father's absence owing either to death or to a marginalized historical role. In re-creating their parents' biographies and the relationship between parent and child, these writers and filmmakers examine the psychopathology of the postwar family and the "parent-effect" in themselves. In many instances, they reveal the desire to regain the parent whom they have lost. Their feelings of loss arise from the sense of abandonment and withdrawal the narrators experienced at an early age while their parents were alive.

For authors such as Christa Wolf and Ruth Rehmann, who grew up during the Third Reich, the investigation of their personal histories entails a more direct confrontation with Germany's fascist

[11]Experiential literature has been widely criticized for its reductive and essentialist argumentation. It proposes a universal patriarchy and woman as the target of oppression. I discuss the merits and shortcomings of this literature in the following chapter.

[12]For additional information on the mother-daughter relationship in German literature see Helga W. Kraft and Barbara Kosta, "Mother-Daughter Relationships: Problems of Self-Determination in Novak, Heinrich, and Wohmann," *German Quarterly* 46 (January 1983): 74–88; Marianne Hirsch, *The Mother/Daughter Plot: Narrative, Psychoanalysis, Feminism* (Bloomington: Indiana University Press, 1989); and Heidy Margrit Müller, *Töchter und Mütter in deutschsprachiger Erzählprosa von 1885 bis 1935* (Munich: Iudicium, 1991).

past and its psychic deposits. Whether these texts explore issues of female subjectivity and gender, or the intersection of personal histories with fascism, or national identity, the act of mourning prevails when these authors speak.

One reason for participating in the process of mourning stems from the loss of the female voice and place in history, as seen in resistance to female authorship throughout the centuries and the complexity of female self-representation. The difficulty begins with women partaking in a literary act that has privileged male subjectivity and defined notions of selfhood, even universalized them, based on the male subject. Autobiographical works by Augustine, Jean-Jacques Rousseau, and Johann Wolfgang von Goethe, to name a few, have long shaped standards, prescribing the canon of autobiographical writing. In its most traditional format, introduced by the emergence of the bourgeoisie in the eighteenth century, autobiography was deemed the textual site of male subjectivity and the story of men's unique transfigurations. The canonized authors often sought to immortalize themselves in their deliveries of public confessions, as well as to legitimate and validate their lives in the mappings of a career or calling. Autobiography, as has often been pointed out in regard to other literary publications, was reserved traditionally for "the universal male."

Consequently, as Nancy Miller suggests, when women write, they are acutely aware of their position as women writers as well as of the discursive domain they enter and the linkage between gender and genre. A distressed relationship between writing and gender historically stems from the perception that writing and womanhood are incompatible. One need only listen to critics' comments on the Austrian writer Ingeborg Bachmann's autobiographically inflected work *Malina* (1971) to fathom the stigma that female authorship has endured. In Elisabeth Lenk's study of the reception of literature by women, she quotes one critic, for instance, who deduced that Bachmann resisted her biological calling—her "natural womanhood"—which meant reproduction and not creation.[13]

---

[13]See Elisabeth Lenk, "Pariabewußtsein und Gesellschaftskritik bei einigen Schriftstellerinnen seit der Romantik," *Wespennest* 44 (1981): 23–32. It is obvious that this critic has limited the concept "woman" to the realm of biological destiny and motherhood. See Lenk's discussion on the various attitudes toward women's writing.

When writing autobiography, women's awareness of the confounding relationship between gender and genre becomes more acute. Sidonie Smith, in her book *Poetics of Women's Autobiography*, most astutely notes that "traditional autobiography has functioned as one of those forms and languages that sustain sexual difference, the woman who writes autobiography is doubly estranged when she enters the autobiographical contract."[14]

In Germany, as in most of Western culture, the problem of female self-representation was compounded by the general difficulty in locating women historically as writing subjects or in finding models. Under these circumstances, the theoretical complexity of female authorship reaches yet another plateau. Even though women become the subjects of their own narrations, these subjects often paradoxically explore their development as engendered objects, their lost sense of self, or their sociohistorical positioning as the "other." Rather than being narratives of independence and autonomy with the protagonist reintegrated into society after a process of maturation, as in the German Bildungsroman, women's personal histories are often melancholic testimonies of "damaged" self-images and loss. Moreover, many women's autobiographies retrace the processes of subjugation and silencing that have been women's cultural legacy.[15] These autobiographers, thus, are faced with writing female subjects into literary identity.

The absence of female authors from the Western literary canon and the subsequent misrepresentations of women's experiences and fantasies have lasted well into the twentieth century, and as it looks, that absence may reach even into the twenty-first century.[16] Surveying the history of cultural productions before the late 1960s,

---

[14]Sidonie Smith, *A Poetics of Women's Autobiography: Marginality and the Fictions of Self-Representation* (Bloomington: Indiana University Press, 1987), 49.

[15]See Gabriele Dietze, ed., *Die Überwindung der Sprachlosigkeit. Texte aus der neuen Frauenbewegung* (Darmstadt: Luchterhand, 1979); Patricia Meyer Spacks, *The Female Imagination* (New York: Alfred A. Knopf, 1972); Eva Meyer, *Zählen und Erzählen*, (Vienna: Medusa, 1983); Elfriede Jelinek, "Begierde & Fahrerlaubnis," *Manuskripte* 26 (1986): 74–76.

[16]In *Getting Personal* (New York: Routledge, 1991), Nancy Miller points to the lag (symptomatic of resistance?) between today's pervasive knowledge of women writers and their underrepresentation in the curriculum at many universities. She states that "the massive work of recovery and reinterpretation has not received more than token recognition in mainstream curriculum" (59).

one readily sees that few women contributed to the archives of knowledge compiled about them. In the European tradition, if women wrote, they often masked their female identities, adopted male pseudonyms, hid themselves inside a male character, or much later, on entering the twentieth century, wrote autobiographies that outlined lives of selflessness complicit with the dominant social expectations.[17] In German literary history, writers and critics regarded letters and diaries as the preferred genres of female expression, since they were thought to be the most subjective of literary forms. During the nineteenth century, letters were even regarded as the most suitable outlet for female spontaneity and sentimentality, which affirmed the notion of a singular female "nature" and reinforced prevailing judgments of women's cultural productions. Most often these documents of self-reflection were either restricted to an intimate realm with one addressee, or they were published posthumously. Once women writers were accepted into the literary establishment, their works were categorically judged sentimental at best and irrational at worst. Subsequently, women's productions, relegated to less-valued categories, tended to entomb women ever more securely into an eighteenth-century "genderology." Such texts as those by nineteenth-century writers Karoline von Günderrode, Bettina von Arnim, Rahel Varnhagen and others were virtually forgotten until feminist literary critics and historians began to chart out an obscured tradition of women writers. Even practitioners of autobiography criticism neglected to address these works, owing to the disparate criteria established to judge works by women.[18]

Letters and journals of early writers have provided an invaluable source of insight into women's attempts at self-representation. These works remain documents of self-disclosure, self-expression,

---

[17]Karoline von Günderrode wrote under the pseudonym Tian; Aurore Dudevant became George Sand; Mary Ann Evans's pen name was George Eliot, and so on. See also Patricia Meyer Spacks, "Selves in Hiding," in *Women's Autobiography*, ed. Estelle Jelinek (Bloomington: Indiana University Press, 1980), 112–32.

[18]For further references, see Domna C. Stanton, ed., *The Female Autograph: Theory and Practice of Autobiography from the Tenth to the Twentieth Century* (Chicago: University of Chicago Press, 1984); and Shari Benstock, ed., *The Private Self: Theory and Practice of Women's Autobiographical Writing* (Chapel Hill: University of North Carolina Press, 1988).

and unrest. Domna Stanton notes that many works by women authors over the centuries have revealed "conflicts between the private and the public, the personal and the professional. There was a systematic tension between the conventional role of wife, mother, or daughter and another, unconventional self that had ambition and vocation."[19] Although she does not include German writers in her discussion, Stanton's conclusions easily apply to German women writers of the same periods. Stifled by the cultural scripting of her gender, Günderrode, for instance, describes the barriers she had to negotiate as a woman:

> Why couldn't I have been a man! I have no feeling for female virtues, for female blissfulness. I only enjoy the wild, great and scintillating. There is an accursed but incorrigible incongruity in my soul; and it will and must remain so, because I am a woman and have the desires of a man, without men's strength. This is why I am in such vacillation and in discord with myself.[20]

The searing movements between two asymmetrical, gendered poles predisposed Günderrode to silence her torment, which meant literally to carry out a social and cultural imperative: to extinguish the female voice and body. She committed suicide in May 1806.[21] Like other writers of her day, Günderrode expressed the desire for self-determination, self-expression, and self-knowledge, goals that have dominated the hermeneutics of the "self." Read today, these personal narratives resist the reduction of women to a single mode of existence.

For contemporary women writers and filmmakers, the exploration of their personal histories has meant the creation of new textual spaces in which to work through the various configurations and dramas of identity and subjectivity formation without imposing a

---

[19]Stanton, *The Female Autograph*, 13. See also Katherine Goodman, *Dis/Closures: Women's Autobiographies in Germany between 1790 and 1914* (New York: Lang, 1986).

[20]*Karoline von Günderrode: Der Schatten eines Traumes, Gedichte, Prosa, Briefe, Zeugnisse von Zeitgenossen*, ed. Christa Wolf (Darmstadt: Luchterhand, 1981), 140.

[21]Wolf, ed., *Der Schatten eines Traumes*, 51. In her introduction, Wolf does not speak of suicide in reference to Günderrode. For her, Günderrode ended a life of perpetual death: "She says herself why she cannot continue to live: She was addicted to life and not to death. She takes leave of 'not-living,' and not from life. The stakes were high; they were herself."

narrative codex. Divergent voices have joined in the trial of writing, reading, and filming themselves into being after centuries of exclusion. For those segments of society that were kept out of the literary establishment or dominant culture, autobiographical production, for the most part, involves working through dispossession. Women, like many marginalized groups, often produce representations that assign new meanings to their positions to counter the fictions that affix them in an asymmetrical binary system. To quote Julia Watson and Sidonie Smith, "They also have the potential to celebrate through countervalorization another way of seeing, one unsanctioned, even unsuspected, in the dominant cultural surround."[22]

In seeking to represent themselves, many women writers and filmmakers first confront self-abnegation and selflessness, traits culturally attributed to women which fall short of the defining criteria cited by critics of normative autobiography.[23] The female "I" in Ingeborg Bachmann's *Malina* (see the epigraph to this chapter) succinctly represents the status of the female subject with which a number of women writers in Germany grapple. Emerging from the negative, the female protagonist views herself in hegemonic terms as supplementary to and supportive of a male figure. Bachmann's rendition of the female subject coincides with feminist discussions in the early 1970s; both made first attempts at a self-definition of woman as "nonbeing." Woman was seen as existing in a negative relation to man, a relation that Simone de Beauvoir explored in her groundbreaking book *The Second Sex*.[24]

[22]Watson and Smith, eds., *De/Colonizing the Subject*, xx.

[23]Various critics have established criteria and definitions of autobiography which inevitably exclude women's works. Georg Misch, in *A History of Autobiography in Antiquity*, trans. E. W. Dickes (Cambridge: Harvard University Press, 1951), for example, refers to autobiography as the documentation of an author's participation in public life. Needless to say, women had no access to the public arena, which reflects the repression of women's speech. Karl Weintraub, in *The Value of the Individual: Self and Circumstance in Autobiography* (Chicago: University of Chicago Press, 1978), defines autobiography as representing the typical or model. Since the male determined the norm, men also became representative of model types. Women had little opportunity to become models.

[24]The female subject, that is, female identity, has been a major topic of feminist theory since the early 1970s and accordingly has gone through various interpretive stages. Yet as early as the 1950s, in *The Second Sex*, Simone de Beauvoir uncovers the position of woman as "Other" in opposition to the male subject. On the basis

Framed by the various epistemologies that have determined woman's identity, the narrator in Bachmann's *Malina* refers to the biblical metaphor of the genesis of woman from Adam's rib and draws on the Freudian allusion to woman as the "dark continent." Bachmann's portrayal of the relationships of the female protagonist touches on the "metanarratives" that define woman in an asymmetrical and binary relationship to man. Significantly, however, the terms of woman's existence as Bachman describes them are set in the subjunctive, the grammatical mode of uncertainty and the unreal. Woman is never located in this text but remains the hidden "I," "the I without guarantees" that Bachmann spoke of in her Frankfurt lectures ten years before publishing *Malina*.[25] Leaving the

---

of a Hegelian and existentialist view, Beauvoir argues that woman is constructed in a negative relation to man to become what man is not, much like the protagonist in *Malina*. Appeals to woman as nature, as the irrational, and as "absolute sex" shrouded and shaped an understanding of female identity. Beauvoir's analysis proceeded to open the doors for further explorations, since as critics of Beauvoir's theory suggest, these philosophical models hermetically lock woman within the systems Beauvoir undertakes to expose. Going beyond Beauvoir's exegesis of gender relationships, Luce Irigaray, for instance, broadens the scope of feminist critique by attempting to emancipate woman from a binary hierarchy and to celebrate difference outside of terms established by a masculinist economy. Woman, she proposes, is repressed and unrepresentable; she is "that sex which is not one," and defies definition. According to Irigaray, woman cannot be located within a phallogocentric hermeneutic. Thus the view of the female subject, promulgated by Irigaray and other like-minded French feminists, is that there has not been such a thing within masculinist discourse: that discourse, because of its own constitution, inevitably negates the female self. For the most part, the specular structure of self-representation within the configurations of male epistemes presupposes a distorted female reflection, a distorted narcissism owing to woman's mediated presence. Many French feminists argue that the female subject consequently resides outside of, and anterior to, traditional epistemologies. According to this scheme, woman is in exile in her own culture and language, the very mediums that serve to construct her. With this tradition in mind, women writing autobiography are predisposed to write against an absence, as well as in resistance to the epistemologies that undermine women's status as subjects.

[25]Irmela von der Lühe, "Ingeborg Bachmann's Frankfurt Lectures on Poetics," *New German Critique* 27 (1982): 31–56. Even though it is suggested here that the poetic "I" Bachmann speaks of in these lectures presented in 1959 is not gender-neutral, the terms that Bachmann attributes to the "I without guarantees" appropriately describes the position of the female writing subject in literature. Thus, *Malina* seems to be the poetic translation of this "I." Von der Lühe also describes Bachmann's distinction between the poetic "I" and the "I" of memoirs. In the latter, "the I of autobiography is always self-assured and unbroken" (43), which indicates Bachmann's understanding of autobiography and the potential adherence to traditional notions of autobiographical writing.

scene of figuratively murderous terms that stifle women's subjectivity and heterogeneity, the female protagonist passes into the wall, entombed. The last sentence—"It was murder"—tragically implicates the gender arrangements that underpin Western culture. In many ways, contemporary women autobiographers re-create these scenes of death in order to restore themselves as subjects. At issue is not only the death of autobiography or that of the author, but the deaths staged within autobiography of selves locked into normative constructs of gender, historical understanding, and more generally, dominant ways of knowing.

Motivated by questions of identity, many contemporary women autobiographers in Germany critically reconstruct significant stages of personal development. By this I mean that numerous autobiographical texts—produced since the women's movement—began to challenge hegemonic assumptions and to analyze the experiences of the writers and filmmakers as women in a conscious effort to uncover the moments in their personal histories which have programmed them for self-effacement, submissiveness, and self-objectification. As Sidonie Smith summarizes, "The [modern] autobiographer begins to grapple self-consciously with her identity as a woman in a patriarchal culture and with her problematic relationship to engendered figures of selfhood."[26] In many self-representations the mirror (refined during the Renaissance and age of Western humanism) that informs and reflects various aspects of identity is still partially formed by dominant culture.

The reconstruction of the past through autobiographical inquiry entails intervention in and resistance to the fictions that have erased gender, race, ethnicity and class distinctions and that have impeded the reading of one's life experiences. Stated another way, through various forms of narrative emplotment, the autobiographers resist their total inscription by cultural practices that have denied diverse modes of identity. By mapping out experiences along with the practices, discourses, and the "technologies of gender," to quote Teresa de Lauretis, many female autobiographers take a close look at how they are shaped as historical subjects, as women in their specificity, and how that specificity is anchored in and directed by sociohistorical formations. Teresa de Lauretis's understanding best

[26]Smith, *A Poetics of Women's Autobiography*, 56.

describes my own use of and reference to experience, as "a complex of meaning effects, habits, dispositions, associations, and perceptions resulting from the semiotic interaction of self and outer world."[27]

The recognition that gender—as an experience of, or relationship to, the "outer world"—is a cultural and not a biological determination has challenged some autobiographers, notably Jutta Brückner and Helma Sanders-Brahms, to isolate and analyze various events that contribute to the social production of gendered identity. Using their own lives as testimony, these autobiographers have worked through the liabilities of essentialism and have unsettled the "truths" that have defined women. In these cases, autobiographical writing functions therapeutically by providing the potential to identify oneself as subject. In addition, the various renditions of women's own lives allow other notions of selfhood and subjectivity to emerge.

Women writers and filmmakers in Germany have begun to stage the dramas of identity at a time when the exploration of subjectivity constitutes a vital defining element in the politics of feminism. Through autobiographies often called "narratives of self-discovery," many authors have made themselves the subjects of their own work and become their own "textual productions." The referent framing the work is their own experience as it is processed, remembered, restaged, and interpreted. It is a second reading of experience, filtered through present needs and desires. Since the past can never be genuinely recaptured or documented, it becomes a series of stories the autobiographer narrates to invest the past with a specific meaning and coherence. As a result, meaning depends on the questions with which the author retrospectively structures her analysis.

The act of writing about oneself involves the construction of identity. With the recognition of a tension between the writing "I" and the written "I," and the schism between past and memory, the autobiographical project slips into a new critical context of self-invention. Key experiences are assembled to reveal the events the autobiographer perceives as central to the formation of her identity.

[27]Teresa de Lauretis, *Technologies of Gender: Essays on Theory, Film, and Fiction* (Bloomington: Indiana University Press, 1987), 18.

Optimally, the autobiographical act may be understood as what Paul Eakin calls "a ceaseless process of identity formation in which new versions of the past evolve to meet the constantly changing requirements of the self in each successive present."[28] Implicit in this process is that autobiography, conventionally an examination and summary of a lifetime, expresses only a phase in an ongoing struggle of self-analysis. The identity created in the text is not fixed, since its interpretation presumably changes, depending on the vantage point or agenda of the narrator. Only one among the many versions of the self is produced, based on a reading of the autobiographer's own life, guided by unconscious desires as much as by conscious interpretive strategies. Like the Freudian projection of screen memories, autobiography conceals as much as it discloses.

The overwhelming presence of autobiographical expression throughout the 1970s and early 1980s in German literature and film by women reveals a need to address questions concerning the multiple axes of identity, particularly national and gendered identity, and to work through productions of subjectivity. The "self" here is not reduced to an essential female identity, and self-representation is not reductively exemplary. To essentialize the self would surely undermine the scope of the autobiographical project because the repertoire of selves elicits a multiplicity of reference points and personal readings, although similarities due to gendered socialization processes and specific cultural and historical contexts cannot be overlooked.

The self discussed here is not a unitary Cartesian self rooted in bourgeois origins, absolute, rational self-consciousness fully present to itself, timeless and above language, but a self decentered and fragmented in time. It is a self intersubjectively constituted, constantly in a state of change, constantly in dialogue with the outer world. It is a subject-in-process whose identity must be continually assumed and then called into question, evading any ideological unity. To challenge the metanarratives, the status of the subject, and the humanist concept of the self and of history are intrinsic parts of these texts. Thus, writing the self in its most sophisticated versions presumes the inclusion of a spectrum of

[28]Paul John Eakin, *Fictions in Autobiography: Studies in the Art of Self-Invention* (Princeton: Princeton University Press, 1985), 36.

voices—the heteroglossia of the novel—that compose and inform its perceptions.

The difficulties that women face when they write autobiography yield a productive tension. They incite a reexamination of the values and ideologies that underpin conceptualizations of selfhood and a redefinition of the autobiographical project as a whole. Today, one must qualify the term *autobiography* and understand its misuse when discussing works by women. As Rita Felski points out:

> The normative criteria of objectivity and distance used to evaluate autobiography in the writings of such critics as Wayne Shumaker and Karl Weintraub are of little relevance in discussing the tradition of women's autobiography, which typically focuses upon the details of domestic and personal life and is fragmented, episodic, and repetitive, lacking the unifying linear structure imposed upon a life by the pursuit of a public career.[29]

A few feminist critics have called for renaming this already dubious genre in order to shift the focus onto female authorship. Domna Stanton uses the term "Autogynography" in her openended exploration of differences between autobiographies by men and women writers. She suggests that before 1968 many female writers were aware of society's stigmatization of female writers and that they "generated a particular self-consciousness about the fact of writing often manifested in a defensive or justificative posture."[30]

---

[29]Rita Felski, *Beyond Feminist Aesthetics: Feminist Literature and Social Change* (Cambridge: Harvard University Press, 1989), 86.

[30]Stanton, *The Female Autograph*, 13. It should be noted that Stanton draws on a wide range of writers. Much autobiography criticism by women has focused on the female autobiographer's awareness of her precarious role as a woman writer, which often placed her in a position of defense. Critics have cited such varied writers as Julian of Norwich, the Duchess of Newcastle, Colette, Simone de Beauvoir, and Anaïs Nin to demonstrate their observation. They reasoned that a woman's constant justification of her writing implies that she watches herself from the outside because she realizes that her readers are mostly men. This mode of self-legitimation is also prominent in Lou Andreas-Salomé's autobiography *Lebensrückblick*, in which she discusses her unwillingness to become a mother. See Nancy Miller, "Writing Fictions: Women's Autobiography in France," and Mary G. Mason, "The Other Voice: Autobiographies of Women Writers," in *Life/Lines: Theorizing Women's Autobiography*, ed. Bella Brodzki and Celeste Schenck (Ithaca: Cornell University Press, 1988), 45–

Contemporary autobiographies, in contrast, reveal an urgency that assumes a right to self-expression. Sandra Gilbert and Susan Gubar choose to emphasize the gendered demarcations of female scripting by referring to the autobiographer as the "Authorgraph."[31]

Even though I use the term *autobiography*—with the understanding of a substantive shift in meaning as it moves from a traditional to a contemporary agenda—I am inclined to refer to autobiographies as "personal histories" as more descriptive of women's autobiographical writing in Germany since the women's movement of the 1970s. First, the term *personal histories* encompasses the transcription of personal experience into language from a subjective viewpoint, which creates a narrative of the self. The subjective viewpoint diverges from the notion of the universal, unitary self exhibited in traditional autobiographies. The subjective viewpoint emphasizes the voice that is speaking inside the text and identifies the voice outside the text by gender, class, race, ethnicity, and historical context. Unlike the personal histories in which female writers, as Stanton states, feel compelled to assert and justify their position as writing subjects, these personal narratives do not question their right to tell.

Second, joining the terms *personal* and *history* calls attention to the dissolution of the traditional boundary between the private and public. It illustrates not only the interdependence between these mistakenly separated spheres but also the artificiality of dichotomizing them. At the same time, the combination of *personal* and *history* highlights the subjectivity of history and the construction of knowledge.

Finally, this designation places autobiography in the tradition of oral histories and attributes to these personal narratives a distinct discursive mode that should not suggest any intrinsic or essentialist female aesthetic. Rather, the difference between autobiographies written by men and by women reflects the cultural engendering

61 and 19–44 respectively; Domna C. Stanton, "Autogynography: Is the Subject Different?" in *The Female Autograph: Theory and Practice of Autobiography from the Tenth to the Twentieth Century*, ed. Domna C. Stanton (Chicago: The University of Chicago Press, 1987), 3–20.

[31]Sandra Gilbert and Susan Gubar, "Ceremonies of the Alphabet: Female Grandmatologies and the Female Authorgraph," in *The Female Autograph*, ed. Stanton, 21–48.

of both sexes manifest, at times, even in the structure of their life stories. In the autobiographies discussed here, the projection of a listener does not serve as a rhetorical device for self-aggrandizement or privilege implying separation and ego, but significantly underscores the act of communing and the establishment of rapport, in addition to highlighting the transfer of cultural information and reflection. The inscribed listener is indicative of seeing oneself both within a community and as part of a historical continuum.

Susan Stanford Friedman offers a poignant theoretical interpretation of what she sees as a contradistinct posture of male and female autobiographers. Her interpretation is based largely on the findings of psychologist Nancy Chodorow and social critic Sheila Rowbotham. Relying on Chodorow's model of the effects of the process of separation and individuation on gender arrangements, Friedman argues that female autobiographies are based on notions of "identification, interdependence, and community" incompatible with the traditional concepts of individualism in autobiographical writing discussed by such critics as Georges Gusdorf and James Olney. Since, as Chodorow shows, female children in much of Western culture experience bonding and dependence, "their experience of self contains more flexible or permeable ego boundaries. . . . The basic feminine sense of self is connected to the world, the basic masculine sense of self is separate."[32] Rowbotham contends that women always have been forced to identify themselves with a group, instead of viewing themselves as unique individuals. "Isolate individualism," Friedman comments, has been "the privilege of power."[33] Owing to the disparate socialization of women, female subjectivities emerging from personal histories by women are apparently not defined in isolation but in relation to others. Mary Mason's research supports the idea of a dialogic structure in autobiographical works by women. Reviewing women's autobiographies over various centuries, Mason, in the words of Bella Brodzki and Celeste Schenck, finds that the attempt at "self-definition in

[32]Nancy Chodorow quoted in Susan Stanford Friedman, "Women's Autobiographical Selves: Theory and Practice," in *The Private Self: Theory and Practice of Women's Autobiographical Writing*, ed. Shari Benstock (Chapel Hill: University of North Carolina Press, 1988), 41.

[33]Friedman, "Women's Autobiographical Selves," 39.

relation to significant others . . . is the most pervasive characteristic of the female autobiography."[34]

In the personal histories discussed in the following chapters, the dialogic structure is a prominent textual strategy. It is notable that a listener or recipient of the speech act is inscribed in these auto-biographical narratives so that discursivity constitutes the primary mode of expression, along with self-reflection. In *Patterns of Childhood*, Christa Wolf's narrator speaks with her daughter; in *Germany, Pale Mother*, Helma Sanders-Brahms, whose film was initially titled *Lene*, addresses her mother, Lene, and then dedicates the film to both her mother and her daughter. Ruth Rehmann's personal history *Der Mann auf der Kanzel* evolves as a dialogue with the narrator's son (her book is dedicated to her children), and *Years of Hunger* by Jutta Brückner implies a collective audience in her address, similar to the confessional or experiential literature published during the 1970s which took part in "collective self-storytelling."[35] The autobiographical renderings discussed here function as a network of dialogues, whether between individuals or among a collective. So when Nancy Miller, in her explorations of autobiographies by women, asks, "What conventions . . . govern the production of the female self as theater?"[36] perhaps the answer is the drama of bonding, of engaging in communication and intersubjective processes, as well as intervening in dominant cultural practices.

Writers Christa Wolf and Ruth Rehmann, who spent most of their youth under the Third Reich, focus on the psychic structures that shaped and were shaped by the historical context. Even though they place less weight on questions of gender as an overarching category of human identity, issues of gender resonate in their work. In contrast, filmmakers Helma Sanders-Brahms and Jutta Brückner, who grew up primarily in the postwar years, more openly explore issues of gender in addition to the historical amnesia that beset Germany.

I have chosen these films and texts in order to illustrate a range of autobiographical expression over the 1970s and 1980s in Ger-

[34]Brodzki and Schenck, eds., *Life/Lines*, 8.
[35]Watson and Smith, eds., *De/Colonizing the Subject*, xxi.
[36]Nancy K. Miller, "Writing Fictions: Women's Autobiography in France," in *Life/Lines*, ed. Brodzki and Schenck, 47–48.

many. The experiential literature as well as all four women's personal histories may be read as sites of struggle for redefining society's relationship to family, history, and the self. These texts represent a conflict between a sociocultural heritage and the desire to come to grips with that inheritance. The question Christa Wolf poses in *Patterns of Childhood*, "How did we become the way we are?" serves as a leitmotif for all four texts. The confrontation with oneself, in the form of the autobiographical enterprise, is a first step in broaching this question. The process of uncovering the past resembles an archaeological exploration much like Gabi Teichert's explorations in Alexander Kluge's film *The Patriot*. In these texts, however, the autobiographer unburies her own personal history, which is ensnared in German history, in order to reinterpret and reassemble the mnemonic shards of the past.

As more women begin to write and to explore the topographies of their lives, the impossibility of reducing the many voices to one becomes evident. My project is not to fix or locate a female self among these authors, but to explore the various ways of self-representation to allow the similarities and differences among these authors to speak for themselves. With autobiographical expression becoming as significant and popular in film as in literature, the register of voices increases. These explorations, as one can imagine, take on new dimensions, especially in terms of female authorship and visual representation. In many ways, however, discussions of filmic autobiography parallel those of its literary sister. At this juncture we should perhaps further extend the discussion to the appearance of autobiographical representation in films by women.

Visual Correspondences

Women filmmakers in particular have prolifically contributed to the reservoir of self-portraiture since their hard-won establishment within Germany's film scene.[37] The sheer number of autobiograph-

[37]Despite Germany's having proportionately more women filmmakers than any other Western nation, women filmmakers cannot be found in most discussions of New German Cinema. In *West German Film in the Course of Time: Reflections on the Twenty Years since Oberhausen* (Bedford Hills: Redgrave, 1984), Eric Rentschler speaks of feminist filmmaking in Germany as "a subject rarely broached in the scrutiny of New German films" (4).

ical films by women again draws attention to autobiography's significance as a popular form of and forum for female expression.[38]
This was especially true in the early phases of women's filmmaking
in the 1970s, when "film after film," as Julia Lesage observes,
"shows a woman, telling her story to the camera."[39]

As in literature, the politicization of the personal sphere became
the sustaining impulse for many films. A number of films produced
in the early 1970s, popularly referred to as "Frauenfilme [women's
films]," are the visual counterpart of "Verständigungsliteratur."
Motivated by a commitment to the women's movement, many
women filmmakers were concerned with examining the institutions
and systems of representation, or "technologies," that consigned
gender differences to a traditional epistemology.[40] Women's daily

[38]One question that has often haunted autobiography criticism is what actually
constitutes autobiographical expression. Within literature, the boundaries and forms
of autobiographical expression continue to remain undefined. Autobiography, especially in its postmodern variation of multiple voices and an infinite number of
presences, has become a literary playground for self-representation and self-
reflection. Any attempt to outline the autobiographical project becomes even more
misguided once autobiography is removed from its literary medium and is translated
into film. For one, filmmaking is a collaborative project, and meaning is produced
by multiple sources. Second, film prevents the integration of the author with her
past persona. Unlike literature, film lacks the immediacy of author and protagonist
because a surrogate performer stages the past self. With the transition from one
medium to another, additional variables must be taken into consideration and new·
strategies of interpretation introduced. See Elizabeth Bruss, "Eye for I: Making and
Unmaking Autobiography in Film," in *Autobiography: Essays Theoretical and Critical*,
ed. James Olney (Princeton: Princeton University Press, 1980). Bruss correctly sus-
pects that the unsuccessful representation of autobiography in film does not necessarily indicate an intrinsic deficiency within the filmic medium, but rather reveals
the rigid conventions that have established themselves within the making and
viewing processes of films. Bruss does not explore this avenue sufficiently. Catherine Portuges points to the gaps in Bruss's argument and shows how films by
women extend the borders of the classic narrative that calls for a unity of subject.
See Catherine Portuges, "Seeing Subjects: Women Directors and Cinematic Autobiography," in *Life/Lines*, ed. Bella Brodzki and Celeste Schenck, 338–50. For an
anthology of auteur theories see John Caughie, ed., *Theories of Authorship* (New
York: Routledge, 1981).

[39]Quoted in Annette Kuhn, *Women's Pictures: Feminism and Cinema* (London: Routledge and Kegan Paul, 1982), 148. See also Renate Möhrmann, "Frauen erobern
sich einen neuen Artikulationsort: den Film," in *Frauen, Literatur, Geschichte: Schreibende Frauen vom Mittelalter bis zur Gegenwart*, ed. Hiltrud Gnüg and Renate Möhrmann (Stuttgart: Metzler, 1985), 434–52.

[40]See Helke Sander, "Feminismus und Film," *Frauen und Film* (1977): 1–3. Here
Sander discusses the need for a feminist critique of cinema. The introduction of the

encounters at home and at work, their relationships to their own bodies, their gendered identities, and their exclusion from historical consciousness—all became explosive topics of inquiry during the 1970s.[41]

The documentary format, or *cinéma vérité* style, first mediated the politicized conceptualization of domestic space that became emblematic of early feminist films especially. Many of these films continued the student movement's leftist focus on the working class but with women as the protagonists; they stood at the juncture of the public and private spheres, a separation that was broken down in these portraits. A few examples of documentary-based films that characterize the early stages of German women's film-making are *Warum ist Frau B. glücklich?* (Why is Mrs. B happy? 1968), Erika Runge's portrait of a female miner whose personal history parallels forty years of German proletarian history; *Macht die Pille frei!* (Does the pill liberate us? 1972), by Helke Sander, on birth control; *Es kommt drauf an, sie zu verändern* (The point is to change it, 1973), by Claudia Alemann, dealing with female factory workers; and Helga Reidemeister's portrayal of a divorced working-class mother in *Von wegen Schicksal* (Who says "fate," 1978). For many directors, personal histories proved the most fertile soil for social analysis and the referent for recasting women's lives.[42]

In the 1980s, many films by women moved beyond the "present tense" representational mode, with a fundamental sociological orientation, into feature films that focused on the past.[43] Questions

---

first issue of the Berkeley-based film journal *Camera Obscura* (Fall 1976) outlines similar objectives: "This kind of analysis recognizes that women are oppressed not only economically and politically, but also in the very forms of reasoning, signifying, and symbolical exchange of our culture."

[41]See early editions of the feminist film journal *Frauen und Film*, of which Helke Sander was one of the co-initiators. Also see the catalogue of films with such subtitles as relationships, the family situation, women and work, the abortion issue, and women's biographies listed in *Der Frauenfilm: Filme von und für Frauen*, Gudrun Lukasz-Aden and Christel Strobel, eds. (Munich: Heyne, 1985).

[42]I do not include experimental or avant-garde films by women filmmakers such as Dore O., Rebecca Horn, Valie Export, or Ulrike Ottinger, even though I would argue that all feminist films during the 1970s were experimental; only the emphasis was different.

[43]One of the reasons for turning to fiction was to attract wider audiences. At the same time, some filmmakers, such as Erika Runge, believed that the documentary format "neglects the utopian elements. . . . I find other possibilities arise from the

about historical process and a gender-determined upbringing led to an examination of women's troubled identity as social, historical subjects. The reconstruction of the past necessarily provoked a confrontation with German history. Films that deal primarily with constructing autobiographical selves include *Tue recht und scheue niemand* (Do right and fear no one, 1975) and *Hungerjahre* (*Years of Hunger*, 1979) by Jutta Brückner; *Deutschland, bleiche Mutter* (*Germany, Pale Mother*, 1979) by Helma Sanders-Brahms; *Die allseitig reduzierte Persönlichkeit* or *Redupers* (*The All-Around Reduced Personality*, 1977) and *Der subjektive Faktor* (*The Subjective Factor*, 1980) by Helke Sander; *Malou* (1980) and *Im Land meiner Eltern* (In the land of my parents, 1981) by Jeanine Meerapfel; and *Peppermint Frieden* (*Peppermint Peace*, 1982) by Marianne Rosenbaum. The female subject and subjectivity became the overriding concerns of many feminist films during the 1970s and 1980s. For the first time, with few exceptions, a female "I" controlled the narrative perspective, signaling a shift in linguistic and specular authority within a system of "signifying practices" traditionally controlled by the male.[44] Set within a feminist framework, these autobiographical representations ventured to investigate female desire and subjectivity.

In these films, women directors focused on their childhoods, the silenced and repressed memories of the past, their parents' lives, and the historical context in which they grew up. As in their literary counterparts, the mother-daughter relationship is the most prominent theme, with other interfamilial constellations following. Characteristic of women's self-representation, the autobiographical persona is deeply embedded in a network of interpersonal relationships and in a social historical world. Rather than portray a single protagonist or hero whose struggle is one of separation,

---

play of emotions in fiction." In Marc Silberman, interview with Erika Runge, "One Brick in a Large House," *Jump Cut* 29 (February 1985): 54.

[44]The only other well-known female filmmaker in Germany before the 1960s was Leni Riefenstahl, who is best known for her propaganda films, in part directly commissioned by Adolf Hitler. It is an acknowledged fact that in the famous Oberhausen Manifesto, in which the beginnings of the New German Cinema were declared in 1962, not one woman's signature is to be found. Even now a constant complaint of women filmmakers is about lack of funding. Today, Margarethe von Trotta and Doris Dörrie are the only two women filmmakers who have gained international recognition. See Julia Knight, *Women and the New German Cinema* (New York: Verso, 1992).

many autobiographical films by women, most often dialogically structured as works of mourning, reveal the desire for proximity, recovery, and reestablishment of a unity, of a relationship with another.

The performance of intergenerational or interpersonal dialogues in Helma Sanders-Brahms's film *Germany, Pale Mother* and Jutta Brückner's film *Years of Hunger* is structurally secured by a discursive filmmaking. The listener, or recipient, in these autobiographical renderings, as in the literary works previously discussed, is either inscribed in the narrative or implied, so that these personal histories, resembling oral histories, function not only as personal explorations but also as means to cement connections and initiate conversations. For example, the opening scene of Helke Sander's autobiographical film *The Subjective Factor* establishes an exchange with Andreas, the filmmaker's son, who brings two books for his mother to peruse. One book documents the student movement and the second women's movement—Sander's own history— whereas the other reflects the political concerns of Andreas's generation with the Wendland, a nuclear-free zone in northern Germany. As Sander narrates the beginning of the women's movement in West Germany, telling Andreas about her past political involvement ("there I am, your mother"), the images come to life. The filmmaker, as storyteller, discursively establishes a heritage of historical knowledge by positioning her son within the open-ended text to assert the continuity of the past with the present. The son stands in for the viewer as partner in dialogue.

Film facilitated the creation of a public space for female expression and for the extension of, in this case, autobiographical dialogue to wide audiences. The production of public space is precisely the effect many filmmakers sought.[45] Through film, they hoped to initiate a widespread grassroots process of consciousness-raising. Personal histories were the private stories turned outward, positioning the female "I" in a recognizable social network. Jutta Brückner explains the intersection between individual and collective experience in relation to her own filmic aspirations: "I may seem to address very personal themes, but these personal problems are

---

[45]Alexander Kluge, "On Film and the Public Sphere," *New German Critique* 24–25 (1981/82): 206–20.

frequently public problems which we have to reconstruct on the screen as such."[46] Like much autobiographical literature of the 1970s, these films staged the communality of female experience by restating women's lives within the interpretive paradigms of second-wave feminism. Such tenuous demands, as those to document authentically and report subjectively, expressed a political agenda that aimed at promoting identification between the female author and the female reader. The question remains whether this format, soon superseded, effected a critical self-understanding.

A female character at the center of the narrative, however, does not guarantee the representation of a subject position. For women, appropriating the subject status in film as well as within the film industry itself, simultaneously calls for countering the classical cinematic language that has powerfully encoded "woman" in a repertoire of images ranging from the femme fatale of the 1930s to the virgin/mother of the 1950s. Even though the subversion of dominant cinematic strategies is not exclusive to the autobiographical enterprise but rooted in the avant-garde, it is essential to the construction of a female subject and to the exploration of an unmediated female gaze—that is, an expression of subjectivity.

In the early 1970s, women filmmakers were acutely aware of the need to create a "new aesthetic," even if it meant simply to counter the traditional positioning of women within dominant cinema. The first issue of *Frauen und Film*, a feminist film journal founded by Helke Sander, articulated the need for images that would allow for new forms of spectatorship and authorship:

> We want to speak to women viewers who are constantly exposed to film images and subject matter which, if not produced by the dominant culture, certainly reproduce it and thereby renew and strengthen it. *Frauen und Film* should give women the courage to escape such brainwashing and admit their own experiences. This is also true of women who work in or with the film medium.[47]

[46]Jutta Brückner, "Conversing Together Finally: Jutta Brückner, Christina Perincioli, and Helga Reidemeister," interview with Marc Silberman, *Jump Cut* 27 (1982): 47.

[47]"Vorwort der Redaktion zum Nachdruck Nr. 1," *Frauen und Film* 1 (July 1975): 2.

Aware of the necessity to resist traditional modes of image production, women filmmakers tested alternative images and repositioned the spectator vis-à-vis the visual narrative.[48] Most important, feminist filmmakers experimented with new possibilities of identification in their cinema of personal experience and with deconstructing women's continued identification with hegemonic structures that erase heterogeneity. Jutta Brückner best describes the challenge feminist filmmakers faced: "Exposed to our collective conformity and at the price of collective repression, the cinema offers us a place to focus our own desires for particular images, to explore our own experience of linguistic and visual absence, for we have always been made into images instead of acquiring our own. We do not yet have this place, but we would like to have it."[49] Autobiographical filmmaking provided a fundamental testing ground for unconventional ways of viewing through its reformulation of a discursive cinema. In addition, "woman" in these stories disperses into a diversity of representations instead of a narrow register of traditional images. *Jeanne Dielmann, 23 Quai du Commerce, 1080 Bruxelles* (1975) by the Belgian filmmaker Chantal Ackermann, *Film about a Woman Who* (1974) by the American Yvonne Rainer, and *Redupers* (1977) by Helke Sander have become classic examples of feminist filmmaking with a preoccupation with women's daily lives. These filmmakers have not only provided new moments of identification, but they have also prepared the ground for new relations of spectatorship.

The rethinking of cinema in feminist terms involves the disruption of existent narrative structures and the codes of mainstream cinema. Because women have a limited tradition of self-representation, the production of images is still based largely on subverting the traditional operations and aesthetics of meaning

---

[48]Classic cinema, Kaja Silverman notes, "projects male lack onto female characters in the guise of anatomical deficiency and discursive inadequacy." Kaja Silverman, *The Acoustic Mirror: The Female Voice in Psychoanalysis and Cinema* (Bloomington: Indiana University Press, 1988), 1. In film, women's identities are predominantly contingent on the male gaze, which female spectators have learned to internalize, just like the prisoner who, according to Foucault, internalizes the surveying gaze of the guard in the Panopticon. The process of learning from images that uphold traditional gender distinctions completes a vicious circle of perceptual incarceration.

[49]Jutta Brückner, "Women behind the Camera," in *Feminist Aesthetics*, ed. Gisela Ecker (Boston: Beacon Press, 1986), 121.

production. For this reason, as film theorist Teresa de Lauretis has stated, contemporary feminist art and criticism for the most part still participate in a process of "deaestheticization":

> So, once again, the contradiction of women in language and culture is manifested in a paradox: most of the terms by which we speak of the construction of the female social subject in cinematic representation bear in their visual form the prefix "de-" to signal the deconstruction or the destructuring, if not destruction, of the very thing to be represented. We speak of the deaestheticization of the female body, the desexualization of violence, the deoedipalization of narrative, and so forth.[50]

Autobiographical discourse in German women's cinema in the 1970s and early 1980s, engages in this process of "de-" in its frequent resistance to habitual meanings and values attached to female subjectivity. The use of a female "authorial" voice-over that locates the perspective from which the story is told, the resistance to woman as spectacle, and the denial of the male gaze are but rudimentary instances. Autobiographical filmmaking engages in the process of "deaestheticization" by breaking through the boundaries of the traditional fictional frame as well. The necessity of breaking through fixed conventions is axiomatic to the feminist project. As Helke Sander says, "Where women are true, they break things."[51]

Many contemporary women's projects with nonpatriarchal aspirations, however, attempt to counter traditional narratives without basing their works on autobiographical material. How do cinematic representations of personal histories differ? Is it enough that the filmmaker's life is thematized, so that the viewer, entering into Philippe Lejeune's proposed "autobiographical pact," accepts the film as a verifiable, subjective rendition of personal experiences?[52] Today this contract, mistakenly or not, is activated whenever a female "I" controls the narrative, so that self-reference or verifiable referents in "reality" are not enough, or are they? If

---

[50]Teresa de Lauretis, "Aesthetic and Feminist Theory: Rethinking Women's Cinema," *New German Critique* 34 (1985): 175.

[51]Helke Sander, "Feminism and Film," *Jump Cut* 27 (1982): 50.

[52]Philippe Lejeune, *Le Pacte autobiographique* (Paris: Edition du Seuil, 1975).

subjectivity and an authorial voice are not cinematically conveyed, then does the autobiographical self not dissipate as the single subject melds with the amorphous masses? How, then, is the autobiographical mode secured by a technology that has been used to efface differences and suppress the source of enunciation?[53]

To begin with, many filmmakers of autobiography have posited a self-referential single subject or perspective, discursively represented by the pronoun "I" that pronounces itself. The use of a voice-over has become the most effective means of establishing a relationship between the subjective viewpoint and the image. It also functions to bridge the gap between the author and her past persona. On a less obvious subtextual, subconscious level, the voice of the author within the filmic interior is invested in such a way that the "I" and the libidinal economy (the desire in the narrative) expressed in the film merge.

In *The Acoustic Mirror*, Kaja Silverman convincingly outlines this process in her reassertion of the existence of the author after his death was proclaimed in 1968. Another type of "author" can indeed be located in experimental films. Besides provocatively arguing, as Nancy Miller does, that the death of the author targets the male author, subsequently disempowering masculine subjectivity as the measure of all epistemologies, Silverman claims that authorial desire and identification can be read in the repertoire and frequent repetition of specific images. She states that "like a dream, the

[53]Bill Nichols, *Ideology and the Image* (Bloomington: Indiana University Press, 1981), 35. The socializing function of institutions such as the film industry has been extensively discussed by French philosopher Louis Althusser, who transposes Lacan's mirror stage in identity formation onto the relationship between individuals and institutions. In Althusser's view, institutions function as "the other" through which we define our identities. In other words, the mirror of dominant cinema serves to create a homogeneous culture by providing identificatory instances between the fictional characters and the spectator. Through operations such as "suturing," whereby the spectator is "sewn into" a film's enunciation through a shot/countershot technique, the spectator effortlessly crosses over into the imaginary realm to become part of the fiction. Thus, the viewer learns to comprehend "the physical world in an [ideologically choreographed] habitual manner" with "the self as subject . . . socially constructed in the imaginary . . . , [which is] the fundamental act of ideology." In many ways, dominant cinema serves to endorse the society and culture that pay for its production. In Western culture, it creates the consumer and attempts to secure a unitary cultural identity and concept of self based on the white male's perception. Only recently has mainstream cinema begun to appeal to minority cultures as a new market.

cinematic text proffers a series of more or less plausible and coherent representations, behind which is concealed the author 'inside' the text, now conceived as an organizing cluster of desires."[54]
The author resides *in* the text, and the author outside of the text
is merely a projection of the voice within.

Silverman proposes two ways in which authorial subjectivity
inscribes itself in the cinematic text: the voice-over—an organizing
first-person pronoun—and the author in the film as iconic representation (for example, Helke Sander plays the protagonist in many
of her films). The construction of the authorial subject inside the
text resembles the construction of the viewing subject outside the
text. Moreover, the authorial subject persistently returns to specific
images, revealing identification, desire, and emotional investment.

Silverman's opening up of what she terms a "theoretical space"
from which female subjectivity becomes audible is extremely helpful in studying autobiographical films. This space assists in seeking
out the sites and revelations of desire in a predominantly visual
medium and in discovering the individual emotional investments
at the base of these autobiographical journeys. The question of
referentiality with the author outside the work directing the read-
ability of the persona inside the text and the question of the creation
of a totalizing unity between author and text are thus surpassed.
Furthermore, the significance of the persona outside the text is
momentarily diminished; the value of the autobiographical project
shifts to the process of reflection and interpretation, and to the
assemblage of a myriad of experiences in which the author chooses
to anchor her existence. The referentiality guaranteed in the retention of the author-function, however, cannot be abandoned, since
it serves as an essential marker of the numerous factors that shape
personal identity. In fact, contemporary women autobiographers
most often insist on these referents because of their involvement
in the politics of identity.

By extending the investigation of autobiographical narration
to various media, women can begin to struggle with self-
representation and to engage in the many different questions that
can be posed when they set out to understand themselves.

[54]Silverman, *The Acoustic Mirror*, 197.

1

Personal Histories

—but no matter how I speak, hesitantly or fluently, whether
I use my own words or the inadequate leftist jargon, as I
offer explanation after explanation trying to clarify, as I send
message after message trying to explain my new life, my
words do not get through to him, they get lost somewhere
before reaching his ears.

I lead a different life, speak another language.
                                        Verena Stefan, *Shedding*

Dear A. . . . Recite all the great names of Western literature,
forget neither Homer nor Brecht, and ask yourself with which
of these mental giants you, as a woman who writes, could
identify. We have no authentic models; this costs us time,
detours, mistakes; but it does not have to be purely a dis-
advantage. Few, very few women's voices have reached our
ears since Sappho sang circa 600 B.C.
                    Christa Wolf, *Cassandra: A Novel and Four Essays*

A Personal Answer to Theory: First Expressions

On 13 September 1968, at a Socialist German Student's Federa-
tion (Sozialistischer Deutscher Studentenbund, SDS) conference in
Frankfurt, Sigrid Rüger, a delegate representing West Berlin, threw
tomatoes at her male comrades. Following the tradition of the Eliz-
abethan theater, she memorably expressed her discontent with the
general male reaction to Helke Sander's epoch-making address,
"Speech by the Action Council for Women's Liberation." Rüger's
gesture, in fact, provoked a heftier reaction than the previous female voice. Taken off guard, the male contingent unmasked itself
by making sneering remarks about women, displaying the sexism
that coexisted with the revolutionary aspirations of the Left. At the
next SDS meeting, in November 1968, women documented their
viewpoint in a flyer produced by the "Weiberrat" (Women's Council),[1] which agitated against the double standard maintained by

---

[1] "Weiberrat" is one of the first organized women's groups that sharply addressed
male sexism and female experience within a patriarchally structured society. This

leftist groups and their perpetuation of traditional "second sex" attitudes toward women. The same oppressive gestures and attitudes of West Germany's power structures, which were minutely analyzed and harshly criticized in the public sphere, were accepted as a natural reflex in the private realm. Visions of a classless society left women in the same state of gendered subordination. Women subsequently realized that they had to take up their own cause.

Among the main themes Helke Sander addressed in her "acte de résistance" was the perpetuation of women's historical silence by the Left's tacit acceptance of the separation between the public and private spheres and its omission of women's concerns. The demands for change advocated by the German Left rarely related directly to women and their new quest for identity and recognition. According to Sander:

> Women are seeking their identity. They cannot achieve this by participating in campaigns which do not touch upon their immediate conflicts. That would be false emancipation. Women can only find their own identity when the social conflicts which have been relegated to private life are articulated; only then will women join together and be politicized.[2]

Her conclusion, "Genossen, eure Veranstaltungen sind unerträglich" (Comrades, your meetings are unbearable), which also appears in her film *The Subjective Factor* (1980), breaks with the theoretical base that repressed the private sphere from political consciousness and reinforced what Hélène Cixous calls the "dual hierarchized oppositions" underlying Western thought.[3]

---

group made its mark on feminist history through its almost legendary flyer that called for freeing the "socialist dignitaries" from their "bourgeois dicks" ("Befreit die sozialistischen Eminenzen von ihren bürgerlichen Schwänzen"). The flyers satirized castration anxieties through cartoons that showed penises hung on plaques and a witch toting a hatchet lounging underneath the wall trophies. The women's movement challenged leftist males to make connections between public and private oppression. On the German women's movement, see Alice Schwarzer, ed., *So fing es an!* (Cologne: Emma, 1981), and Herrad Schenk, *Die feministische Herausforderung* (Munich: C. H. Beck, 1981).

[2]Helke Sander, "Speech by the Action Council for Women's Liberation," in *German Feminism: Readings in Politics and Literature*, trans. and ed. Edith Hoshino Altbach (Albany: State University of New York Press, 1984), 307–10.

[3]Hélène Cixous refers to these dualities and wonders where "woman" is to be

Leftist theories, at least in the way they were interpreted during the student movement, seemed to provide no room for a personal language. In *Den Kopf verkehrt aufgesetzt*, a personal eyewitness testimony of the late 1960s and beyond, Michael Schneider observes that the aversion toward psychology at the time reflects the repression of individuality:

> The New Left's development of theory betrays a dissociation between political rationality and personal needs. This was reflected in the Left's ongoing, rekindled animosity toward psychoanalysis, even toward psychology in general, which was denounced as a "bourgeois illness." During this period, there was as yet no women's movement to function as the champion of the repressed sensual-emotional sphere. If women even hoped to compete with men, they had little choice but to yield to the new political morality of achievement.[4]

Documentaries and "factual" reports were called upon to produce "objective" blueprints of power relations—the emphasis was on an empirical analysis of society and class structures. Yet empirical analysis neglected to take gender relations, subjectivity, and the personal into account. Individuality and individual needs, which

---

found within this paradigm. Through a coupling of oppositions, woman retains a subordinate position. These oppositions are not neutral. They are gendered and culturally evaluated.

[4]Michael Schneider, *Den Kopf verkehrt aufgesetzt, oder die melancholische Linke: Aspekte des Kulturzerfalls in den siebziger Jahren* (Darmstadt: Luchterhand, 1981), 49. Schneider offers a very insightful résumé of this period. Unfortunately, however, a questionable tone prevails when he discusses the participation of women who adopted the Left's theoretical base as enthusiastically as men did. It seems that when taken out of their "natural habitat," that is, the emotions, these women turn into grotesque figures or anomalies. I continue the quote that appears in the main text. His words simulate a firsthand, eyewitness news form of address: "For many [women] who appropriated 'Critical Theory' in seven-league boots, it led to grotesque forms of masculinization. They talked about their emotional needs, if they mentioned them at all, in an ironic tone, and if they happened to fall in love, then most certainly with the most militant comrade, who stood tall at the podium, stormed the rector's office and bared his chest to the water cannons of the Berlin police even at five degrees below zero" (49). In the descriptions that follow, no further mention of women is made. In fact, in speaking of "bourgeois sons," Schneider completely omits women from his historical summary of the late 1960s and the 1970s.

Schneider strangely seems to imply were women's responsibility, were seen as mere devices of bourgeois institutions. The personal was excluded, just as women had been excluded from the historical process and repressed by what Foucault has called the "fellowship of male discourses."

It is not surprising, then, that a discussion of the private and personal and of the contradictions that accompany the separation between the public and private spheres was widely initiated by women. For them, it was an existential question. It meant illuminating the sphere of female identity and experience. The private sphere, which was traditionally perceived as a constant, immutable, and impermeable shrine, underwent rigorous analysis for the first time. As a result, the "politicization of the private sphere," an appeal that lies at the heart of Sander's speech, became a slogan of the women's movement. The curtain was drawn back as many women began to take a good look at what goes on behind the scenes not only in Germany but in many Western countries. Emphasis on child-rearing, on power relations within the family, and issues of gender marked the new focus of attention. Analysis for the first time was striking home.

Autobiographical writing and textualizations of the self and of personal experience in West Germany flooded the literary market and dominated various literary forms. The prevalence of self-exploration during the 1970s is a manifestation of the perspectival shift that followed the turbulent years of the student movement. Once the movement had lost its momentum and dispersed into myriad directions, a rechanneling of analytical energies occurred. Introspection, fashionably neglected by Marxist theories, became acceptable in the 1970s. Those critics who had comfortably focused on the proletariat, on breaking radically with a bourgeois past and the family, on ignoring personal emotional development and, specifically, German history, were finally themselves challenged. Personal and national identity, themes long neglected, could no longer be repressed. One's coming to terms with one's own sociohistorical development as male or female in these years was a necessary sequel to the Marxist 1960s. Trivializing this surge of self-exploration, Reinhard Baumgart remarks: "Every new book season is filled with fathers, mothers, aunts, daughters, trips to Paris, marital crises, student years or years on drugs; continuously new yet rather similar biographical fragments serve as reproaches or pretexts for novels."[5] The relationship between the self and the sociohistorical context was the new focus of inquiry, with interpersonal relationships, self-expression, and subjectivity as cardinal motifs.

A number of trends during the 1970s fertilized the ground for autobiographical expression, including a declining allegiance to objective theoretical approaches, the resurgent popularity of psychology, the widespread formation of encounter groups, a renewed interest in the repressed German past, an emphasis on the history of daily life, and, above all, a growing women's movement. In literature, the nimbus surrounding this decade was termed the "New Subjectivity." Functioning as a linguistic marker coined by journalists, New Subjectivity was diagnosed as opposing the impulses that drove the textual ambitions of the late 1960s and Hans Magnus Enzensberger's well-known proclamation of the death of literature in the first *Kursbuch* published in 1968.

New Subjectivity signaled a reorientation from politically engaged literature based on documentary formats and attempts to render reality objectively to a self-reflective literary format with the reintroduction of narrative writing. Erika Runge's "Überlegungen beim Abschied von der Dokumentarliteratur" (Reflections upon leaving documentary literature, 1976) exemplifies the shift that many writers underwent in the years between 1968 and 1976: "If I were to begin a novel, I would like to . . . include my experiences, my needs, my feelings. I would want to voice my wishes. Maybe there will be others, maybe they will voice their own then."[6] The intervention and inclusion of the subject suggest the attempt to establish a rapport with the reader and provide possibilities of initiating the reader's confrontation with her or his own makeup.

---

[5]Reinhard Baumgart, "Dem Leben hinterhergeschrieben," *Die Zeit*, 5 October 1984, p. 72.

[6]Erika Runge, "Überlegungen beim Abschied von der Dokumentarliteratur," *Kontext* 1 (1976): 99. Before shifting to a more subjective style of prose, Runge, like many leftist writers at the time, turned to the working class to record the voices of the oppressed. The compiled interviews appeared as the *Bottrop Transcripts* (1968) with a foreword titled "Berichte aus der Klassengesellschaft" by Martin Walser.

To include the subject also means that the person who performs the interpretation claims the perspective. At the same time, this literary reorientation insists on the relevance of subjectivity in cognitive and conceptual processes, whereby the social subject is the acknowledged filter of perspective.[7]

The concept of "objectivity," a vestige of nineteenth-century positivism, was quickly invalidated by the acknowledgment of subjective relativity and by a postmodern cynicism that exposed the ideological interests that determined "findings." Autobiographical writing was an effective way of countering "objective" capitalizations on meaning by dispersing one story into a plurality of stories or voices. In addition, autobiographical representations were invested with strategies that sought to combine curiosity about the self and the demand for "authenticity" with the interest in documentary representations cultivated in the late 1960s. The autobiographical impulse in the mid-1970s partially grew out of the focus on documentary renderings and the trend against professional writing.

In his summation of 1970s literature and New Subjectivity, the conservative literary critic of the *Frankfurter Allgemeine*, Marcel Reich-Ranicki, distills their common denominators: "Self-observation, self-exploration, self-representation."[8] Yet despite the

[7]In literary criticism, it is also the time in which reception theory made its breakthrough. The reader became the focal point. Interpretations were deemed dependent on the perspective from which interpretations are performed. In contemporary parlance, this means an investigation into "where the reader is coming from." Since the text carries with it a plurality of meanings, it can be read in numerous ways, depending on the information the reader brings to the text—information based on class, race, gender, cultural background, and so on.

[8]Marcel Reich-Ranicki, "Anmerkungen zur deutschen Literatur der siebziger Jahre," *Merkur* 33 (1979): 169–79. For further discussions of New Subjectivity, see Helmut Kreuzer, "Neue Subjektivität: Zur Literatur der siebziger Jahre in der Bundesrepublik Deutschland," *Deutsche Gegenwartsliteratur: Ausgangspositionen und aktuelle Entwicklungen*, ed. Manfred Durzak (Stuttgart: Reclam, 1981), 77–106; Klaus Scherpe and Hans-Ulrich Treichel, "Vom Überdruß leben: Sensibilität und Intellektualität als Ereignis bei Handke, Born, und Strauss," *Monatshefte* 73 (1981): 187–206; Johann August Schülein, "Von der Studentenrevolte zur Tendenzwende oder der Rückzug ins Private," *Kursbuch* 48 (1977): 101–17; Hinrich Seeba, "Persönliches Engagement: Zur Autorenpoetik der siebziger Jahre," *Monatshefte* 73.2 (1981): 140–54; Leslie Adelson, "Subjectivity Reconsidered: Botho Strauss and Contemporary West German Prose," *New German Critique* 30 (1983): 3–59; and David Roberts, "Tendenzwenden: Die sechziger und siebziger Jahre in literaturhistorischer Per-

seemingly obsessive focus on the self, such terms have connotations that vary according to the motives for self-analysis. Even though an overlap exists, a clear difference in agenda between most male and female enunciations during this time is evident. For many men who participated in the student movement and joined the extraparliamentary opposition (Außerparlamentarische Opposition, APO) fathered by Rudi Dutschke, New Subjectivity meant withdrawing from the public political arena because of the realization that political and social changes as radical as those they had wished for would not come about. According to one critic, the fundamental tenor of the time was "self-criticism, resignation, mel-

---

spektive," *Deutsche Vierteljahresschrift* 56 (1982): 290–313. See also Richard W. McCormick's excellent discussion in *Politics of the Self: Feminism and the Postmodern in West German Literature and Film* (Princeton: Princeton University Press, 1991). Ernst Jandl wittily captures the self-absorbed, narcissistic sentiment that has often been seen as characteristic of the 1970s in his poem "vergessen, erinnern":

ich setze mich auf mich
ich entleere mich
ich spüle mich in mich
ich verströme mich
ich vergesse mich
ich erinnere mich an mich
ich beschaffe mich
ich bereite mich zu
ich schlinge mich in mich
ich verarbeite mich
ich vergesse mich
ich erinnere mich an mich

I sit down on myself
I empty myself
I rinse myself in myself
I flow through myself
I forget myself
I remind myself about myself
I constitute myself
I prepare myself
I devour myself
I process myself
I forget myself
I remind myself about myself

(Ernst Jandl, *die bearbeitung der mütze gedichte* [Darmstadt: Luchterhand, 1981], 31; my translation.)

ancholia, and mourning."[9] These sentiments transformed into a concern with one's immediate emotional sphere; within the personal sphere, the boundaries of political involvement receded. Peter Handke's statement, "Es geht mir darum, meine Realität zu zeigen" (I am concerned with showing my own reality), is certainly much tamer than the lacerating accusations found in his play *Publikumsbeschimpfung* (*Offending the Audience*), which premiered in 1966.[10]

Yet the disillusionment, also diagnosed by Michael Schneider, that wafted through the Left, plunging it into a general malaise, seems more indicative of the sentiments of its male contingency. One look at *Nach dem Protest: Literatur im Umbruch* (After the protest, literature in transition), edited by Martin Lüdke, as well as other summations of new subjective writing, supports this observation, since women are conspicuously absent from the roster of authors cited; nor do they appear as contributors in Lüdke's anthology describing the literature of the time. This omission may not necessarily be another example of exclusion, but rather an indication that many women, still carried by a euphoria of discovery and political intent, had already broken with the student movement in order to rechannel their efforts into the women's movement. It is no coincidence that in the works of Peter Handke, Peter Schneider, and Botho Strauss, three key male authors of New Subjectivity, the male protagonists are abandoned by their female lovers, and that in films by Wim Wenders, who is often designated as part of this trend, male bonding in the absence of women constitutes his focus of attention.[11]

Gender distinctions are rarely taken into account in most discussions of New Subjectivity. Consequently, the already inflated term New Subjectivity (continuously recycled in literature courses and publications) has come to signify everything and therefore nothing.[12] Moreover, this designation only obscures the many ten-

---

[9]Roberts, "Tendenzwende," 298.

[10]Peter Handke, "Gegen den tiefen Schlaf," *Die Zeit*, October 1976.

[11]See Peter Handke's *Der kurze Brief zum langen Abschied: Erzählung* (1972, *Short Letter, Long Farewell*) and *Die Stunde der wahren Empfindung* (1975, *A Moment of True Feeling*), Peter Schneider's *Lenz* (1973), and Botho Strauss's *Die Widmung* (1977, *Devotion*).

[12]Karen Ruoff Kramer, "New Subjectivity: Third Thoughts on a Literary Discourse" (Ph.D. diss., Stanford University, 1983).

dencies in literature of the 1970s that maintained the critical and political edge of the student and women's movements. These movements paved the way for social changes that challenged the core of most social structures and Western attitudes. The political implications of autobiographical works by women, which were far too easily catalogued under the heading New Subjectivity owing to women's historically imposed affiliation with subjective expression, hardly found approbation. Instead, the value of these works was constantly diminished by the derisive attributes often imputed to them, such as self-indulgence, egocentrism, myopia, and separatism—undoubtedly leaving a pejorative impression. I would even venture to say that placing into the category of New Subjectivity women's texts that perform self-explorations into female identity and subjectivity in the 1970s is a gross misrepresentation. The potentially liberating effects of self-discovery are again repressed by the umbrella term.

The inoperability of this term in relation to writings by women, or so-called women's literature, is clear when, for example, a feminist critic such as Sigrid Weigel awkwardly presents "New Subjectivity" as a subheading in *Die Stimme der Medusa* (The voice of the Medusa), a review of works by contemporary women, and then proceeds to discuss "weibliche Subjektivität" (feminine subjectivity), certainly a category in and of itself in its specific focus on works by women.[13] Renate Möhrmann, in fact, is one of the few who keenly distinguishes between male and female literature of the 1970s:

> If the construction of the male "I" was spoken of in terms of withdrawing [Rück-Zug], then the textualization of the female "I" could literally be referred to as a coming out [Vor-Zug]. There is no evidence of a nostalgic retreat into privacy, but rather a move to make century-old injuries public and to retract the resentment that has become normative. Reflecting on one's "characteristic features" is not a solipsistic process of withdrawing, but rather the gateway to a new kind

[13]Sigrid Weigel, *Die Stimme der Medusa* (Dülmen-Hiddingsel: Tende, 1987). The term "women's literature" specifically refers to particular texts that were produced in the 1970s. At the center of these texts was the quest for an autonomous, emancipated female identity. These writings were motivated primarily by the telos of the women's movement and followed its agenda programmatically.

of social interaction in which the relationship between genders is no longer determined by hierarchy, but rather by a dialectic equality.[14]

Women's self-reflective writing marked a political consciousness on the rise. Turning toward the private sphere was not a retreat, but rather an engaged and active stepping out. The problem, then, of packing a period into a term—since a term hardly can sustain the variety of impulses constituting a decade—is evident once the many exceptions break away from the rule.

In literature by women, the new preoccupation with the self had to be approached with different analytical tools. Since the self as female subject and agent had no historical precedent, language presented the first barrier. For some authors, the problem began with the use of the first-person pronoun "I," since the female "I" in literature was seldom self-referential. When women wrote, they spoke through the male "I" to mask themselves as female authors, except, of course, in autobiographical sketches, letters, and diaries. Consequently, feminist writers, or what Nancy Miller refers to as self-conscious women writers, were faced with what Christa Reinig in 1976 described as a "tough male enterprise that has lasted three thousand years. Every female author must sense that, when she uses the word 'I.' From that point on, you really can't continue."[15] The lack of or the unfamiliarity with a female tradition of literary self-representation resulted in the awareness of a grammatical schizophrenia. Radical feminists orthographically highlighted their alienation by hyphenating or dissecting the sign. French writer Monique Wittig explains her use of the disjunctured j/e ("I") in *The Lesbian Body*: "The 'I' who writes is alien to her own writing at every word because this 'I' [Je] uses a language alien to her; . . . J/e poses the ideological and historic question of feminine subjects. If I [J/e] examine m/y specific situation as subject in the language, I [J/e] am physically incapable of writing 'I' [Je], I [J/e] have no desire to do so."[16] Although few autobiographical texts written in Ger-

[14]Renate Möhrmann, "Feministische Trends in der deutschen Gegenwartsliteratur," in *Deutsche Gegenwartsliteratur: Ausgangspositionen und aktuelle Entwicklungen,* ed. Manfred Durzak (Stuttgart: Reclam, 1981), 341.

[15]Christa Reinig, "Das weibliche Ich," *Frauen Offensive* 5 (1976): 50.

[16]Monique Wittig, *The Lesbian Body,* trans. David Le Vay (Boston: Beacon Press, 1975), 10–11. See also Wittig's interview "Sich selbst leben: Ein Gespräch in Paris," *Emma* 3 (1986): 40–41.

many by women actually dissect the sign, they do provide a microscopic view of female objectification and linguistic marginality.

Women's personal answer to theory was to document their experiences, thereby challenging traditional epistemologies and scripts, either by disbanding them through women's life stories, or subverting them through counterperspectives. By focusing on women's experiences and female identities, women writers hoped to diverge from male paradigms and to write themselves free.

The Language of Experience: Firing the Canon

The avalanche of protocols and experiential literature written by women in the mid-1970s perfunctorily titled "Verständigungsliteratur" (literature of self-discovery) reveals a widespread need for the investigation of female identity and the recording of women's perspectives, anxieties, and fantasies.[17] The call to document one's life during this time grew into a veritable movement with a multiplicity of texts that countered the years of silence and the toll they took. The first meeting of "writing women" took place in Munich in 1976. In the same year, a series of workshops sprang up all over the Federal Republic. In West Berlin, the "Berliner Autorentag des Verbandes Deutscher Schriftsteller" sponsored a symposium for women writers. Its title, "Schreib das auf, Frau!" [Write that down, woman!], reverberated throughout the women's movement. Feminist journals such as *Courage* and *Emma*, both founded in 1976, offered further outlets for female expression, as did the series "The New Woman" introduced by Rowohlt in 1977.[18] Such publications were among the first to solicit female voices to establish a public sphere. In addition, several publishing houses and bookstores run by women were founded. The act of writing as a vehicle of self-expression and outreach became a communal event.

[17]Beginning protocols most often deal with the mother-daughter relationship: Barbara Franck, *Ich schau in den Spiegel und sehe meine Mutter* (Hamburg: Hoffmann and Campe, 1979); Roswitha Fröhlich, *Ich und meine Mutter: Mädchen erzählen* (Ravensburg: Maier, 1980); Monika Sperr, ed., *Liebe Mutter Liebe Tochter: Frauenbriefe von heute* (Munich: Rogner and Bernhard, 1981); and Signe Hammer, *Daughters and Mothers: Mothers and Daughters* (New York: Signet, 1976).

[18]Weigel, *Die Stimme*, 47–48.

Writing played a major role in the transformations many women underwent. By producing their own stories, women interested in self-discovery had to translate their experience into language, to learn to articulate their needs, and to decipher themselves in relation to their positions within the social order. Christa Wolf explains the role writing plays for women: "For women, writing is a medium which they place between themselves and the world of men."[19] Encouraged to document their lives, women produced texts that were momentous and unprecedented acts of breaking the silence synonymous with women's exclusion from the public sphere as well as from the historical process. Culturally rooted psychological inhibitions and intimidations were among the many obstacles that preceded the shattering of the barriers of silence. The act of writing was seen as a means of gaining authority and of dealing with internalized cultural biases that generally inhibited women's speech and creative productions. Studies in publications such as *Women's Ways of Knowing* show that these obstacles are not self-imposed but derive from attitudes toward women's speech in Western culture. The authors conclude that "one common theme" underlies many women's experiences: "that women, like children, should be seen and not heard."[20]

The production of texts, then, based on women's own life stories—a remnant of the interest in documentary literature of the late 1960s—catalyzed a learning process that entailed the assertion of linguistic authority, a demand for respect and attention. Writing, like film, provided a format for self-exploration, raising the consciousness of women as they reassessed their lives in new terms. Through writing, the narrating "I" could draw closer to herself by constructing a self to counter the program of self-abasement and the sense of powerlessness traditionally seen as the female mode. Women, in fact, secured a position in the network of social discourses and became visible by placing themselves in the text. French feminist Hélène Cixous promoted writing precisely for this reason: "I shall speak about women's writing: about *what*

---

[19]Christa Wolf, "A Work Diary, About the Stuff Life and Dreams Are Made Of," in *Cassandra: A Novel and Four Essays*, trans. Jan van Heurck (New York: Farrar, Straus and Giroux, 1984), 232.

[20]Mary Field Belenky et al., eds., *Women's Ways of Knowing: The Development of Self, Voice, and Mind* (New York: Basic Books, 1986), 5.

it will do. Woman must write her self: must write about women and bring women to writing, from which they have been driven away as violently as from their bodies—for the same reasons, by the same law, with the same fatal goal. Woman must put herself into the text—as into the world and into history—by her own movement."[21] To include oneself in the text, as Cixous suggests, was seen as a way to take control of one's life. On a more sophisticated level, Cixous aimed at the recasting of cultural scripts by including new perspectives and subjects. Yet, in order to create a space for female subjects, existing systems of representation needed to be challenged. New meanings could emerge if the repetition of the past negation, not only of female writers, but of female representation was avoided. At the time, Cixous's idea of "écriture féminine" was accompanied by the call for "writing the body."[22] For Julia Kristeva and Luce Irigaray, as for Cixous, the process of writing facilitates the enunciation of the unconscious synonymous with the site of woman and the repressed, alterior to the meta-narratives of Western culture. "Writing the body," they believed, signified a return to a time of preverbal, pre-oedipal identification with the mother to rediscover unprohibited, uncensored forms of female pleasure. In psychoanalytic terms, women's libidinal economy, seated in a pre-oedipal phase, preempted women's entrance into the Law of the Father, through which their bodies (and thus sexual pleasure) are appropriated by a male symbology in language. The desire to release the buried and pregendered constituted the core of the French feminist program, which strongly influenced feminist analysis in the 1970s and mid-1980s. Such theories motivated many explorations of female identity and subjectivity that led to a utopian and essentialist analysis.

These analyses predictably created general models of gender difference that were abstract and ahistorical. Such studies, however, began to wedge women out of definitions that erased them

[21]Hélène Cixous, "The Laugh of the Medusa," *Signs* 1.4 (1976): 875.

[22]See Elaine Marks and Isabelle de Courtivron, eds., *New French Feminisms* (New York: Schocken Books, 1981); Leslie W. Rabine, "Écriture Féminine as Metaphor," *Cultural Critique* (1988): 19–44; Ann Rosalind Jones, "Writing the Body: Toward an Understanding of l'Écriture Féminine," in *The New Feminist Criticism: Essays on Women, Literature, and Theory,* ed. Elaine Showalter (New York: Pantheon, 1985), 361–77.

and to prepare for plotting the complex interplay between the social and material conditions that affect women's lives. The studies attempted to repossess "woman" by suggesting an unmarked conceptual space in which to represent a female subject. The purpose was to extend boundaries to include an undefined territory called "woman." The conceptualization of this space in terms of a metaphoric insistence on alterity so as to provide freedom of movement beyond dominant theories and to suggest transformative implications has become axiomatic for deconstructionist feminism.

Bearing the theoretical flaws of this literature in mind, one still could say that "Verständigungstexte," or experiential literature, as narratives of constructed self-discovery, inhabit the space outside the canon and mainstream representations of women. For their time, they represented what Alice Jardine calls "delinquent" narratives. Moreover, the marginalization of these texts exposed the literary establishment's continued efforts to enforce a canonical standard. The establishment's resistance only confirms the significance and vitality of these documents.

This space outside institutions has had various names, yet as many feminist critics in the meantime have shown, an elaboration of "woman" as a universal female self blatantly erases differences. The conflation of culturally and historically diverse voices into one melting pot called "woman" has led to gross political misrepresentation. The depiction of female subjectivity in all of its diversity thus began to constitute a vital aspect of the feminist project, particularly since the 1980s with the inclusion of a wide range of voices. Through personal stories, women deviated from classical narrative scenarios in which, as Tania Modleski observes, "woman," codified as temptress or angel, must die, be killed, or be domesticated for order to be restored.[23] Many women's self-conscious representations inevitably challenged the dominant fictions as well as the cultural patterns that reinforce them. Women began to author their own dramas without recycling the scripts that turn Jocasta into a commodity shared by father and son.[24]

A new perspective on both women's social position and the

[23]See Tania Modleski, *Loving with a Vengeance: Mass-produced Fantasies for Women* (New York: Methuen, 1982).

[24]Roland Barthes, *The Pleasure of the Text*, trans. Richard Miller (New York: Hill and Wang, 1975), 47.

cultural meaning attributed to her affected women as writers, film-makers, readers, and spectators. The analytical foundation laid in the early stages of feminist criticism offered a coherent interpretive basis, one that was sometimes admittedly restrictive in scope. Nevertheless, the wave of writing at the beginning of the second women's movement was a manifestation of an acute need for women to come to terms with themselves as gendered social subjects. It set the stage for women to perform their own dramas.

A cursory survey of experiential literature reveals that topics such as motherhood, sexuality, pregnancy, the mother/daughter relationship, suicide, disfigurement, and fear of abandonment define the topography of textual confrontation. The publication of women's own viewpoints challenged old assumptions of gender issues. For example, motherhood, which had been ideologically shielded from criticism and regarded as one of the most sacred institutions of Western culture, became one of the many subjects extensively scrutinized.[25] A major part of the agenda accompanying narratives of self-exploration was a direct and spontaneous documentation of personal experience, however tenuous this project seems now. The demand for "authenticity," which paradoxically often turned into exemplification, called, not for reporting "the way it was" in the sense of an objective history, but rather for a more subjective rendition of the way "I saw and felt it."

Subjectivity was valorized over the "objective" parameters that maligned female identity. Feminist theorists showed that women's perspectives traditionally had no place in the field of objective discourse. The insistence on subjectivity appeared as a strategy as well as an indication of an immense curiosity about women's perceptions and processes of representation, owing to an awareness that whole areas of knowledge were yet to be discovered. The

[25]The debate actually produced two diverging movements. One was a critical confrontation with the social meaning of motherhood and the ways in which it affects women's position within society. Some women admitted they did not want to be mothers; others confronted their roles as mothers and reassessed them. Among the more critical literature, one finds Adrienne Rich's groundbreaking book *Of Woman Born: Motherhood as Experience and Institution* (New York: Bantam, 1976). See also Elisabeth Badinter, *Motherlove: Myth and Reality* (New York: Macmillan, 1981); Julia Kristeva, "Stabat Mater," in *The Kristeva Reader*, ed. Toril Moi (New York: Columbia University Press, 1986), 160–86; and E. Ann Kaplan. *Motherhood and Representation: The Mother in Popular Culture and Melodrama* (New York: Routledge, 1992).

boundaries of institutional authorship were transgressed, with each person's story considered equally important in furnishing the many missing pieces of information. Along with other movements that represented the disenfranchised and encouraged them to put themselves on the linguistic map (such as efforts to produce workers' literature), feminism led to an unequaled proliferation of texts in which the separation between life and text gave way to the publication of what journalists called "oneself as a document."[26]

Despite the debate surrounding the actual literary value of these texts, which some critics called naive outpourings of unreflected emotion and others referred to as dogmatic feminist narratives, the historical significance of Verständigungsliteratur in the 1970s must be seen primarily in relation to its creation of a public forum.[27] Women's texts facilitated a support system and provided a realm for personal confrontation. *Verständigen* means "to inform or communicate." Unlike traditional confessional writing, which peaked in the eighteenth century with the Pietists who produced minute, fastidious entries to serve as a seismograph of spiritual stirrings, the authors of contemporary experiential literature were engaged in a direct dialogue with others. To use Nancy Miller's words, they created "un sujet à aimer." By contrast, as Miller points out, women reading "woman" in traditional texts find no one to like or identify with in the text and thus no place in the text.[28] Women writers in particular were faced with an absence of adequate models. The literature of self-discovery gave rise to a political community and initiated a dialogue among women, who enthusiastically greeted the transformation of inhibiting social practices. Besides introducing a female viewpoint, these texts generated a basis for solidarity among women, altering their awareness of themselves as gendered

[26]Workers' literature promoted by the "Werkkreis Arbeiterliteratur" provided workers with a public forum for their own experiences, thus fulfilling the same function for workers as "Verständigungsliteratur" did for women in the 1970s. Max von der Grün, a writer who concentrated on the factory milieu, was one of the more accomplished proponents of workers' literature.

[27]See Rita Felski, *Beyond Feminist Aesthetics: Feminist Literature and Social Change* (Cambridge: Harvard University Press, 1989). Her chapter "On Confessions" is an excellent survey of this genre of literary self-reflection.

[28]Nancy Miller, "Changing the Subject: Authorship, Writing, and the Reader," in *Feminist Studies/Critical Studies*, ed. Teresa de Lauretis (Bloomington: Indiana University Press, 1986), 109.

persons. Women began to examine self-negating concepts of womanhood in relation to sociohistorical contexts rather than as personal shortcomings and deficiencies. Evoking a commonality of experience among these women, who for the most part shared a similar cultural background, these texts drew women out of their isolation to discuss their lives. The editors of *Frauen, die pfeifen*, a collection of Verständigungstexte predominantly by amateur writers, defined their project as: "simply to use literature as a medium for communicating our experiences, difficulties, fantasies, and thoughts in order to emerge from isolation; as a means of publicizing our personal and social situation in a process of transformation."[29]

Encouraging women to write had a significant yet seldom mentioned motivation: hope of unleashing creativity. The brief biographical sketches in *Frauen, die pfeifen* show that many of the women wrote only when they could afford a respite from their daily routines. The public dialogue ensuing from these texts also played a major role in initiating the consciousness-raising processes quintessential to the women's movement. The overwhelming popularity of these texts unsettled many critics, who either became anxious about the sudden exhibition of female self-expression or failed to recognize the historical significance of these texts and unduly feared the subordination of literature to the purposes of an encounter group. Reinhard Baumgart's sardonic yet observant description of the resurgence of autobiography as self-therapy during the 1970s inevitably includes works by women. He exclaims despairingly: "Only things that are readily accessible, things from one's own past, seem to attract authors as tangible and comfortable topics, so that an intimate confessional and conversational tone pervades literature, and a disconcerted and sympathetic nodding has spread among readers as though our literary establishment had changed into an encounter group."[30]

Verständigungstexte produced a situation similar to psycho-

---

[29]Ruth Geiger et al., eds., *Frauen, die pfeifen: Verständigungstexte* (Frankfurt am Main: Suhrkamp, 1978), 11.

[30]Reinhard Baumgart, "Das Leben—kein Traum? Vom Nutzen und Nachteil einer autobiographischen Literatur," in *Literatur aus dem Leben: Autobiographische Tendenzen in der deutschsprachigen Gegenwartsdichtung*, ed. Herbert Heckmann (Munich: Hanser, 1984), 13.

analysis, with the energy and dialogue between a movement and its participants resembling the process of transference between analyst and analysand. In one sense, writing became a public expropriation of individual culpability through outpourings of personal anguish and anger in an often naive and unreflected format. A sophisticated analysis was usually lacking, which appeared to trivialize expression and at times promote an unendurable melodrama.

Guided by a feminist agenda, similar realms of experience were highlighted, enabling a basis for identification. The body of textual selves formed a collective "I," and the voices that employed the first-person pronoun became both the product and process of its representation. One of the main criticisms against the women's movement was that the "I" deceptively represented white, middle-class women. Differences of race, ethnicity, sexual preference, and class gained recognition only much later. The collective quality of the "I" that resulted from the wave of the West German "literature of self-discovery" underscores the fundamental interaction between individual and collective identity in the early phases of the second women's movement. However, the misdirected appeal of early feminism to create a monolithic female self constituted an important defining element of the politics of the women's movement.

Once again, the notion of New Subjectivity fails to address the dynamics behind the production of texts by women. Delf Schmidt makes the distinction between the withdrawn "I" in the literature of New Subjectivity and the public "I" of the women's movement: "The 'I' that is articulated in a group that perceives itself as a collective subject does not express a private, isolated form of interaction, but something qualitatively different from the so-called New Subjectivity."[31] Women's autobiographical sketches often served as outlets for rage and affliction. These texts developed their own eccentric dynamic propelled by the momentum of many unifying voices. A discursive process, singular and unprecedented, was fueled by an excessive proliferation of texts.[32] Only later, after the

[31]Delf Schmidt, "Gegen die Placebo-Literatur," *Literaturmagazin* 11 (Reinbek: Rowohlt, 1979): 15–16.

[32]There are many theories of the novella that could be superimposed onto Verständigungsliteratur, which I see as a discursive happening. In attributing novelistic

initial public catharsis evolved into a more self-reflective mode, did this surplus of self-expression spend itself. As the author Ursula Krechel astutely notes, the writers who based their texts so closely on personal experience soon depleted their resources, particularly since many women were only between the ages of eighteen and thirty.[33]

Publishing houses played a major role in advancing Verständigungsliteratur. Exploiting new markets, publishers catered to the needs of the newly politicized female public; they encouraged "confessional" or "experiential" writing and selected it over other submitted texts. "The public, with its expectations and needs, is the true author of these texts, thematically as well as aesthetically," some critics noted.[34] An intricate relationship of dependency between writer and reader arose; virtually undiscovered until the late 1970s were other women writers, such as the Austrians Ingeborg Bachmann and Marlen Haushofer, whose works of the fifties and sixties did not resonate with the confessional literature of the day. On the basis of the overwhelming popularity of "Verständigungsliteratur," one can infer that these narratives of self-discovery filled a specific historical need acutely felt by both writers and their audiences. For example, *Shedding* (*Häutungen*, 1976), Verena Stefan's first work, which explores social and sexual aspects of a young physical therapist's relationship to men and to the Left, sold more than two hundred thousand copies by 1980.

The novelty of a female perspective inspired the female readership. The pleasures derived from these texts reflect what Roland Barthes calls "hysterical readings." In *The Pleasure of the Text*, he asks rhetorically:

> Why do some people, including myself, enjoy in certain novels, biographies, and historical works the representation of the "daily life" of an epoch, of a character? Why this curiosity about petty details: schedules, habits, meals, lodging, clothing, etc.? Is it the hallucinatory

---

qualities to this type of literature, I particularly refer to Goethe's definition of the novella as "an unheard-of event." The novella is defined as a story with a compact, pointed plot, which seems to describe many of these narratives.

[33]Ursula Krechel, "Leben in Anführungszeichen: Das Authentische in der gegenwärtigen Literatur," *Literaturmagazin* 11 (Reinbek: Rowohlt, 1979): 80–107.

[34]Baumgart, "Das Leben—kein Traum?" 73.

relish of "reality" (the very materiality of "that once existed")? And is it not the fantasy itself which invokes the "detail," the tiny private scene, in which I can easily take my place? Are there, in short, "minor hysterics" (these very readers) who receive bliss from a singular theater: not one of grandeur but one of mediocrity (might there not be dreams, fantasies of mediocrity)?[35]

Perhaps women did experience bliss while viewing singular theaters that addressed their own daily lives; perhaps they found Nancy Miller's "sujet à aimer" within these texts. For many readers, a sense of recognition and understanding affirmed their own existences. Perhaps the reading of these texts produced the excitement of self-recognition in the gestures represented as well as the possibility of self-discovery in the text. Since the theater of grandeur, valor, and heroism was performed without women, a female audience was often left to view dramas cast in a syntax that was different from their own. In classical texts, for instance, the only form of heroism attributed to women is self-sacrifice.

The 1970s concentrated on facilitating identification and mirroring recognizable episodes. Both readers and writers became "minor hysterics" who delighted in "communing" through texts to affirm their own feelings and perceptions. For the first time, stories about daily lives were circulated, which meant that every woman could tell her story and be sure of an audience. The enthusiastic reception of these stories and the public dialogues that ensued were the key, since without them most of the texts would never have been written.

Aimed at triggering a metamorphosis, the implicit feminist agenda of these textual explorations invites criticism. Some of the consequences of coupling the autobiographical project of Verständigungsliteratur with a feminist telos may be illustrated by such works as Verena Stefan's *Shedding* and Svende Merian's *Der Tod des Märchenprinzen* (Death of a fairy tale prince, 1980), both of which long influenced popular understanding of "women's literature" and caused women writers to distance themselves from this provisional typecasting.[36] These texts have since aroused controversy,

---

[35]Barthes, *The Pleasure of the Text*, 53.
[36]Sigrid Weigel, "Frau und 'Weiblichkeit' Theoretische Überlegungen zur feministischen Literaturkritik," *Argument-Sonderband* (1984): 103–13.

with some critics dismissing them as effusively didactic, prescriptive, and contrived to stage a feminist rebirth.

Jutta Kolkenbrock-Netz and Marianne Schuller point out that the euphoria that carried the women's movement not only animated these autobiographical accounts but determined their forms of representation.[37] In addition, the problem with many of these personal portraits influenced by the women's movement is their resolute desire to affirm "woman" and to describe ways to effect change. The linear progression of these narratives adheres to autobiographical conventions promoting autonomy and independence as the teleological goals of literature. The linear format also reproduces traditional male paradigms and effaces the multiplicity of potential female representations across lines of race, class, and gender. For example, in *Shedding*, the protagonist progressively constitutes her identity by finding herself in relation to other women; she learns to identify with women by immersing herself in what she calls "women's culture." Yet the nature imagery at the end painfully recycles romantic and reductive stereotypes of woman as nature. Kolkenbrock and Schuller argue that this propensity for producing stereotypes duplicates normative social assumptions.

Predominantly directed toward a female audience predisposed to applaud women's personal struggles against the male "enemy," experiential literature fostered an exclusionary women's community with all the advantages and disadvantages of membership in an exclusive club. Kolkenbrock and Schuller suggest that these texts evolve into dramas of vehement accusations and vituperative indictments that obscure rather than promote an understanding of "gender politics." The patriarch is only vilified and therefore doomed to lose. Kolkenbrock and Schuller state that "instead of radically exposing obsessive submission as cultural oppression and as a male-generated disciplining of pleasure, [the text], apart from its dolorous and stereotypical complaints, actually only makes what has hitherto been hidden public."[38] Because these

[37]Jutta Kolkenbrock-Netz and Marianne Schuller, "Frau im Spiegel," *Argument* (1982): 154–74.
[38]Ibid., 165.

works lack an analytical edge, they tend to reproduce women's passive, suffering role. However, because they aimed at breaking taboos and identifying gendered experience, they also served to intervene in traditionally male texts and to challenge a literary hegemony.

Despite the eagerness of publishing houses to sensationalize personal conflicts in order to provide for their newly discovered market, these literary confrontations with personal identities had a significant function that should not be overlooked. For one, the female voice could no longer be neglected. Second, many women had their first encounter with naming their own experiences, hence the feeling of urgency in these texts, wherein many women made initial attempts at self-definition. Linking themselves to and identifying with a larger social group, women gained support and assistance in deprivatizing personal experience. Third, these texts invested in the creation of a public forum that called for social change. They elicited a discussion and encouraged many women to articulate their experiences and perceptions. The initial susceptibility to dogmatic formulas may be symptomatic of the centuries of silence women endured. In Germany, feminism was the only movement that unequivocally addressed women's experiences and provided new paradigms to explicate their realities. A feminist jargon served as but a first linguistic scaffold with which to build.

Only now, with the increasing availability of women's writings, are we able to criticize these autobiographical undertakings in which traditional literary representations surrendered to formulaic though explosive renderings of personal stories. In all fairness, the corpus of experiential literature, which the Austrian writer Elfriede Jelinek calls "the first phase, the phase of lamentations," must be read in reference to a specific historical period and respected as a phase that called for struggle.[39] These texts were written at a time when female productions were either scarce or absent, not only from the literary curriculum but also from the literary canon. These texts, like their cinematic counterparts, also formed an "opposi-

[39]Elfriede Jelinek, interview, *Deutsche Bücher* 15, ed. Ferdinand van Ingen (Amsterdam: Rodopi, 1985), 78.

tional public sphere" that destabilized the ideologically motivated representations of female existence and, with them, primary social fixtures. At the very beginning of a groundbreaking experiment, these autobiographical narratives prefaced the more complex attempts at self-representation that followed in both literature and film.

2

Christa Wolf's
Patterns of Childhood

[One] casts the net of memory, throws it over oneself and
pulls oneself in, predator and prey all in one, over the threshold of time, the threshold of space, in order to see who we
were and who we have become.

Ingeborg Bachmann

What's the point of remembering? Live now! Live now! But
I am only remembering so that I can live now.

Elias Canetti

The Poetics of Experience

Any critical look at autobiography in German literature inevitably
must treat Christa Wolf's *Kindheitsmuster* (*Patterns of Childhood*,
1976), one of the most provocative and complex literary self-
portraits to date. Wolf's novel is a dense, multilayered investigation
of the self which transgresses the traditional borders of autobiography anchored in liberal humanism. Wolf engages in a dialogue
of tenses. She breaks through the borders that traditionally divide
past and present, public and private, event and perception, which
are all woven together to compose a life. In *Patterns of Childhood*,
Wolf not only retraces sixteen years of childhood during the Third
Reich but also confronts the capabilities and assumptions of autobiographical expression, including such notions as authentic representation and the mechanics of memory. She reflects on the
limitations, the liberating potential, the necessity, and the deceptions of memory.[1] Wolf tells a "story" and simultaneously contem-
plates the impossibility of telling that story. In view of Germany's
fascist past, her task of autobiography is not easy.

Wolf places the autobiographical project in jeopardy from the

[1]See Gayle Greene, "Feminist Fiction and the Use of Memory," *Signs* 16 (1991):
290–321.

outset by prefacing her memoir with a disclaimer as to the verifiability of events and persons. The preface raises several theoretical and practical issues concerning autobiographical representation, including the difficulty, if not the impossibility, of capturing experience through writing. "All the characters in this book are the invention of the narrator," Wolf says in her preface. "None is identical with any person living or dead. Neither do any of the described episodes coincide with the actual events." With this statement, she unsettles the "autobiographical pact" that Philippe Lejeune sees as an implicit contract of reference and the mainstay of autobiographical writing. Her disclaimer, however, is not a denial of verifiability, since self-referentiality (the autobiographical mode) is secured on the first page when she addresses herself in the second person. Instead the disclaimer serves as an acknowledgment of the limits of autobiographical composition, an admission that writing and imagination alter characters and events, and that only one version or interpretation of the self is ultimately produced.[2]

Throughout her work, Wolf struggles with the complexity of representation and the mediation of experience and the past. The narrator wonders:

> The past—whatever the continuously accumulating stack of memories may be—cannot be described objectively. The two-fold meaning of the word "to mediate." To be the mediator between past and present—the medium of a communication between the two. In the sense of reconciliation? appeasement? smoothing out? Or a rapprochement of the two? To permit today's person to meet yesterday's person through the medium of writing? (*Patterns of Childhood*, 164)[3]

As many contemporary critics suggest, the autobiographical self emerges through language and its operations of naming, defining,

---

[2]See Peter Handke, *Gewicht der Welt* (*The Weight of the World*) (Frankfurt am Main: Suhrkamp, 1982). In his autobiographical ramblings, he writes: "Tell me a story about myself; it may not be right—but tell me about myself! I need a version of myself" (194).

[3]Christa Wolf, *Patterns of Childhood* (formerly *A Model Childhood*), trans. Ursule Molinaro and Hedwig Rappolt (New York: Farrar, Straus and Giroux, 1980). All page numbers refer to this edition.

and interpreting.[4] The self that unfolds in autobiography is inevitably a very selective portrait imbued with a perspective that is anchored in the moment of writing. In Peter Handke's portrayal of his mother and his own biography in *Wunschloses Unglück* (*A Sorrow beyond Dreams*, 1972), the author addresses the alterations that occur during the process of writing (the process of remembering). Both Handke and Wolf abandon the possibility of reconstructing the self in the historicist sense of reproducing objective documents of the "way it was," with sepia photographs (coinciding with a nineteenth-century understanding of history and empiricism), as a deceptive and deficient means of entering the past. They both completely dismiss the notion of memory as a static principle that has the potential to freeze-frame an event.

Still, Wolf admits to her obsession with documenting the moment, with nostalgically fixing a memory or a fragment of time, even as she realizes that the immediacy of experience dissipates in the act of representation:

> Ideally, the structure of the experience coincides with the structure of the narrative. This should be the goal: fantastic accuracy. But there

---

[4]See Roland Barthes, *Roland Barthes by Roland Barthes*, trans. Richard Howard (New York: Hill and Wang, 1977). Barthes writes: "This book is not a book of 'confessions'; not that it is insincere, but because we have a different knowledge today than yesterday; such knowledge can be summarized as follows: What I write about myself is never the last word: the more 'sincere' I am, the more interpretable I am, under the eye of other examples than those of the old authors, who believed they were required to submit themselves to but one law: authenticity. Such examples are History, Ideology, the Unconscious. Open (and how could they be otherwise?) to these different futures, my texts are disjointed, not one of them caps any other; the latter is nothing but a further text, the last of the series, not the ultimate in meaning: text upon text, which never illuminates anything" (120). See also Roland Barthes, "From Work to Text," in *Textual Strategies*, ed. Josué V. Harari (Ithaca: Cornell University Press, 1979). Here Barthes discusses the properties of the text in relation to the work. The text, he writes, is plural, decentered, without closure, metonymic, derives from intertexts, and forms a network of tissue with the author functioning as the "guest." The author "is no longer the privileged and paternal, the locus of genuine truth, but rather ludic. . . . There is a reversal, and it is the work which affects the life, not the life which affects the work: the work of Proust and Genet allows us to read their lives as a text. The word 'biography' reassumes its strong meaning, in accordance with its etymology. At the same time, the enunciator's sincerity, which has been a veritable 'cross' of literary morality, becomes a false problem: the I that writes the text is never, itself, anything more than a paper I" (79).

is no technique that permits translating an incredibly tangled mesh, whose threads are interlaced according to the strictest laws, into linear narrative without doing it serious damage. To speak about super-imposed layers—"narrative levels"—means shifting into inexact no-menclature and falsifying the real process. "Life," the real process, is always steps ahead; to catch it at its latest phase remains an un-satisfiable, perhaps an impermissible desire. (*Patterns of Childhood*, 272)[5]

Many journal-like entries in *Patterns of Childhood* serve as temporal and spatial markers that secure a tangible present, the time of writing which began 3 November 1972 and ended 2 May 1975.[6] Wolf's recording of episodic memory is an attempt to counter for-getting as a form of repression.[7]

Besides challenging the autobiographical ideal of transcribing life into text, Wolf's autobiography follows a postmodern agenda. To quote Linda Hutcheon, Wolf "puts into question that entire series of interconnected concepts that have come to be associated with what we conveniently label as liberal humanism."[8] Wolf interro-gates such concepts as authority, uniqueness, and unity. Under-mining authority by decentering her position as author, Wolf employs the freedom of narrational movement to examine the dif-ferent ways of representing a troubled past. Throughout her self-reflexive narrative, she transgresses the arbitrary boundaries that define meanings and values in a world of which she has reason to be suspicious. Many genres appear in her text only as vestiges: a date or inner monologue signals a diary; a fact recalls historical or

[5]Heinz Dieter Weber, *Über Christa Wolfs Schreibart* (Konstanz: Universitätsverlag Konstanz, 1984), 19–20. Weber has discovered that Wolf's reference to "fantastic accuracy" is a quote taken from the heart of Robert Musil's *The Man without Qualities*. Quoting Musil, Weber comments: " 'Accuracy as a human attitude,' this is what we read in chapter 62, in which the 'utopia of essayism' is developed." A similarity between Musil's project and Wolf's own way of writing is particularly visible in Musil's concept of writing: " 'Fantastic Accuracy' is a 'conscious human essayism,' which is in the position to make it possible to see the real in the light of that which has not yet come true, to see human beings as the 'essence of their possibilities,' 'the unwritten poetry of their being.' "

[6]Therese Hörnigk, *Christa Wolf* (Göttingen: Steidl, 1989), 165.

[7]See Elizabeth F. Loftus et al., "Who Remembers What?: Gender Differences in Memory," *Michigan Quarterly Review* 26.1 (1987): 72.

[8]Linda Hutcheon, "Decentering the Postmodern: The Ex-Centric," in *A Poetics of Postmodernism: History, Theory, Fiction* (New York: Routledge, 1988), 57.

journalistic documentation; and her interpretive inquiry suggests an essay. Her title also departs significantly from the implicit and traditional expectation in autobiographical writing that the subject is unique. The designation "patterns" in the title emphasizes sameness, rather than the singularity of experience that the critic of autobiography Georges Gusdorf insists on in his delimitation of autobiographical representation as "a conscious awareness of the singularity of each individual life."[9] The "patterns," as Wolf calls them, are culturally and historically specific; they imprint "culture," which Clifford Geertz identifies as a network of meaning through which people define and shape their experiences.[10] For the most part, these patterns of identity are organized by multiple variables.[11] For girls of Wolf's generation—she was born in 1929— gender was strictly defined, and the possibilities of subverting that definition were virtually nonexistent.[12] Wolf largely elides questions of her gendered socialization. Instead, she explicitly addresses the patterns imposed on adolescents who grew up in Germany during the Hitler years and who experienced the rigorous socialization processes transmitted in the private sphere or in the public sphere by such organizations as the Hitler Youth (Hitlerjugend, HJ) or League of German Girls (Bund deutscher Mädchen, BDM), which functioned much like extended families.

Wolf's depiction of this period in terms of patterns seems appropriate since it stresses the uniformity imposed by the Third Reich. To promulgate homogeneity and stability, the Nazi Party transmitted its commitment to uniformity through rigid codes of conduct, formally expressed in the parades, in congresses, and in

[9]Georges Gusdorf, "Conditions and Limits of Autobiography," in *Autobiography: Essays Theoretical and Critical*, ed. James Olney (Princeton: Princeton University Press, 1980), 8–9.

[10]Clifford Geertz, *The Interpretation of Cultures* (New York: Basic, 1973).

[11]Wolf thought that the translation of "Muster" as "patterns" rather than "model" more appropriately suited her text.

[12]It is interesting to note here that among the many objections to the "Volkszählung" (the national census, revived by Chancellor Helmut Kohl's government in 1987), opponents cited the possibility of easily "reidentifying" citizens by matching data and geography, even though the information collected was anonymous. In one population pool, researchers ascertained, it would be difficult to distinguish individual people due to the similarity of their lives. Those in this pool are women who were born in the early twentieth century and who became mothers and wives as a full-time career.

the aestheticization of the political (as Walter Benjamin described it), which can be seen in Leni Riefenstahl's monumental propaganda film *Triumph of the Will* (1934). Yet these patterns are only outward manifestations of deep-seated sociocultural practices and assumptions. Wolfgang Emmerich notes that underneath the veneer lie various discourses and institutions that brought forth destructive forms of behavior and damaged perceptions. These he credits Wolf with portraying insightfully: "Fear, hatred, lack of compassion, subterfuge, deception, and other forms of mimicry, obedience and loyalty and duty, without respect of persons, are presented—along with many other patterns of behavior that damage individuals and their sense of perception, warp them, and leave them to the discretion of a political system such as fascism."[13]

The narrator's life appears typical of her time. In many ways, Wolf's emphasis on the commonality of experience among her peers reflects the social structures that inhibited and persecuted difference: "Anyone believing that he detects a similarity between a character in the narrative and either himself or anyone else should consider the strange lack of individuality in the behavior of many contemporaries. Generally recognizable behavior patterns should be blamed on circumstances" (*Patterns of Childhood*, preface). Wolf heightens the ambiguity of autobiographical representation when she alerts the reader to the conditions that eventuated in a lost sense of individuality. Life during the Third Reich, from 1933 to 1945, enforced a similarity of experience that poignantly unites her generation. Wolf's personal history functions as a mirror and a collective autobiography.

Are Wolf's de-emphasis of individual experience and her decentered position results only of the time during which she grew up? In an essay on women's autobiography, Susan Stanford Friedman remarks that women's identities often reflect an awareness of their marginalization in a society dominated by men. Drawing on a psychoanalytical model developed by Nancy Chodorow, Friedman notes that women autobiographers, because of their upbringing in a different psychosocial context, display a concept of selfhood different from that of writers who are men. "We can anticipate finding

[13]Wolfgang Emmerich, "Der Kampf um die Erinnerung," in *Christa Wolf: Materialienbuch*, ed. Klaus Sauer (Darmstadt: Luchterhand, 1979), 119.

in women's texts a consciousness of self," she writes, "in which 'the individual does not oppose herself to all others,' nor 'feel herself to exist outside of others,' 'but very much with others in an interdependent existence.' "[14] Wolf's identification with a community in her work is not with a specific gender (except for her identification with her daughter), but with a generation. The form of address she selects also illustrates a relational understanding of selfhood as opposed to a self that is separate and detached. Perhaps this positioning of the self among a network of subjects accounts for the absence of both an authorial overview and a claim for full, conscious narrative control that often "drives inexorably toward unity, identity, sameness," as Shari Benstock suggests.[15]

My discussion of Wolf's reformulation of autobiographical writing does not aim at establishing a "feminine aesthetic." Instead, it proposes that women's works are informed by experiences anchored in the way women are culturally situated. Women's different sociocultural position may elicit different perspectives and methods of delivery.[16] Wolf, who has been asked on several occasions about the possibilities of a feminine aesthetic, asserts:

[14]Susan Stanford Friedman, "Women's Autobiographical Selves: Theory and Practice," in *The Private Self: Theory and Practice of Women's Autobiographical Writings,* ed. Shari Benstock (Chapel Hill: University of North Carolina Press, 1988), 41.

[15]Shari Benstock, "Authorizing the Autobiographical," in *The Private Self: Theory and Practice of Women's Autobiographical Writings,* ed. Shari Benstock (Chapel Hill: University of North Carolina Press, 1988), 19.

[16]A wealth of literature, some of it very provocative, addresses the question of a feminine aesthetic. For example, Elfriede Jelinek writes, "It seems to me that a female dramatic theory is not just directed toward purposeful telling to get to the end of a story; women fall more in love with subplots, with reflected dramatic plots that are more static, that do not stride head on, but are elliptical or circular" (Elfriede Jelinek, interview, *Deutsche Bücher* 15, ed. Ferdinand van Ingen [Amsterdam: Rodopi, 1985], 17). In *Why Is There Salt in the Sea? (Wie kommt das Salz ins Meer,* 1979), Brigitte Schwaiger presents the protagonist's grandmother's way of storytelling, which resembles Jelinek's belief. Schwaiger says: "It is rare for father to listen to grandmother's stories. They are all intricate and entangled like life itself. No beginning and no end. Meandering, always losing the thread. Grandmother doesn't want to leave out anything essential that comes along, and at the end she sits there and asks us if we remember what she wanted to tell us" (45). Schwaiger's representation does not preclude an essentialist feminine aesthetic but can be examined as an expression of women's ways of experiencing time and the many services they offer and the needs they often attend to. See also Helen Fehervary, "Autorschaft, Geschlechtsbewußtsein und Öffentlichkeit," *Argument* 92 (1982): 132–53; Sonja Hilzinger, "Weibliches Schreiben als eine Ästhetik des Widerstands," *Neue Rundschau* 96 (1985): 85–102.

To what extent is there really "female writing"? To the extent that for historical and biological reasons women experience a different reality than men do and express this. To the extent that women do not belong to the rulers, but rather to the ruled, for centuries, to the objects of the objects . . . ; to the extent that they stop wearing themselves out attempting to integrate themselves into the prevailing system of insanity. To the extent that through writing and reading they are intent on autonomy.[17]

Her autobiographical account presents the subject as emerging from historical experience and as influenced by existing institutions and discourses. On the basis of this premise, a feminine aesthetic (just as "woman") is not an essential category, ahistorical or universal, but is rather dependent on a network of contexts, as is the subject. Wolf shows how the social subject is contingent on historical and intersubjective experiences and how the subject enters into a dynamic exchange with its various contexts.

To look at *Patterns of Childhood* as autobiography requires placing this work in the context of recent discussions of autobiography that have vastly changed the face of autobiographical identity and notions of referentiality.[18] Michael Schneider, in *Die erkaltete Herzensschrift*, offers one explanation for this change: "In the twentieth century, the autobiographical text leaves the symbolic territory of truth. It breaks with the precept that once seemed to dictate its movements: the author forgoes the notion that he [*sic*] is presenting

[17]Christa Wolf, *Cassandra: A Novel and Four Essays*, trans. Jan van Heurck (New York: Farrar, Straus and Giroux, 1984). Wolf here undermines attempts to polarize male and female productions. Just as in memory research psychologists have shown that male and female ways of remembering and things remembered are not empirically distinguishable, so too Wolf shows that if gendered similarities are visible, they can be attributed to similarity of experience anchored in a historical context. This allows for change and alteration, since these categories are viewed as the effect of sociohistorical constructions.

[18]Some theorists have gone so far as to diagnose the end of autobiography altogether, since the poststructural self is seen solely as an effect of language without a referent. See Paul de Man, "Autobiography as De-facement," *Modern Language Notes* 95.5 (1979): 919–30; Michael Sprinker, "Fictions of the Self: The End of Autobiography," in *Autobiography: Essays Theoretical and Critical*, ed. James Olney (Princeton: Princeton University Press, 1980), 321–42. For a discussion of *Patterns of Childhood* as autobiography, see also Sandra Frieden, " 'In eigener Sache': Christa Wolf's *Kindheitsmuster*," *German Quarterly* 54.4 (1981): 473–87.

an authentic or truthful portrait of himself [*sic*]."[19] Schneider attributes the loss of autobiographical veracity to the introduction of other technologies that have surpassed autobiography in documentary potential. He charts a progression in which script has been displaced by photography and then by film as the medium of memory. (Wolf herself uses the metaphor of film to describe memory.) Yet with the obsolescence of logocentric thinking and its claim to truth, authenticity, and objectivity, documentary reliability has no absolute medium. In fact, Wolf manipulates autobiography to create her own aesthetic of self-exploration. In an interview with Hans Kaufmann, Wolf introduces the concept of "subjective authenticity" as the guiding impulse of autobiographical representation. She defines it as "a subject who is ready to surrender itself to its subject matter . . . without restraint; to take upon itself the myriad of tensions that become unavoidable; to be curious about the transformations that both subject matter and author then undergo. One sees a different reality than before."[20]

For Wolf, the text becomes a working station, a fabric, an arrangement of dialogues with herself; the author becomes a postmodern *bricoleur*.[21] By forging a polyvalent network of voices, Wolf not only expands narrative space, but allows for unforeseen configurations that comment on one another to produce novel insights.[22] Subjective authenticity necessitates surrendering oneself

[19]Michael Schneider, *Die erkaltete Herzensschrift: Der autobiographische Text im 20. Jahrhundert* (Munich: Hanser, 1986), 14.

[20]Christa Wolf, interview, "Subjektive Authentizität," *Die Dimension des Autors II* (Berlin: Aufbau, 1986), 324.

[21]Roland Barthes, *The Pleasure of the Text*, trans. Richard Miller (New York: Hill and Wang, 1975), 64. Here Barthes presents the function of the text: "Text means Tissue; but whereas hitherto we have always taken this tissue as a product, a ready-made veil, behind which lies, more or less hidden, meaning (truth), we are now emphasizing, in the tissue, the generative idea that the text is made, is worked out in a perpetual interweaving; lost in this tissue—this texture—the subject unmakes himself, like a spider dissolving in the constructive secretions of the web."

[22]Christa Wolf, "Erinnerte Zukunft," in *Lesen und Schreiben* (Darmstadt: Luchterhand, 1977), 220. Wolf often refers to her work as looking toward the future while looking at the past. Prose provides the space in which these two movements are simultaneously possible. Wolf states, "Prose can further extend the borders of knowledge about ourselves. It preserves the memory of a future in us from which we dare not divorce ourselves on pain of our destruction. It supports the development of a human being into a subject. It is revolutionary and realistic: it seduces and gives courage to achieve the impossible."

to the text in order to discover. As Wolf says, the chemical process of memory can be explained scientifically, but each individual combines and interprets memories differently. "If this were not so," she writes, "some people's assertions would be accurate: documents could not be surpassed; the narrator would therefore be superfluous" (*Patterns of Childhood*, 69). These documents or recordings are not static, absolute, objective sources that speak for themselves; they must be brought into contact with one another and read. As with every text, the reader (also as writer) produces its meaning. The document is thus incomplete without its storyteller. Engaged in an interpretive process, the narrator enters into dialogue with a number of texts and creates a narrative through combining and exploring alternative meanings. Through what Wolf calls "epic prose"—a term that places her work in the tradition of Bertolt Brecht's "epic theater"—the text becomes the site of discovery and provocation, with social change as its overriding project.

The problem of authenticity that Wolf grapples with throughout her work suggests a means of exploring and unearthing the various personal interests that direct and influence memory. The reproduction of authentic autobiographical materials usually entails negotiating unverifiable realms of subjective knowledge and sentiment. The child Nelly (the name Wolf gives to her autobiographical persona) believes that no one loves her. This personal experience is contrasted with publicly verifiable events like a recorded speech by Goebbels, the minister of propaganda, which can be linked directly to a certain historical time and place (*Patterns of Childhood*, 164). Juxtaposing psychological and historical events, Wolf addresses the conflict that autobiographers face in representing both kinds of events as equally valid and authentic records of the past.[23] Since the personal sphere is not tangible, it escapes empirical verification; yet it contributes most significantly to defining the author's notion of self.

By delving into what Wolf calls the substratum of consciousness, or the "Tertiär"—a geological metaphor meaning tertiary formation—she tries to locate the child she once was in order to under-

---

[23]Rolf Tarot, "Die Autobiographie," in *Prosakunst ohne Erzählen*, ed. Klaus Weissenberger (Tübingen: Niemeyer 1985), 27–43.

stand her "present-day" emotional constitution. She stages her past as in a play (she refers to "directing" Nelly through events), to relive the past at a distance, in order to observe and analyze it, a process that Freud describes as "remembering, repeating, and working through." "Working through" the past frequently occurs through mimesis: re-enactment through remembrance and articulation. Autobiographical writing then provides an analytic space in which the author can explore the past and take part in a personal work of mourning for the lost or repressed child.[24] Bernhard Greiner refers to the therapeutic, reconstructive function of Wolf's prose: "Christa Wolf's writing is writing against the ego as consciousness, for the sake of an ego that does not expend its energy resisting the repressed, but rather comes alive and becomes viable by learning to address what is oppressed and repressed in its own history."[25] Through writing, Wolf challenges many borders simultaneously, including those of her own country's memory and of historical representation.

Patterns of Childhood is structured by the tension between remembering and forgetting, a tension that partially results from recalling a period that resists memory. In her autobiographical exposé, Wolf strips away layers of time and the various shields that guard against the past. She relies on the imagination to fill in gaps. Wolf shies away from the traditional structure of narrative linearity—a source of chronological distortion—that suppresses memory. Realizing that the concerted simultaneity of events escapes consideration, she avoids a causality that leads only to perfunctory resolutions.[26] Organized as a network of lines, *Patterns of Childhood* performs "life" in its fragmentations, interruptions, and

[24]Sigmund Freud, "Remembering, Repeating, and Working Through," in *The Complete Psychological Works*, trans. and ed. James Strachey (London: Hogarth Press and the Institute of Psychoanalysis, 1966), 12: 147–66.

[25]Bernhard Greiner, " 'Mit der Erzählung gehe ich in den Tod': Kontinuität und Wandel des Erzählens im Schaffen von Christa Wolf," in *Erinnerte Zukunft*, ed. Wolfram Mauser (Würzburg: Königshausen and Neumann, 1985), 120.

[26]Christa Wolf, interview, "Dokumentation: Christa Wolf: Ein Gespräch über Kassandra," *German Quarterly* (1984): 109. Wolf discusses the plethora of events and memories in the course of a single day. To reproduce them is impossible, as she states: "One could hardly get enough paper to write down all the experiences and memories that take place in one day in the life of any fairly complex person. I am seeking to capture how a person's inner experience occurs."

recollections, with the self as the nodal point of departure and arrival. The text performs the "switches" that Jean-François Lyotard has identified as symptomatic of the postmodern condition by moving from one event to another through various temporal and spatial territories all connected by the narrator.[27] Wolf describes the act of composing her self-portrait: "When one begins, one writes, for example, in a linear manner. In my opinion that was very thin—'thin' in the sense that: space was not being filled. It was a line, but not space."[28] The nonlinear montage allows for the juxtaposition of scenes that comment on one another and leave room for conjecture and associations, or the expression of "the eerie" ("das Gespenstische"), as the German writer Heinrich Böll notes in referring to the Third Reich.

Wolf not only engages in the work of memory, she concomitantly structures her text according to the associative ways in which memory works. Memory itself, along with childhood, becomes the object of intense investigation. Wolf views the properties and functions of memory from a variety of angles: etymological, denotative, scientific, and artistic. She compares memory to a computer, discussing the uncertainty of it and its role in structuring and defining societies and civilizations. Moreover, autobiographical memory produces self-awareness.[29] It secures identity; without memory, the self would continuously dissipate with each passing second and therefore remain without a history or past, without orientation. The self, so to speak, is a composition of past tenses that memory stores. The autobiographer comments: "The present intrudes upon remembrance, today becomes the last day of the past. Yet we would suffer continuous estrangement from ourselves if it weren't for our memory of the things we have done, of the things that have happened to us. If it weren't for the memory of

[27]Jean-François Lyotard, interview, "Der Appell des großen Anderen," *Tageszeitung*, 22 March 1986, p. 11. For a catalogue of the different levels of narration in *Patterns of Childhood*, see Christel Zahlmann, "*Kindheitsmuster*: Schreiben an der Grenze des Bewußtseins," in *Erinnerte Zukunft*, ed. Wolfram Mauser (Würzburg: Königshausen and Neuman, 1985), 143.

[28]Christa Wolf, "Erfahrungsmuster," in *Die Dimension des Autors* II (Berlin: Aufbau, 1986), 353.

[29]For a discussion of memory and autobiography as well as a chapter on *Kindheitsmuster*, see Barbara Saunders, *Contemporary German Autobiography: Literary Approaches to the Problem of Identity* (Leeds, England: W. S. Maney and Sons, 1986).

ourselves" (*Patterns of Childhood*, 4).[30] Memory is the archive of self-knowledge where images are stored, catalogued, retouched, revised, reinscribed, and repressed. They cannot be retrieved verbatim. Even if the events they encapsulate are preserved by technology, memories pass through a filter of emotional and referential "investments." As Wolf recognizes, memories are tendentious, enmeshed with wishes, desires, and fears; they are remembered and thus recomposed with each changing reference point. Above all, they are dependent on the autobiographer's present-day questions and concerns. Sigmund Freud, Richard King says, was among the first to point out "the terribly complicated and intimate connection between present and past, reality and fantasy. . . . What Freud came to see was that 'interest'—the interweaving of desire and defense—put memory in its service; behind all the rigorous probings of memory stood the wish. . . . There are no disinterested registrations of the perceptual present nor disinterested memories of the past."[31]

Wolf selects divergent events to interpret the effects on her present and future life of her ideological upbringing under fascism. The central questions are: "How did we become what we are today?" (*Patterns of Childhood*, 209), what lasting effects are passed from generation to generation, and what psychic structures formed? The task of answering these questions is immensely difficult for Wolf, since the memories she attempts to release are not the nostalgic materials of some autobiographies, but rather events and sentiments that produce shame and discomfort in the present. The difficult questions of how to enter the past in order

---

[30]Luis Buñuel, *My Last Sigh*, trans. Abigail Israel (New York: Alfred Knopf, 1983), 4–5. The filmmaker Luis Buñuel, best known for his provocative surrealist films, reflects: "You have to begin to lose your memory, if only in bits and pieces, to realize that memory is what makes our lives. Life without memory is no life at all, just as an intelligence without the possibility of expression is not really an intelligence. Our memory is our coherence, our reason, our feeling, even our action. Without it we are nothing. . . . Our imagination, and our dreams, are forever invading our memories; and since we are all apt to believe in the reality of our fantasies, we end up transforming our lies into truths. Of course, fantasy and reality are equally personal, and equally felt, so their confusion is a matter of only relative importance."

[31]Richard King, "Memory and Phantasy," *Modern Language Notes* 98.5 (1983): 1197–98.

to remember the revealing moments and how to flesh out the patterns of behavior transmitted by the ideologies of the Third Reich are compounded by Wolf's emotional reservation about the child Nelly. In other words, Wolf confronts the additional problem of awakening the child in herself, whom she actually dislikes, and who has in part been repressed. Her memories are tinged with ambivalence.[32] "The closer she [Nelly] gets to you in time, the less familiar she becomes," she reflects, "or do you think that one can understand someone one is ashamed of? To protect someone one mistrusts in order to defend oneself?" (*Patterns of Childhood*, 211). The narrator struggles to apprehend the child whom the adult has avoided and tried to forget. The memories Wolf endeavors to recall have been buried, preferably to be forgotten, not only by the individual but by a whole nation. Years later the child is being revived.[33]

Despite the preface, Wolf never denies the autobiographical status of her work. On the contrary:

Nowhere do I conceal that this deals with so-called autobiographical material, this has not been kept secret. However, this "so-called" is important, since there is no identity there. But there is—this is one of the peculiarities of my biography—but maybe others in my age group feel the same way—a feeling of estrangement toward this time. Not from a particular day on, but certainly beginning with a precise moment within a space of time, the feeling of no longer being this person. I no longer have the feeling that I was the one who thought, said, or did that. And that is what I wanted to express by using the third person. In other words, I had to, because I would not have gained access to the material otherwise, as I found out through experimentation.[34]

[32]Margarete Mitscherlich, "Die Frage der Selbstdarstellung," *Neue Rundschau* 91.2/3 (1980): 308–16. Mitscherlich observes that when Wolf undertakes her autobiography at the age of 45, she is motivated perhaps by the realization of her own mortality through her mother's death, which occurs shortly before she begins to confront her own past. This supports my belief that many autobiographies are written in a time of crisis.

[33]See Bernhard Greiner, "Die Schwierigkeit, 'ich' zu sagen: Christa Wolfs psychologische Orientierung des Erzählens," *Deutsche Vierteljahresschrift* 55 (1981): 333–43.

[34]Christa Wolf, "Erfahrungsmuster," 358.

Wolf's attempt to locate the child so distanced (pushed so far away) from her heightens the anguish of claiming her past. Like the child in Pablo Neruda's poem "Book of Questions" (which is an epigraph to Wolf's autobiographical exploration), the protagonist Nelly is allegedly deceased metaphorically. Yet the patterns Nelly has learned during her most formative years cannot be extinguished, much in the same way that history cannot be severed from the present or future. The child's voice "speaks," unrecognized and undetected; it is part of the inner psychic structure, even if the author feels dissociated from this past self. Wolf realizes the necessity of reclaiming the child in herself who has been exiled into the subconscious, disowned and abandoned, since she continues to influence the adult's gestures, perspectives, and reactions. In an interview given years after the publication of *Patterns of Childhood*, Wolf explained how these patterns persist if they are not dealt with, despite any heightened self-awareness.[35]

The successful identification of the patterns permits their release from the subconscious and the conflation of the second- and third-person pronouns. The integration of these voices is ultimately expressed with the pronoun "I." "The final point would be reached," Wolf writes, "when the second and the third person were to meet again in the first or, better still, were to meet with the first person. When it would no longer have to be 'you' and 'she' but a candid, unreserved 'I' " (*Patterns of Childhood*, 349). This conflation, tainted by the nostalgic hope of a future unity of subject, as Wolf conditionally reflects, will hardly be achieved. Although the author gains access to the past by using the third person, her use of it exhibits the continued disparity of past and present and, more important, allows for distance between the subject and object of inquiry. The third person in autobiography, Philippe Lejeune suggests, "is more often used for internal distancing and for expressing personal confrontation. [It] brings both relief and tension to the text."[36] The second- and third-person pronouns may well be the only forms of address viably sustained within the contemporary autobiographical project. Use of the third person functions as a more honest auto-

---

[35]Christa Wolf, "Unerledigte Widersprüche," in *Im Dialog* (Darmstadt: Luchterhand, 1990), 25.

[36]Philippe Lejeune, "Autobiography in the Third Person," *New Literary History* 9 (1977): 28–29.

biographical practice, since the subject-in-process is virtually always changing; the subject is always repositioned within a dynamic historical context and therefore can never be the same as the past self. The resort to the third person at the same time shows the subject to be admittedly fragmented and undermines traditional notions of the autobiographical self as whole and virtually "all-knowing." Through Nelly, Wolf gains access to the past and journeys into the "Tertiär."[37]

Wolf's unorthodox appropriation of autobiographical representation, implied by her disclaimer, by her self-referential discussion of memory, as well as by the reference to fiction throughout her text and the designation "novel" in the West German edition, resembles a postmodernist defiance of boundaries. Perhaps, however, the cautionary tone underlying Wolf's autobiographical inquiry is more indicative of the changes that occurred after World War II and of a profound mistrust of perception experienced by those who lived during the Third Reich.

A Dialogue of Tenses

When Freud first analyzed repression in 1915, he identified it as a reflex that shields the ego from "undesirable guests" by "rejecting and keeping something out of consciousness."[38] Of course, long before the emergence of psychoanalytic discourse, language had already provided a means of such escape from the undesirable or the uncomfortable. Language provided one with the means to neutralize confrontation, to bury the past, and to look forward without looking back, lest, like Lot's wife, one were turned into salt.[39] One

[37]Christa Wolf, "Gedächtnis und Gedenken Fred Wander: *Der siebente Brunnen*," in *Lesen and Schreiben* (Darmstadt: Luchterhand, 1980), 187. Wolf quotes a woman as saying: "Fascism—that for me is 'Tertiär' " (187). It becomes an interesting insight for Wolf, since she sees her generation's subconscious as having been structured by fascism.

[38]Sigmund Freud, "Repression," in *General Psychological Theory* (New York: Macmillan, 1963), 110–11.

[39]Theodor W. Adorno, "Was bedeutet: Aufarbeitung der Vergangenheit," in *Eingriffe: Neun kritische Modelle* (Frankfurt am Main: Suhrkamp, 1963), 128. Adorno, speaking in psychological terms, addresses the negative connotation of guilt. Western culture sees the "healthy" personality, Adorno postulates, epitomized in the Faust figure who forges ahead, leaving the past behind. In fact, Mephistopheles' main goal is revealed as the destruction of memory.

way to armor the conscious is through "forgetting," a process consciously or unconsciously activated and used by both individuals and societies. Jane Flax describes repression as "an ongoing process in which knowledge about the self or its relations to others becomes inaccessible to consciousness. For Freud, repression is an active, repetitive process designed to insure that this knowledge or material remains inaccessible, is split off from and unavailable to the mind's capacity for recall, thought, and memory."[40] Repression is not a casual or conscious act of forgetting. As psychoanalytic critics have insisted, memories are deliberately "screened" off from consciousness, so that we, as Flax reminds us, "forget that we 'forgot' something."[41] Repression allows human beings to function, but only tenuously. Ultimately, the greater the refusal to face the past, the more disabling and debilitating it becomes, because of the energy expended in sequestering the forgotten and keeping it dormant. The repressed continues to reside in the unconscious and "to have a powerful effect on our internal experience and sense of self."[42] Since repressed material never disappears, the possibility of its emergence hauntingly persists.

As Freud explains in his lectures, detecting the repressed is often a matter of glimpsing its fleeting manifestation. The narratives of the repressed often betray themselves through incidental remarks, transferences, "Freudian slips," or speechlessness (aphasia). Often the stories that resist being told are those most likely to signal the tip of an iceberg. It is precisely the censored slippages or unnatural absences that lead to discovery. Quoting from Virginia Woolf's diary, Shari Benstock shows that the autobiographer is often aware of another stratum of consciousness which does not find any direct outlet, but manifests itself in "invisible presences."[43] In reference

[40]Jane Flax, "Re-membering the Selves: Is the Repressed Gendered?" *Michigan Quarterly Review* 26.1 (1987): 94.

[41]Ibid.

[42]Ibid. Freud's structural theory of repression shows that the subject does not have full control of itself and is not the "master of its own house." Consciousness is always influenced, determined or being upset by repressed forces and conscious memory, as well as our feelings and desires. These forces can never be fully known.

[43]Benstock, "Authorizing the Autobiographical," 27. She points out that Virginia Woolf is referring to women's stories that are suppressed in literary history. See also Jane Gallop, "The Father's Seduction," in *Daughters and Fathers*, ed. Lynda E. Boose and Betty S. Flowers (Baltimore: Johns Hopkins University Press, 1989), 97–110.

to her own collection of autobiographical entries, Virginia Woolf notes: "As an account of my life they are misleading, because the things one does not remember are as important; perhaps they are more important."[44]

Christa Wolf, in her own self-analysis, sets out to probe the events overlooked. Recapitulating her recent visit to L. (her birthplace, Landsberg an der Warthe, today in the Polish province Gorzów), she reflects on the nausea she experienced when she left a café and remembered that the Hitler Youth headquarters had been located down the street. At the time, she neglected to visit this place that she often frequented as a child. She later interprets her oversight as unconscious avoidance, triggered by the effect the house used to have on Nelly. Retrospectively, Wolf concludes, "Nelly never walked into that house without being overcome with fear, and never walked out without a feeling of relief" (*Patterns of Childhood*, 232). Recognition of the omission appears to have opened a door to the forgotten, to lead Wolf closer to excavating the memories of her childhood. As she acknowledges, there are many blind spots that obstruct perception and self-knowledge, and create absences. Once one resituates oneself, to extend Wolf's metaphor, a clear view opens that allows for valuable insight. Is it not possible that precisely these hidden and forgotten pasts are often those that wield the most power?

Everyone finds out, if they ever find out about themselves—that they have a blind spot in every phase of their lives. Something they do not see. It is linked to their ability to perceive, to their personal history. And a society or a civilization has a blind spot as well. This spot is precisely what produces self-destruction. The point is not to circumscribe it but to go into it, into the eye of the hurricane, so to speak: in my opinion, this is the task of literature. This often takes the form of self-exploration, because I, you, every one of us, due to our upbringing and socialization, are a part of this civilization. The Enlightenment neglected this spot because it concentrated only on reason.[45]

[44]Benstock, "Authorizing the Autobiographical," 27.
[45]Christa Wolf, "Dokumentation: Christa Wolf: Ein Gespräch über Kassandra," 114.

The blind spot is registered in the subconscious, which literature, in its utopian aspiration, illuminates. Through her writing, Wolf persistently attempts to push beyond the borders of consciousness to release memories that are stifled by fear and guilt.[46]

The investigation of blind spots or lacunae is symptomatic of her work in general. In *No Place on Earth* (*Kein Ort. Nirgends*, 1979), for example, an imaginary meeting between the Romantic writers Karoline von Günderrode and Heinrich von Kleist leads to the articulation and contemplation of what Wolf refers to as the "feminine and intellectual elements" that are sequestered and exiled to the borders of societies.[47] In *The Quest for Christa T.* (*Nachdenken über Christa T.*, 1971), Wolf reflects on the damage caused by adapting or conforming to social norms at the cost of forfeiting personal hopes and desires and the loss of individuality. In *Cassandra* (1983), she rewrites the Cassandra legend by restoring the prophetess's power of speech and credibility, which Apollo revoked after giving her the gift of foretelling the future. Wolf revives the voices that have been socially suppressed because of their resistance to oppression, dehumanization, and destruction.[48] In *Patterns of Childhood*, it is suggested that neglect of the blind spot fosters complicity with the ideologies of fascism. For Wolf, the stories that need to be examined are those that explain the coming of the Third Reich and its twelve-year duration.

In *Patterns of Childhood*, Wolf attempts to break down what she figuratively refers to as the fortifications that surround individual memory, or the storehouse of personal histories. She looks behind the "Medaillons," or legends that have become pat explanations

---

[46]See Christel Zahlmann, "Kindheitsmuster: Schreiben an der Grenze des Bewußtseins," in *Erinnerte Zukunft*, ed. Wolfram Mauser (Würzburg: Königshausen and Neumann, 1985).

[47]Christa Wolf, interview, "Culture Is What You Experience," *New German Critique* 27 (1982): 90. Wolf began *No Place on Earth* in 1976, a time of intense and open artistic repression in the former GDR, culminating in the expatriation of songwriter Wolf Biermann, the arrest of writer Jürgen Fuchs, and the house arrest of scientist Robert Havemann, a vocal critic of the former GDR government. Authors such as Reiner Kunze and Sarah Kirsch moved to the West around the same time. Although *Patterns of Childhood* was relatively well received, Wolf admits her sense of isolation and the pressure she felt in being marginalized and turned into an outsider.

[48]See Ortrud Gutjahr, in "Erinnerte Zukunft," in *Erinnerte Zukunft*, ed. Wolfram Mauser (Würzburg: Königshausen and Neumann, 1985), 53–80.

of the past. They are often calcified images that constitute a personal repertoire of the self as well as historical understanding.[49] A state of embattlement is implied in the image of fortifications, which hints at blocking and silencing memories that destabilize equilibrium and threaten the status quo. The fortification called consciousness guards and preserves the self, fossilizing patterns of behavior, and imprisons one within its walls along with the past. Dreams, which Wolf profusely records, deliver one possibility of slipping past the borders of consciousness. Yet what would happen if these threatening memories were released, Wolf provocatively asks?

> But twenty-nine years later you have to ask yourself how many encapsulated vaults a memory can accommodate before it must cease to function. How much energy and what kind of energy is it continually expending in order to seal and to reseal the capsules whose walls may in time rot and crumble. You'll have to ask what would become of all of us if we allowed the locked spaces in our memories to open and spill their contents before us. But memory's recall—which incidentally varies markedly in people who seem to have had the exact same experience—may not be a matter of biochemistry, and may not universally be a matter of choice. (*Patterns of Childhood*, 69)

Wolf argues that it is essential, no matter how painful, to search for the voices that have escaped language. For her, they are embodied in Nelly. They are the child buried in the unconscious who has been repressed and banned by collective and individual memory. When the adult narrator asks, "What are we to do with the things that are engraved in our memories?" (*Patterns of Childhood*, 309), the answer that Wolf pursues lies in bringing the patterns to an analytical level of awareness by remembering and working through them. Memory here serves as a strategy of resistance.[50]

---

[49]Christa Wolf, "Medaillons," in *Lesen und Schreiben* (Darmstadt: Luchterhand, 1980), 23–27.

[50]The process of remembering is a way of creating an identity. See Margaret Lourie et al., eds., "Women and Memory," *Michigan Quarterly Review* 26.1 (1987): 3. According to the editors of the special issue entitled "Memory and Women," "the practice of remembering, as the emblem of the Women's Studies enterprise, marks the desire to bring to consciousness all that the symbolic system represses

For those who grew up under Germany's fascist regime, resuscitating past scenes means confronting a period in history which has been disavowed and sealed off from public and private consciousness.[51] Wolf points out the extent to which the mechanisms of repression have been activated within her generation and preceding generations: "Love and death, illness, health, fear and hope left a deep impression in one's memory. Events that have been poured through the filter of a consciousness that is not sure of itself—sieved, diluted, stripped of their reality—disappear almost without a trace. Years without memory which follow the beginning years. Years during which suspicion of sensory experience keeps growing. Only our contemporaries have had to forget so much in order to continue functioning" (*Patterns of Childhood*, 387).

Wolf stands before a past that has been collectively kept at bay, forgotten, disowned, and avoided until the 1970s, when the work of mourning became a discursive event, more in West Germany than in the former German Democratic Republic.[52] A probe of the unconscious involves a highly subjective confrontation with the narrator's own biography in which she endeavors to illuminate not only the blind spot in her own psychic structure (the work of

---

in order to maintain and perpetuate itself: a return of the repressed, as Julia Kristeva has pointed out, that has the power to disturb, subvert, and transform the existing paternal order."

[51]Language of avoidance assists the process of "forgetting," or erasure. For example, Wolf points to the ideological motivation behind the terminological change of "Flüchtlinge" (refugees) to "Umsiedler" (resettlers) to describe the floods of people who left the northeastern parts of Germany for sanctuary in the West (*Patterns of Childhood*, 297). In "Was bedeutet: Aufarbeitung der Vergangenheit," Adorno also mentions that there is an inevitably neurotic relationship to the past, with the development of defense mechanisms where there is no attack and a euphemistic language designed to shield (deny?) what happened in German history. Adorno points to the usage of the term "Kristallnacht" ("night of broken glass") as such a circuitous transcription. Ironically, the fall of the Berlin Wall in 1989 shares the same date–November 9–with the Kristallnacht.

[52]Christa Wolf, interview, "Dokumentation: Christa Wolf: Eine Diskussion über Kindheitsmuster," *German Quarterly* (1984): 91. When asked why so many works of the 1970s in what used to be both Germanies dealt with the Third Reich and why such works were not written sooner, Wolf responded that it took a long time to recover from the shock of 1945. Even though she was a child at the time and never directly involved in the atrocities that occurred, her generation was too deeply affected to be able to confront the topic of Nazi Germany right away.

psychoanalysis) but also the blind spot of society (the work of history). West Germany's symbolic "Zero Hour" in 1945 allegedly signaled a rebirth during which the experiences of the Third Reich were excised from consciousness, but past tendencies were only hidden behind proclamations.[53]

In Wolf's own country, the former German Democratic Republic, a similar disavowal took place. East Germany's legitimization rested on being the antifascist German state because of a more stringent de-nazification program and an official allegiance to the Soviet tradition. German fascism was henceforth conveniently projected onto the West. Marc Silberman notes that "finally, West Germany is considered to be the legal historical and ideological heir to the forces which led to fascism—namely, monopoly capitalism."[54] The former GDR's detachment from Germany's fascist past is shown by the omission of such names as Adolf Eichmann and the chemical corporation I. G. Farben from the history book studied by Lenka, the narrator's daughter. Wolf also draws attention to the lack of sensitivity toward the past exhibited by workers walking within the grounds of Auschwitz with blaring transistor radios. Beginning with her own biography, the indispensable point of departure for her, Wolf tries to release repressed remembrances within herself and to initiate a dialogue with others.

Patterns of Childhood is one of the first works written in the former GDR to break through the long tradition of silence and denial of the National Socialist past. Works such as Hermann Kant's *Der Aufenthalt* (The sojourn, 1977), Karl Heinz Jacobs's *Wilhelmsburg* (1979), or Heiner Müller's *Germania Tod in Berlin* (Germania death in Berlin, 1977) also belong to the so-called second wave of literature that dealt with the fascist past. Their authors set themselves off from the prescribed ideological format that previously marked the GDR's literary tradition of antifascism and what Marc Silberman calls its "established pattern which lays out motivations, causal

---

[53]In the film *One, Two, Three* (1961), the German-born filmmaker Billy Wilder parodies the artificiality of Germany's de-nazification program and pokes fun at the seductions of capitalism. Filming was briefly interrupted by the building of the Berlin Wall.

[54]Marc Silberman, "Writing What—for Whom? Vergangenheitsbewältigung in GDR Literature," *German Studies Review* 10.3 (1987): 528.

connections and evidence of the rise of fascism."[55] The conventions of the social-realist tradition stressed enlightened transformations: a soldier or one-time supporter of the Nazi party becomes a deserter, or else the narrative of resistance is celebrated. As Wolf observes, the canon of postwar GDR literature neglected to address her own experiences.[56] Because the normative literature was based on producing memory in support of a national myth of resistance and party-line politics, the effects of the repressed everyday mechanisms of fascism continued to exert hidden pressures. Wolf's work contrasts with the normative literature by situating the individual within the historical process and the petty bourgeois milieu of her family and by examining the various exchanges between and among individuals, family, and society.[57] Wolf portrays neither the heroes nor the exceptions; instead the focus of her autobiographical portrait is a child who lived within family structures distinctly formed by historical experience.

Wolf explores the structures that influenced her psychological development. Efforts to homogenize and regiment Germany's youth, she concludes, laid a precarious emotional foundation. Messages of Spartan obedience, discipline, and subservience promoted self-denial, self-deception, and the eventual loss of individuality.[58] The connections between emotional debility and a youth spent under the regimens of the Third Reich are illustrated in scenes that range from Nelly's realization that "obeying and being loved amount to one and the same thing" (*Patterns of Childhood*, 14–15)

[55]Ibid., 534. See also Peter Hohendahl and Patricia Herminghouse, eds., *Literatur der DDR in den siebziger Jahren* (Frankfurt am Main: Suhrkamp, 1983).

[56]Christa Wolf, "Erfahrungsmuster," 351: "I am a little bothered that many of our books dealing with these times end with heroes who quickly change, with heroes who actually even arrive at important and correct insights during the time of fascism, both politically and in a humanitarian sense. I do not want to challenge any other author's experience. But my experience was different. I found that it took a long time before tiny insights at first and then later more far-reaching changes became possible."

[57]Weber, "Über Christa Wolfs Schreibart," 39.

[58]Christa Wolf, "Tabula rasa," in *Lesen und Schreiben: Neue Sammlung* (Darmstadt: Luchterhand, 1980), 18–23. Other controlling mechanisms were censorship and surveillance. In the entry titled "Tabula rasa," Wolf refers to the dearth of literature caused by strict controls and a more oppressive inscription of patterns consistent with one doctrine.

to enactments of overtly aggressive and hostile teachings of nationalism and anti-Semitism.[59] As Wolf shows, both the private sphere and the public sphere structure the subject for either denial or disguise. Nelly learns not to cry; she ought to be brave and to practice self-control. The narrator mentions the difficulty of attaining clarity and the unresolved moral conflicts the child experiences. Fear and anxiety are among the most powerful emotions that impede self-exploration and compassion. For example, the autobiographer remembers Nelly's feelings after witnessing Jews escaping from burning synagogues on Kristallnacht, the "night of broken glass," when Jewish homes, businesses, and synagogues were attacked: "It would not have taken much for Nelly to have succumbed to an improper emotion: compassion. But healthy German common sense built a barrier against it: fear" (*Patterns of Childhood*, 160–61).

Wolf describes other barriers, too. When Nelly in a fit of rage against her teacher destroys a number of flower pots, her mother admonishes her to be reasonable. The narrator turns the phrase around. Rather than interrupt introspection and deaden curiosity (which "be reasonable" has come to mean), she calls for heightened self-reflection in order to overcome the alienation from her feelings: "Understanding and listening to reason. Thus: come to one's senses. (Come to your senses!)" (92). The parenthetical imperative signals the voice of the present-day author who desires to know herself and to examine her situation as subject within the historical experience of the Third Reich, thereby regaining the ability to mourn. Such impulses as remembering and mourning that potentially intervene in (historical) repetitions were prevented, if not

[59]Child-rearing practices particularly common during the first half of the twentieth century came under scrutiny in the 1970s. Autobiographical texts assisted in revealing the strict and often brutal measures that were traditionally used to raise children and, more important, the effects of this upbringing. Much of this tradition stems from Lutheran teachings based on the concept "Spare the rod, spoil the child." German psychoanalyst Alice Miller has done extensive work on what she calls "Schwarze Pädagogik" or "poisonous pedagogy." See Alice Miller, *For Your Own Good: Hidden Cruelty in Child-Rearing and the Roots of Violence*, trans. Hildegard Hannum and Hunter Hannum (New York: Farrar, Straus and Giroux, 1983), and *Thou Shalt Not Be Aware: Society's Betrayal of the Child*, trans. Hildegard Hannum and Hunter Hannum (New York: Meridian, 1986). Also see Guntram Vogt, "Kindheit und Jugend im Faschismus. Zur literarischen Verarbeitung eines Wirklichkeitsverlusts," *Diskussion Deutsch* (1986): 271–91.

subsumed, by what Alice Miller calls the "poisonous pedagogy" that played an integral role in the oppressive child-rearing process in Germany. Wolf remarks upon the slow calcification of emotion: "You realize that the emotions which you have suppressed will take revenge, and you understand their strategy to the last detail: they apparently withdraw, taking related emotions with them. Now it's no longer just the mourning and pain that are non-existent but regret and, above all, memory, as well. Memory of homesickness, mourning and regret. Taking an ax to the root. Emotions are not yet fused with words: in the future emotions will not be governed by spontaneity but—no use avoiding the word—by calculation" (*Patterns of Childhood*, 275). The progressive internalization of ideological structures contributed to her losing trust in her own ability to judge, see, and feel.

Repression, then, commonly associated with the harvest of the postwar years is the result of a way of living cultivated during the Third Reich. Wolf wonders: what conditions fostered this disavowal? What grids were imposed upon experience that made the blind spots more pervasive than at any other time? How could a whole population plead amnesia, and how does it deal with its conscience? She calls this lived forgetting a chronic blindness. Many closed down their senses and stopped seeing, disregarding their everyday experiences and censoring their own speech and actions. Wolf is interested in remembering the events shrouded in silence. When Nelly's mother, Charlotte Jordan, supplies a Ukrainian prisoner of war about to give birth with strips of sheets to clothe the baby, she discovers that many men and women in the labor camps are dying. Nelly quickly senses from the atmosphere and her mother's expression that the subject is taboo. "Nelly knows what is expected of her," Wolf writes; "she plays deaf and dumb. And that's what she became" (68).

Wolf describes the nuances that separate knowing from not knowing. She recounts the death of her aunt Jette, a victim of Germany's euthanasia program, and remembers the stifled reactions of her family. Yet, repression often finds physical expression, as when Jette's twin sister Lucie experiences violent migraine headaches and vomiting. Even Nelly's mother, who is characterized as straightforward and outspoken, maintains a strict silence, although for a fleeting moment her face betrays alarm and fear. Such dis-

turbing events widen the blind spot until their occurrence is
blocked out of sight—that is, out of mind. When a Communist
who survived the concentration camp wonders, "Where on earth
have you all been living?" (39)—a sentence that brands itself in
Nelly's memory—he refers to an obstructed and a selective perception. The narrator's daughter, Lenka, born long after the war,
cannot comprehend the issue of the simultaneity of knowing and
not wanting to know, of being there and not being there. Wolf
calls this phenomenon of seeing while not seeing "the ghastly
secret of human beings in this century" (42). For her, the ability
to experience this duality is no less of an enigma. "Anyone who
later affirmed that he had not known about the concentration
camps," she asserts, "had completely forgotten that their establishment had been reported in the papers. (A bewildering suspicion: they really had forgotten. Completely. Total war: total
amnesia)" (39). Through autobiographical inquiry, the narrator reviews what the child learned not to see, much less understand:
the tension between her parents, the forbidden words, the burning
synagogues, and later the deep silences of people released from
concentration camps. She seeks to articulate the unspeakable in
order to prevent its recurrence.

Wolf shows how Nelly's upbringing predisposes her to avoid
and deny, a tendency that continued despite the contradictions
within the self that increased toward the end of World War II,
when the slogans and promises one had learned to obey and believe
in lost their meaning. Ideals, beliefs, and behavior had to be re-
routed and another identity adopted. For those like Wolf, who to
an extent identified with the fatherland and its figurehead, the
dogma and gestures they had learned were hardly rehabilitated or
forgotten after a certain date or with a changed border. As many
writers point out, attitudinal shifts resulted from defeat by outside
forces, not changes in personal desires and needs. Right after the
war, when Germans were caught between fronts, allegiances became strategies of survival, often dependent on the politics of the
occupied zone and on opportunism. In his review of Horst Bienek's
Earth and Fire, Andreas Huyssen observes that the fall of the Third
Reich marked not a change of consciousness but rather a change
of costume.[60] Since the effects of fascism had settled into every

[60]Horst Bienek, *Earth and Fire*, reviewed by Andreas Huyssen, *New York Times
Book Review*, 15 January 1989, p. 26.

gesture and into the banalities of daily life, self-censorship and repression continued. Nelly's need to learn another form of greeting to replace the Nazi greeting she used when growing up illustrates both the changes and the way ideology had become a natural reflex.

The trauma of loss and disillusionment, as well as the need to reconstruct a new identity, was not addressed publicly in either East or West Germany. In *The Inability to Mourn* (*Die Unfähigkeit zu trauern*), Alexander and Margarete Mitscherlich comment on the unsettling absence of a psychological reaction to the end of the war in 1945 and speculate on the emotional vacuum that must have followed the loss of Hitler, the object of desire and narcissistic identification. I quote a passage from the Mitscherlichs' book to illuminate the psychic processes that have become the focus for much discussion:

> To millions of Germans the loss of the Führer . . . was not the loss of someone ordinary; identifications that had filled a central function in the lives of his followers were attached to his person. As we said, he had become the embodiment of their ego-ideal. The loss of an object so highly cathected with libidinal energy—one about whom nobody had any doubts, nor dared to have any, even when the country was being reduced to rubble—was indeed reason for melancholia. Through the catastrophe not only was the German ego-ideal robbed of the support of reality, but in addition the Führer himself was exposed by the victors as a criminal of truly monstrous proportions. With this sudden reversal of his qualities, the ego of every single German individual suffered a central devaluation and impoverishment. This creates at least the prerequisites for melancholia.[61]

When Nelly is faced with the overwhelming realization of the war atrocities committed by a government (a leader) to which she had devoted herself, her inner world collapses. Yet, Nelly cannot mourn, for the work of mourning requires that one separate from the person (or object) mourned. Nelly's fall into melancholia and illness suggests a strong identification with and even an internal-

---

[61]Alexander Mitscherlich and Margarete Mitscherlich, *The Inability to Mourn: Principles of Collective Behavior*, trans. Beverly R. Placzek (New York: Grove Press, 1975), 26.

ization of the figure and principles she had learned to believe in.[62] The following years are spent rechanneling and repressing the premises on which she bases her identity. Yet the acts of forgetting and suppressing manifest themselves in the body through migraine headaches and sleeplessness. Nelly's father, Bruno Jordan, reacts with resignation after returning from a Soviet prisoner-of-war camp. He silently shakes his head when he hears of the heinous crimes committed.

Working through such personal histories is a long, arduous process that few have undertaken even today. Theodor Adorno contends that Germany's thwarted work of mourning stems from the sociopsychological mechanisms he sees rooted in Germany's history. The structures hauntingly persist even more acutely in the former GDR, where one authoritarian system was exchanged for another and what playwright Heiner Müller calls "the Stalinist fiction of socialism" prevailed.[63] Patterns of Childhood confirms that Adorno's 1963 observation still applies: "National Socialism continues to live on and even today we do not know whether only as the specter of what was so monstrous that it appeared at the moment of its own demise; the question is whether the readiness to commit the unspeakable festers in human beings and in the relations that they embrace."[64] Wolf's autobiography speaks to the necessity of understanding oneself within a historical process. She begins her exploration by acknowledging the continuity of history and thus rejecting the ideological notion that 1945 was a year of total renewal. The first sentence of the narrative, a leitmotif of her project, reads: "What is past is not dead; it is not even past. We cut ourselves off from it; we pretend to be strangers" (Patterns of Childhood, 3). The past shapes the present.[65] As the narrator shows,

[62]Heinrich Böll, "Wo habt ihr bloß gelebt?" in Christa Wolf Materialienbuch, ed. Klaus Sauer (Darmstadt: Luchterhand, 1979), 10. Böll describes Nelly's pledge of loyalty in her diary and declaration of unyielding devotion to the "Führer" following Germany's defeat and the impending trauma of loss. Regarding the process of mourning in Christa Wolf's work, see Roland H. Wiegenstein, "Kassandra hat viele Gesichter," Merkur 74 (1977): 989–1006, and Uwe Wittstock, Über die Fähigkeit zu trauern (Frankfurt am Main: Athenäum, 1987).

[63]Heiner Müller, "Plädoyer für den Widerspruch," Neues Deutschland, 14 December 1989, p. 5.

[64]Adorno, "Was bedeutet: Aufarbeitung der Vergangenheit," 125.

[65]Christel Zahlmann, Christa Wolfs Reise "ins Tertiär": Eine literaturpsychologische

an emotional continuum inevitably exists for those who grew up under the Third Reich and for the generations that follow.[66]

Wolf belongs to the generation that, according to Germany's chancellor Helmut Kohl (born in 1930), was privileged with "the blessing of being born late" ("Gnade der späten Geburt"). This generation was spared the historical guilt of having participated in the Third Reich. Moreover, the phase implicitly absolves those who grew up during twelve years of fascist rule from any responsibility for its deeds. Kohl's absolution, however, summarily dismisses the traces inevitably left on children whose formative years were spent under the Hitler regime. It appears to be yet another effort to disavow the past and to deny its impact on personal development. Addressing Germany's fascist past and remembering her own childhood in her acceptance speech for the Scholl Prize, Wolf dissociates herself from Kohl's claim: "The memory of the horror that haunted me for many years also reappeared once I had grasped what my contemporaries and I were reared and ordained for. I have never been able to feel anything like 'blessed' by the late timing of my birth, or anything like an absolution from responsibility, but only this horror at the ability to be seduced by an insane system of inhumanity."[67]

Wolf is acutely aware of the dangers inherent in neglecting and even disowning a past that needs to be uncovered if history is not to repeat itself. At the end of the *Tractatus Logico-Philosophicus*,

---

Studie zu "Kindheitsmuster" (Würzburg: Königshausen and Neumann, 1986), 88. In her psychoanalytical analysis of *Patterns of Childhood*, Zahlmann detects manifestations of "Nelly" in the present-day writer. For example, the manner in which scenes are discussed and the events highlighted reveals a specific psychogram: "The emotional participation in descriptions of violent acts is striking, the thorough and precise detail, and in part the strong identification, particularly with victims of violence." Although an interesting analysis, at times Zahlmann draws conclusions that seem too causal and sweeping.

[66]The "evidence" of continuity is still present. For example, in January 1989 a right-wing group won a surprisingly large number of votes and eleven seats in the parliament of West Berlin. The trend has continued on into the 1990s, with the "Republikaner" winning seats in other provinces of Germany such as Baden-Württemberg. Their platform calls for the expulsion of foreigners. One of the group's spokespersons is a former SS officer. Neo-Nazi and right-wing attacks on foreigners seeking asylum, especially since Unification, are another tragic sign of historical continuity and the return of the repressed.

[67]Christa Wolf, *Ansprachen* (Darmstadt: Luchterhand, 1988), 75.

Ludwig Wittgenstein writes, "We must remain silent about the things we cannot speak about." Wolf, in effect, inverts Wittgenstein's statement, arguing for the necessity of finding forms to articulate the experiences long silenced.[68] She contends that one must break the silence, especially on subjects that defy articulation. The burden of her own history makes this contention even more urgent, even though years passed before she could take the first step in formulating her childhood experiences.

Realizing the possible repetition of the past, and evoking the Nietzschean snake swallowing its own tail as a symbol of the eternal recurrence of the past, Wolf writes of "history's accursed tendency to repeat itself: we must brace ourselves against this" (*Patterns of Childhood*, 170). The task of counteracting both the cyclical motion of history and the neurosis of cultures that is inherent in the repetition compulsion calls for participating in a dialogue in order to remember. Wolf emphasizes the need to establish a dialogical connection between the tenses to change the approach to historical understanding. Wolf scrutinizes not only the past but also the time of writing, from 1971 to 1975, and her own views on various contemporary events, such as the war in Vietnam and the assassination of President Salvador Allende and the subsequent dictatorship in Chile. Wolf deliberately lays these events out like the pieces of a mosaic in which past and present resonate. In doing so, she links the various tenses and demonstrates a process of historical interpretation, in a way reminiscent of Walter Benjamin's emphasis on the present in historical constructions. Benjamin believed, on the basis of historical materialism, that historical representation should be dealt with as a construct. "History," he said, "is the subject of a structure whose site is not homogeneous empty time, but time filled by the presence of the now [Jetztzeit]."[69]

Traditional historiography, rooted in the nineteenth century, offers a chronology of hermetically sealed events told by an omniscient narrator. In other words, the perspective from which the story is told remains unstated. This type of representation communicates an inevitability, as though history were moved by internal laws

[68]See also Ingeborg Bachmann, *Die Wahrheit ist dem Menschen zumutbar* (Munich: Piper, 1981), 7.

[69]Walter Benjamin, *Illuminations: Essays and Reflections*, trans. Harry Zohn (New York: Schocken Books, 1978), 261.

outside human agency or personal responsibility. It represses knowledge and creates further blind spots that impede recognition of the dynamic relationship between past and present.[70] Traditional historical narration also elides the interdependence between the public and private, allowing for normative interpretations, such as the argument that the Germans were seduced by Hitler, to help perpetuate a psychology of victimization.[71] A major accomplishment of *Patterns of Childhood* is that Wolf wrote against the traditional, dominant historical inquiry that promotes the concept of history "out there," intangible, propelled by an insular dynamic, independent of its negotiators and agents, and defying personal access. Arguing that "it is the person who remembers—not memory," she shows that people make and interpret a history that is profane, not providential (*Patterns of Childhood*, 118). She endorses the didactic function of autobiography by illustrating how present events must be evaluated in relation to the past, for if they escape our field of vision and analysis, we again become mourners of "inevitable" pasts.[72] To intervene in the cyclical movement of history and its fatalistic recurrence is the utopian aim of her work. As Hesiod's depiction of Mnemosyne, the goddess of memory or remembrance in Greek mythology, suggests, it is the task of memory to see past, present, and future simultaneously.[73] Wolf emphasizes the strong interdependence that exists between all three temporalities.

To end such cycles, one must confront the very structures that

[70]The traditional understanding of history in some ways produces history as a commodity. Through sets and costumes, history serves only as a backdrop for romance or as an impulse for fashion, recycling the accoutrements of the past. A headline in the *San Francisco Chronicle* that read "Lots of History for Sale" referred to a major auction. Clearly, such treatments of history neglect a critical self-reflexive relationship to the past.

[71]In Hans Jürgen Syberberg's film *Hitler: A Film from Germany* (1977), the filmmaker represents Hitler as a projection of a population's wishes and desires, rather than as an evil force that singularly consumed a nation. See Anton Kaes, *From Hitler to Heimat: The Return of History as Film* (Cambridge: Harvard University Press, 1989).

[72]Christa Wolf, "Selbstinterview," in *Lesen und Schreiben: Neue Sammlung* (Darmstadt: Luchterhand, 1980), 55.

[73]Lourie, "Women and Memory," 1. "In Greek mythology Mnemosyne was the goddess of memory and the mother of the Muses, and thus the patroness of all intellectual and artistic endeavors. In Hesiod's *Theogony*, for instance, she grants power through her daughters to 'tell of what is, and what is to be, and what was before now' (line 38)."

promoted them. Personal memory calls the unconscious to the surface so that it is not left to its own devices. Through the work of memory, the autobiographer can intervene to effect changes. "One cannot overcome the murder of six million Jews," Wolf contends: "The task is not to 'overcome' the fact that twenty million Soviet citizens were murdered, but rather to force open the patterns of that time through writing, to arouse emotional affliction, compassion, and mourning instead of arousing feelings of guilt that provoke a renewed desire to repress and forget."[74] The past cannot be "overcome," but the patterns that continue to live on in its subjects can be addressed. Wolf believes that writing potentially creates a public space, a place for memory that may trigger personal confrontations. Personal histories and subjective recordings have contributed importantly to discussions of the past in Germany.

Consequently, Wolf designs an inner dialogue that conveys a process-oriented mode. She refers to herself as "you" in order to create, inquire, remember, speculate, and draw associations. The second-person informal pronoun engages the autobiographer in a dialogical format. It also acknowledges Nelly outside the present tense. On occasion, "you" is the form of enunciation that reproduces the voices directed at the child—an imperative that calls the child to attention.[75] Yet the narrator's voice does not remain within the text. Through her self-reflexive address, autobiography becomes the site where "inner monologue and literary communication mingle" instead of remaining concealed as they do when an "I" is introduced.[76] This mode of enunciation, as Lejeune remarks, heightens the exchange between writer and reader, since it implicates the reader as addressee.

> One notices the mingling when the autobiographer unfolds the enunciation by writing "in the second person." This procedure makes evident, on the one hand, the co-presence in the enunciation of an

[74]Wolf, "Erfahrungsmuster," 372.

[75]Jeanette Clausen, "The Difficulty of Saying 'I' as Theme and Narrative Technique in the Works of Christa Wolf," *Amsterdamer Beiträge zur neueren Germanistik* 10 (1980): 330. The address in the second person appears to have the additional function of reproducing the voices that addressed Nelly. Jeanette Clausen calls it "the 'inner voice' of the self . . . [which] is composed of the internalized voices of many who have addresssed her."

[76]Lejeune, "Autobiography in the Third Person," 30–31.

"I" (now implicit), a "you," and a "he" [sic] (hidden beneath the "you"), all three referring to the same individual. On the other hand, we become aware of the double nature of the receiver; if I speak to myself as "you," I nonetheless offer this enunciation as a spectacle to the auditor or reader, who is present at a discourse destined for him [sic], even if it is no longer addressed to him [sic]. The enunciation has been theatricalized.[77]

Indeed, it is an invitation to participate in the text, to include one's own memories, and to interact with the author. This type of "writerly" text, to borrow Roland Barthes's designation, calls on the reader to co-produce the narrative. By using the second-person form of address, the autobiographer also increases the number of those addressed and creates an intimacy at the same time. Besides the readers, a "listener" is inscribed directly in the text: Lenka, the narrator's daughter. In the tradition of oral histories, the narrator transmits her experiences and the sites of their occurrence so that her daughter, who is approximately the same age Nelly was at the end of the war, develops an awareness of her own historical heritage and its lessons. Lenka is encouraged to see her own life in relation not only to the present but also in relation to her mother's life and to Germany's past. The next generation embodies history's continuity.[78] Only such connections make historical studies meaningful.

Like many autobiographies, *Patterns of Childhood* places the private sphere and invisible histories at the center of investigation. Contained in "master narratives," historical writing has traditionally focused on major events and movements and has tended to document narrowly conceived notions of politics. Only since the 1960s has this view of history been successfully challenged by al-

[77]Ibid. See also Jean Starobinski, "The Style of Autobiography," *Autobiography: Essays Theoretical and Critical*, ed. James Olney (Princeton: Princeton University Press, 1980); Sandra Frieden, *Autobiography: Self into Form: German Language Autobiographical Writings of the 1970s* (New York: Lang, 1983), and "A Guarded Iconoclasm: The Self as Deconstructing Counterpoint to Documentation," in *Responses to Christa Wolf: Critical Essays*, ed. Marilyn Sibley Fries (Detroit: Wayne State University Press, 1989), 266–77.

[78]See Ingeborg Drewitz's novel *Gestern war Heute*, in which she depicts three generations of women and the continuum visible within three lives. See also Werner Brettschneider, "*Kindheitsmuster: Kindheit als Thema autobiographischer Dichtung*" (Berlin: Erich Schmidt Verlag, 1982).

ternative histories that represent daily life or present a so-called decentered view. Bernd Engelmann, a leftist historian, was one of the first in the Federal Republic to popularize a more social-historical perspective; he was followed by such historians as Norbert Elias, Lutz Niethammer, and Carlo Ginzburg. Oral histories and autobiographies have added new reservoirs of information, established the interdependence of private and public spheres, and, more important, made identification with historical narration possible. These narratives have significantly contributed to public self-reflection, since they often represent rarely recorded, though commonly shared, experiences. They become relevant documents that interact with people's lives. Since history shapes consciousness and memory through the systems of meaning it imposes, it is necessary to include rather than to detach and repress multiple perspectives. This inclusion is particularly important since "collective memories" often tend to restructure personal knowledge. Maurice Halbwachs writes: "Collective memory . . . encompasses individual memories, but does not meld with them. It develops according to its own laws and even if certain individual memories occasionally penetrate it, they change as soon as they are embedded in a totality that is no longer a personal consciousness."[79]

A single perspective can never embrace the subjective interpretations of experience necessary for developing a critical sensibility in society. As Wolf ascertains, the damaging effect of preserving only one perspective is evident throughout the history of Western culture, particularly in the continued disenfranchisement of large portions of the population. Consequently, certain areas of knowledge never become a part of public memory; they have no public arena for articulation or reflection. For instance, Wolf speaks of the history of flight from Germany's eastern regions as Russian troops marched in toward the end of World War II, and she points out the remarkable absence of these stories among normative histories: "For instance, few descriptions exist of 'the flight.' Why? Because the young men who later wrote books about their experiences had been soldiers? Or because there is something dubious about the subject? The term itself later disappeared" (*Patterns of Childhood*,

[79]Maurice Halbwachs, *The Collective Memory*, trans. Francis J. Ditter and Vida Yazdi Ditter (New York: Harper and Row, 1980), 35.

321). In view of the homogeneous perspective afforded by the mass media as well as their near monopoly of historical interpretation, subjective remembrances provide additional material and consequently expand interpretive frameworks. Historical knowledge, as a result, becomes inclusive. The communal yet plural act of remembering allows for the polyphony of voices that may bring us closer to ways of knowing the past that have not yet been deciphered. The opening up of the text of history through personal viewpoints is a key to the autobiographical project. However, the sequence of remembering and of breaking long-standing taboos inevitably calls forth defensiveness, an attitude that reviews of *Patterns of Childhood* in the former GDR powerfully display.[80]

In *Patterns of Childhood*, history is present not as a means of explaining absolute, uncontested relationships of cause and effect but rather as a field of discourses that intersect and shape a time period and the persons living in it. Wolf examines the voices and moments whose traces are absent from cultural or social memory. She looks at the persons who are absent from written histories, even though they are its bearers and participants, even though their gestures may reveal as much as official records, if not more. For the narrator, the excavation of episodes and the retention of split seconds of recognition not included in official memories joins the present, the past, and that which has been repressed. The author looks at the details of daily life within the microcosm, from which she can deduce behavior rather than relying on foreclosed interpretive structures that discredit what the filmmaker Helke Sander has called the subjective factor.

Through Wolf's discursive representation of the past, established by the self-reflexive autobiographical mode, the montage of events, and the enunciation of an "I-you" relationship in which the source of enunciation is stated, the past becomes living material from which to learn and to negotiate adjustments for the future. The

---

[80]See Hans Richter, "Moralität als poetische Energie," *Sinn und Form* 29 (1977): 667–78; Annemarie Auer, "Gegenerinnerung," *Sinn und Form* 29 (1977): 847–78. See also Therese Hörnigk, "Das Thema Krieg und Faschismus in der Geschichte der DDR-Literatur," *Weimarer Beiträge* 5 (1978): 73–90; Alexander Stephan, *Christa Wolf* (Amsterdam: Rodopi, 1980); Gerd Krieger, "Ein Buch im Streit der Meinungen: Untersuchung literaturkritischer Reaktionen zu Christa Wolfs 'Kindheitsmuster'," *Zeitschrift für Literaturwissenschaft, Ästhetik und Kulturtheorie* 1 (1985): 56–75.

past, according to Wolf, provides essential knowledge that must be recalled and preserved, particularly in times like these when everything moves so quickly.[81] The danger in losing sight of or repressing the past is the possibility of sacrificing the future. Wolf writes: "In the age of universal loss of memory (a sentence which arrived in the mail the day before yesterday) we must realize that complete presence of mind can be achieved only when based on a clear past. The deeper our memory, the freer the space for the goal of all our hopes: the future" (*Pattern of Childhood*, 153). For Wolf, historical monuments are reminders. Her most immediate reminder was the Berlin Wall, which was close to her apartment before its dismantling in 1989.[82] Wolf's autobiographical task begins and ends with questions; particularly in view of present-day political events in Germany and unification, her work is still uncompleted.

[81]See Paul Virilio, *Ästhetik des Verschwindens* (Berlin: Merve Verlag, 1986).

[82]Alfons Heck, *The Burden of Hitler's Legacy* (Frederick, Colo.: Renaissance, 1988). See also Peter Sichrovsky, review of *The Burden of Hitler's Legacy*, by Alfons Heck, *New York Times Book Review*, 18 September 1988, p. 34. There are other autobiographical reviews and rewritings of history that are less probing and even resemble a discourse on Germany's wartime victimization. For instance, Heck illustrates the power of Hitler's propaganda machinery, particularly over unsuspecting and innocent youth, and its ability to create fanatical supporters. He notes that he himself was a high-ranking leader in the Hitler Youth, age seventeen, when his career ended with Germany's defeat, a defeat which, Heck confesses, "I accepted only intellectually in 1945. It took another 30 years to accept it publicly and without reservation." However, in a display of extreme audacity, Heck goes so far as to set those who grew up under Hitler's regime on a par with victims of concentration camps and heinous persecution. Referring to the Nuremberg Trials and the verdict submitted against Baldur von Schirach, the leader of the Hitler Youth, Heck writes, "He had been convicted only on count 4, Crimes against Humanity, primarily for his deeds as Gauleiter of Vienna, but his seduction of Germany's youth, to my way of thinking, killed many more people than had the deportation of 60,000 Jews. The fanaticism he had inculcated led to the death of millions of German adolescents" (36). Heck's lack of self-reflexivity and his disturbing, moralizing tone threaten to rewrite history. Moreover, his interpretation of history is insular and lacks the least hint of doubt. It is an absolute recollection that seems to push the past further away instead of bringing it closer. Perhaps this type of shield promotes the continuation of the past of which Wolf is so suspicious.

3

Ruth Rehmann's *Der Mann auf der Kanzel: Fragen an einen Vater*

> Our fathers did not kill any father, but we killed or tortured
> fathers until they gave up or surrendered. Fathers used to
> be the strongest. That is over. Everything goes on without
> them now. That is just like us. Fathers ranted, shouted, and
> lashed out. They left the house when they couldn't take it
> anymore. We cursed them and hoped they would come back.
> Fathers knew it. That is why they left, and that is why they
> came back. We killed those who knew nothing about any-
> thing, and now we are in for it. It is over. The angels are
> extinguishing anything that smells like father.
>
> Bodo Morshäuser, *The Fathers Are Dead*

Returning to Remembered Sites

The events of the past are bound by time and space, although
the effects slip beyond these borders and leave their traces on each
present movement. For many autobiographers, symbolic reentry
into the topography of the past entails the restaging of events, the
questioning and probing of their course, and, most important, the
analysis of the marks they have left on the present. Moving between the present and the past involves a journey fraught with
insecurities, many of which are unique to the situation in postwar
Germany. In the 1970s and 1980s, this journey literally takes place
by visiting the sites of one's beginning. In *Patterns of Childhood*,
Christa Wolf travels to her native L., in what is today Poland. In
Such Sad Tidings (1976), Elisabeth Plessen, the first German female
writer to explore the father-daughter relationship, comes to terms
with the ambivalence she feels toward her father while traveling
to her native Schleswig to attend his funeral. Her journey is com-
pleted before arriving; she works through their relationship and
symbolically takes leave of him. The route represents the staging
of a personal farewell, a process of mourning without social ritual
or precedent. In *Der Mann auf der Kanzel: Fragen an einen Vater* (The

man in the pulpit: Questions for a father), Ruth Rehmann finds herself in Auel, a small town in the Palatinate, the place of her childhood. Reviewing her past, she attempts to piece together a portrait of her father and to question his role as a pastor during the Third Reich. Like the accounts of many other personal histories explored in Germany since the mid-1970s, Rehmann's (auto)biographical novel turns into an investigation of Germany's fascist history. Her work reveals the psychic structures that may have made possible the emergence of a fascist state. More significantly, the remarkable resemblance between father and daughter appears precisely in the strategies of repression and denial the daughter writes about and with which she judges her father's life.

In literature, the return to the fathers gathered momentum in the early 1980s with a sudden abundance of autobiographical texts. As with all obvious literary trends, this literature was grouped, reviewed, and labeled. "Väterliteratur" or "literature of the fathers" was described by critics as the "literary sensation of the season."[1] These autobiographies explore the personal relationship between father and child with all the profound psychological needs and desires harbored within it. In *Nachgetragene Liebe* (Love in the aftermath), Peter Härtling confesses his wish to establish a connection to the father he always avoided: "I have always run away from you, father, and now I'm running after you."[2]

These texts have an elegiac tenor of loss, and they also take issue with the historical legacy and the psychic structures handed down to successive generations. As most of these narratives reveal, an investigation of Germany's fascist past entails a confrontation with the father. The father, as active or passive participant in the Third Reich (in gesture, or by default, if not in spirit), is placed on the witness stand and retried. In one sense, these autobiographical novels uphold a traditional perception of a public-private schism, especially since the revival of interest in the father frequently implies a confrontation with the "fatherland," nationalism, and national identity. Mothers are conspicuously absent in these texts. Although feminist historiographers since the 1970s have taken a

---

[1]Reinhardt Stumm, "Vater-lieber Vater," *Die Zeit*, 22 February 1980, p. 17.
[2]Peter Härtling, *Nachgetragene Liebe* (Frankfurt am Main: Büchergilde Gutenberg, 1980), 173.

closer look at the role women played in the Third Reich, critical examinations of late are just beginning to assess women's involvement.[3] During the 1980s, many authors turned their attention to the father, which raises the question of what channels suddenly opened to permit this interest and to counteract the hitherto marginal role the father played in postwar literature.

Significantly, all the texts in the genre "literature of the fathers" appear after the father's death. Rolf Hauble contends that death reminds these authors of their own mortality.[4] A psychological mechanism is triggered; a consciousness of legacy and continuity to the next generation is aroused. Moreover, it seems that for many of these authors, death represents the end of hope for paternal attention and the fulfillment of primal needs. The authors express melancholia and mourning. With their fathers' deaths, an ultimate, irrevocable disappointment surfaces. The children bear the realization of never again being able to return to their fathers, either to gain the acceptance and recognition many clearly yearned for or to establish a relationship based on mutual understanding and openness. The awareness of finality is often met with bitterness, resentment, and grief. In an imaginary letter to her dead father, Brigitte Schwaiger in *Lange Abwesenheit* writes: "When would you have taken the time to talk to me? When I realized that you were going to die, I held it against you that you simply went away, without ever having been there for me."[5]

The long absence of the father signals a damaged relationship not only within the private sphere but also to the father as an emblem of the state and of German national identity. In many ways, the literature of the fathers could more appropriately be called the literature of mourning, since a sense of loss and emotional impoverishment feeds these narratives. The work of mourning is for the victims of Germany's horrific crimes, but it is also for the lost or tainted image of the father. Both daughters and sons have begun to revisit the paternal to probe his or her own formation as subject, perhaps in order to confront the denied or disturbed

---

[3]See Claudia Koonz, *Mothers in the Fatherland: Women, the Family, and Nazi Politics* (New York: St. Martin's Press, 1987).

[4]Rolf Haubl, "Das Gesetz des Vaters," in *Die Sprache des Vaters im Körper der Mutter*, ed. Rolf Haubl et al. (Giessen: Anabas, 1984).

[5]Brigitte Schwaiger, *Lange Abwesenheit* (Hamburg: Rowohlt, 1980), 8.

link to the fathers in their own lives. Each author creates an imaginary realm in order to gain access to the father, which actually means to deal with the voice of the father within the author.

It is no surprise that much of this literature came after the film *Holocaust* was shown on television in 1979; heated debates on national identity, historical and personal responsibility, and the repression of Germany's fascist past resulted.[6] Many authors who contributed to the genre "literature of the fathers" responded by trying to find a psychosocial predisposition for the politics of the Third Reich within their own families. History, they found, manifests itself in gestures circulated in the private realm and in the persons who raised them and whom they grew to love—and despise? Ruth Rehmann asks: "Why the father? Why just now? Why so many? . . . in this case it is the father, key figure of our own existence in time and society, the cause of many effects that cannot be understood without him."[7]

Michael Schneider extensively analyzes the rift between generations that marked German society from the late 1960s through the 1980s. In his article "Fathers and Sons, Retrospectively: The Damaged Relationship between Two Generations," he provides a symptomatic reading of the "literature of the fathers" and speculates on its unifying traits. Even though he focuses on the father-son relationship, his observations address the father-daughter relationship as well. The authors of this literary genre, he contends, generally represent a postwar generation whose fathers tried to restore their psychological losses within the family. Returning from the war defeated, their ideals shattered, these fathers often brutally sought to regain control, to reassert their authority, and to boost their depleted sense of self in the only sphere in which they were able to exercise unlimited power. They desperately reassembled their broken identities, often at the expense of their children. Besides being influenced by the ravages of war, these fathers, as Klaus Theweleit elaborates in his book *Männerphantasien*, were also trained in the spirit of such Prussian ideals as obedience, discipline,

---

[6]Michael Schneider, "Fathers and Sons, Retrospectively: The Damaged Relationship between Two Generations," trans. Jamie Owen Daniel, *New German Critique* 31 (1984): 3.

[7]Ruth Rehmann, "Die Väter bitten um eine neue Sicht: Folgen einer Rezeption," *Süddeutsche Zeitung* 85 (1982): 130.

and self-control.[8] In the postwar era, these rigorous principles (which, in Schneider's estimation, facilitated the older generation's surrender to fascist orthodoxy) often persisted privately in the dealings of fathers with their own children. Schneider succinctly comments: "As much of the Germans had been 're-educated' by the victorious Allies, they remained true to themselves as teachers and parents. They continued to raise their children in accordance with the age-old Prussian pedagogical maxims, which dictated that a child's will had to be broken, and that a child had to be beaten and punished in order to 'temper' it."[9] Consequently, emotional turmoil and a sense of abuse and denial are worked out in these narratives.

As many of these authors have recognized, the psychic legacy of the Third Reich has engulfed their lives. The historical continuity remained, despite the feeble, albeit momentous Zero Hour (1945), intended to be a break with the past and the ostensible turning of a new leaf in German history with the introduction of a democratic state. Repressed from the public sphere, the past became anchored in the private realm and in the gestures of daily life. The roster of titles that, coincidentally or not, all appeared about 1980 include Ruth Rehmann's *Der Mann auf der Kanzel* (1979); Heinrich Wiesner's *Der Riese am Tisch* (The giant at the table, 1979); Jutta Schutting's *Der Vater* (The father, 1980); Christoph Meckel's *Suchbild: Über meinen Vater* (Image for investigation: About my father, 1980); Peter Härtling's *Nachgetragene Liebe* (Love in the aftermath, 1980); Sigfrid Gauch's *Vaterspuren* (Traces of father, 1979); Brigitte Schwaiger's *Lange Abwesenheit* (Long absence, 1983); and Ludwig Harig's *Ordnung ist das ganze Leben: Roman meines Vaters* (Order is the essence of life: Novel of my father; 1985).[10]

These personal accounts, as Ruth Rehmann notes, reveal a need to broach this period in order to comprehend one's own heritage. She dedicates her book to her children in an awareness of historical continuity. In *Stranded Objects: Mourning, Memory, and Film in Post-*

[8] Klaus Theweleit, *Männerphantasien* (Hamburg: Rowohlt, 1980).

[9] Schneider, "Fathers and Sons," 26.

[10] The father-child constellation has also been explored in such films as Thomas Harlan's *Der Wundkanal* (*Wound Passage*, 1985), in which Harlan stages an inquisition of his father, the famous Third Reich filmmaker Veit Harlan, played by a convicted mass murderer. Thomas Mitscherlich's *Vater und Sohn* (Father and son, 1984) is an autobiographical confrontation that places the authority of his father in question.

war Germany, Eric Santner discusses the importance of such an undertaking, especially for the generations removed from the historical context of fascist Germany. He cites Alexander and Margarete Mitscherlich's study *The Inability to Mourn* (originally published in 1967) in order to launch a discussion of what he calls the "rhetoric of mourning" that underlies contemporary critical theory and writing and, within the German context, "the apparent absence of any sustained emotional confrontation with the Nazi past in postwar German society."[11] Santner superbly argues that the following generations do not inherit guilt, as Chancellor Helmut Kohl implied in the phrase "the blessing of being born late," but rather, they inherit the psychic structures that impeded their parents' and grandparents' work of mourning. Discussions of the effects of the psychic legacy of the German past have appeared in numerous interviews and books in the 1980s.[12] The literature of the fathers thus lends valuable insight into the intersection of history and the private sphere.

Moreover, the polyphony of explorations undermines the pos-

---

[11] Eric L. Santner, *Stranded Objects: Mourning, Memory, and Film in Postwar Germany* (Ithaca: Cornell University Press, 1990), 1.

[12] I recommend the following readings that expand on this topic: Peter Sichrovsky, *Born Guilty: Children of Nazi Families*, trans. Jean Steinberg (New York: Basic Books, 1988); Adolf Muschg, "Die Ungnade der späten Geburt," *Frankfurter Rundschau*, 21 February 1987; Wieland Elfferding, "Unversöhnte Unschuld, *Tageszeitung*, 11 April 1987, p. 17; Dietrich Strothmann, "Die Kinder der Mörder," *Die Zeit*, 10 April 1987, p. 20. Of course, the extent to which children are affected by their parents' pasts largely depends on their parents' degree of involvement in the Third Reich. Setting out to investigate the scars that this twelve-year period left on succeeding generations, Peter Sichrovsky in *Born Guilty* interviewed fourteen men and women whose fathers actively participated in war crimes. Although each child deals differently with her or his inheritance, for most of the "children," it is the cause of a deep-rooted crisis. In fact, it appears to be the overriding factor that informs their identities. Some either openly resent their fathers or try to protect and support their family members. Niklas Frank, son of a former SS officer, engages in a more turbulent confrontation with his heritage in *Hitler's Children: Sons and Daughters of the Third Reich Talk about Themselves and Their Fathers*, ed. Gerald L. Posner (New York: Random House, 1991). Frank savors thoughts of his father's execution for crimes against humanity and lashes out against the memories of his father. The perspective Sichrovsky explores dwells on the children in these texts—they are texts of affliction different from autobiographical novels representative of "literature of the fathers" in which the father is somewhat compassionately represented. Inadvertently, these texts produce testimonies of another type of war "victim," namely, the children of these parents.

sibility that any single story can cast the image of Germany and the conditions from which fascism emerged. The denominators are irreducible as each personal history, each "father story," unfolds. Ruth Rehmann observes: "The period—Nazi period or Third Reich—[is] diversely mirrored and refracted in the various father images."[13] Indeed, these autobiographical renditions open up the historical text and, as Michael Schneider writes, they "lend new insights into the psychological processes which permitted the bourgeois fathers either to become Nazis or to 'go along' with them, and in the telling of these life stories, the authors provide a more differentiated understanding of the conformist problematic of fascism."[14]

Expressionists such as Walter Hasenclever, in his play *The Son*, and Arnoldt Bronnen, in his play *Parricide*, fiercely attacked the patriarchal father, who was emblematic of a repressive, absolutist Wilhelmine society. Unlike authoritarian fathers in early twentieth century texts, the fathers in many contemporary texts have lost their footing. As Christoph Meckel writes, "The children are tormented by [the father's] brokenness (they did not yet know that this fatherhood—the dethroned despot—was characteristic of a whole generation). The fact that he loved them made it worse."[15] Influenced by questions posed during the student movement of the late 1960s, which assailed the suppression of Germany's fascist past from public and private discourses, many authors lashed out against the historical amnesia that beset Germany, and they forced the nation and their parents to remember.[16] Yet, this undertaking proved complex. Attempting to confront their fathers as historical subjects, many authors were faced with the painful conflict of loving and supporting someone who, at times, seemed morally objectionable, if not reprehensible. The search into the past often produced a hidden history, in turn followed by intense disappointment and estrangement.[17]

---

[13]Rehmann, "Die Väter," 130.

[14]Schneider, "Fathers," 16.

[15]Christoph Meckel, *Suchbild: Über meinen Vater* (Düsseldorf: Claasen, 1980), 134.

[16]Ulrich Greiner, "Söhne und ihre Väter: Über die Studentenbewegung als Konflikt der Generationen," *Die Zeit*, 6 May 1988, p. 14.

[17]Reading his father's diary, Christoph Meckel describes the shock of seeing his father as a stranger: "I found the notes of a person I did not know. It was not

The emotions disclosed appear more ambivalent than the unconditional denial of the father during the 1960s or the staging of the father-son relationship in Expressionist drama, in which the father is figuratively killed by the son's unmitigated hatred. The fathers in the works discussed here are rewritten from the perspective of a new epistemological era when children are interested in uncovering the traces their fathers have left on their lives and identities.[18] In contrast to the literature of the early twentieth century, daughters have entered this discursive terrain. Traditionally absent from discussions of the family, daughters, in an unprecedented undertaking, have begun to map their fathers' roles in shaping their identities.

Retreat or Confrontation?

Ever since the late 1960s, certain questions have loomed over Germany like a cloud signaling the onset of an inner storm, questions that stir memories many would prefer to leave at the sites of their origins. For Germany's children, questions about their parents' participation in the Third Reich have indeed become an integral part of learning about themselves, their beginnings, and their family histories. The investigation has inevitably turned into an existential even though threatening necessity, as Reinhardt Stumm notes. "The contributing authors had to ask themselves, at some point in their existence, whose creatures they actually are, what their dependencies look like, whether these are controlled or unconscious. The relationship to the father as disciplinarian who

---

possible to know this person, to believe that he is possible—unthinkable" (*Suchbild*, 64).

[18]See the following review articles dealing with this literature: Heinz Beckmann, "Der Torhüter vor der eigenen Welt," *Rheinischer Merkur*, 28 March 1980, p. 33; Karl Krolow, "Annäherung an den Vater," *Berliner Tagesspiegel*, 17 February 1980, 45; Manfred Rieger, "Die Väter und ihre schreibenden Kinder," *Basler Zeitung*, 11 April 1981, p. 43; Heinrich Vormweg, "Eine sanfte Art von Mord?" *Süddeutsche Zeitung*, 11–12 April 1981, p. 130; Dörte von Westernhagen, "Die Kinder der Täter: Deutsche Geschichte als Familiendrama: Selbstzweifel, Zwiespaltigkeit, Haß und Schuldgefühle," *Die Zeit*, 28 March 1986, p. 17.

points the way, forms or deforms, bends and shapes [them] needs to be clarified."[19]

For such authors as Ruth Rehmann, whose relationship to the father is rooted in the war years, these questions involve an additional dimension. They entail reproducing a family portrait that in some way stands at odds with their own childhood memories and desires as well as family history. Especially when a selectively cultivated pool of "official" family memories or stories that play a vital role in defining oneself are at stake, such mnemonic excursions pose danger. As the teacher, Limbach, in Rehmann's narrative *Der Mann auf der Kanzel* (1979), remarks: "It would be interesting to pursue how such a family memory functions, . . . what it passes on and what it avoids; and to ask oneself why" (15).[20] He challenges the author to look at the gaps and fissures as well as the underlying structures of the information that shape the body of personal histories.

In her autobiographical narrative, Rehmann sets out to examine family memories by opening up private texts and intersecting them with their historical context. She removes her father, a Lutheran pastor, from the shrine of family memory in order to question his role as a pastor during the Third Reich. The collective amnesia of a nation makes this task exceptionally complex, since the autobiographer releases voices that memory has long resisted and repressed. The narrator's brother symptomatically illustrates the open hostility toward confronting Germany's past and, more personally, one's parent's involvement in the Third Reich. When the autobiographical narrator visits her brother in order to recapitulate times predating her birth, he becomes defensive and accuses her of meddling in affairs that do not concern her. Escaping into religion (much like his father) to cover his unwillingness to face family history, the brother blames his nephew, the narrator's leftist son, Thomas, for provoking his mother's inquiry and patronizingly asks, "Are the two of you working through the past again? Isn't it starting to come out of your ears? To have an awareness of

[19]Stumm, "Vater-lieber Vater," 17.

[20]Ruth Rehmann, *Der Mann auf der Kanzel: Fragen an einen Vater* (Munich: Hanser, 1979). All quotations are taken from this edition. This book has not yet been published in English translation. Translations here are my own.

personal guilt, when I think in those terms, is part of being Christian anyway: we are all sinners" (64). He relativizes notions of guilt, disencumbers himself from historical responsibility, and redeems himself by calling upon a Christian heritage.[21]

As the narrator finds out, family recollections are obstructed by the events that shaped German history during twelve years of fascism. It becomes especially painful when one is called on to associate one's parents with this unwanted period of German history. The narrator confesses:

> Family memory [Familiengedächtnis] no longer works, I said. There is a bad connection: Nazi period, war, collapse. How do you talk about fathers who were neither Nazi criminals nor resistance fighters? How does one get them one by one alive through the mill of generalizations and wholesale judgments? How can we protect them from being distorted by horrifying images or ideals? How does one explain the difference between experienced time and retrospection without falling into that apologetic refrain of lament, the refrain, "I was too young, I did not see anything, I was not a part of it?" (*Der Mann auf der Kanzel*, 15)

The problem, as the first-person narrator admits, is to decide on a point of entry and a perspective from which to revive and interpret family history during that period The problem grows when one

[21]The sympathetic tone in many narratives of "Väterliteratur" suggests not only the problems of German national identity but also a shift in perspective. These works reflect a continuing tendency to rewrite history in order to restore a vision of Germany from which Germans can regain pride in themselves. This tendency finds its strongest expression in the historians' debate (Historikerstreit), ignited by historian Ernst Nolte at the Free University of Berlin, who attempted to relativize Nazi war crimes by comparing them to the Soviet gulags, and Jürgen Habermas's reply. Here, it becomes quite obvious that the revisionist historian stands in as a therapist of the collective in creating an analytical space for uncovering the effects of the Third Reich on the German population. The focus has turned toward Germans as individuals and away from a general, collective profile that permitted the repression of personal memory. The indictment of Germans as "culprits" is diminished, because in many cases the dilemma of conformity is individualized and a basis of identification with the individual facilitated. Also, the ambiguities of the era make it easier to accept that some avoided taking a stand. Claudia Koonz warns of the danger in losing sight of the "real" victims when rewriting the paradigm of guilt ("Schuldparadigma"). On the "historians' debate," see the special issue of *New German Critique* 44 (1988) and Richard J. Evans, *In Hitler's Shadow: West German Historians and the Attempt to Escape from the Nazi Past* (New York: Pantheon, 1989).

must deal with gray zones riddled with ambiguity and paradox. The difficulty of evaluating a person who lived through this time fills the project with uncertainty. In addition, as Judith Ryan observes, "The inadequacy of memory, the limitations of subjective perception, the lack of appropriate literary models, the discrepancy between what had actually happened and what one might have wished to have happened"—all are elements that haunt this literature.[22]

Interestingly, the narrator's inquiry is not self-initiated. As she says, she would have preferred to drive through to Holland to begin her vacation rather than spend the night in her hometown. Her inquiry is launched by the next generation, her daughters, who later recede into the background, leaving the son in the role of the significant interlocutor. The protagonist's son, Thomas, appropriately studies history and belongs to the generation that first pried into their parents' memories. The intergenerational dialogue compels the author to reflect on her own father, long deceased.

Describing the circumstances that led to her crucial reckoning with the past, Rehmann recounts, "Our discussion began at the top of the Siebengebirge, lengthy and controversial as usual in this family without a father, without a voice of authority" (9). Since this genre consists of novels written mostly after the father's death, not always as a consequence thereof, but certainly with the father's death as its precondition, it implies that the "voice of authority" must be displaced for an investigation to commence.[23] Otherwise, the entrance into the volatile terrain of the past is impeded and defended by the institutionalization of "safe" discourses or buffers of silence.[24]

Despite Thomas's provocation, the narrator is the one who is called on to interpret her father's life beyond family remembrance.

[22]Judith Ryan, *The Uncompleted Past: Postwar German Novels and the Third Reich* (Detroit: Wayne State University Press, 1983), 13.

[23]See Rolf Haubl, "Das Gesetz des Vaters," *Die Sprache des Vaters im Körper der Mutter*, ed. Rolf Haubl et al. (Giessen: Anabas, 1984).

[24]Peter Härtling in *Nachgetragene Liebe* produces a valuable image to express the type of inaccessibility associated with the patriarch: "Father walls himself in with bookcases. In his office alone there are four or five; in the hall three more. The bookcases pile up next to him, black and dark brown, monsters with glass doors, behind which books stand in rows, or boxes of decorative essays like crowns, bulging with achievement and aspiration" (13–14).

As prefigured by the author's initial obsequious posture, this confrontation indeed ends as it begins, with the narrator succumbing to powerlessness. She does not place herself in critical opposition to the language of authority or history in the way Christa Wolf does but continues to submit to it despite her son's unrelenting inquiry: "The clerics had played a highly questionable role, except for Niemöller. What was your father's opinion of Niemöller?" (11). Attempting to protect her father from harsh generalities, she replies: "He was apolitical. . . . He followed his conscience" (11). The narrator pursues the possibilities of remaining apolitical and following one's conscience in the midst of a political climate that impinged on everyone's life.

To a certain extent, *Der Mann auf der Kanzel* is an exception to the autobiographical subgenre of "literature of the fathers," since Ruth Rehmann, born in 1922, does not belong to the generation of war babies who later indicted their fathers for an emotionally vacuous postwar upbringing. Like Christa Wolf's narrator, the autobiographical author experienced the war years. Her relationship to her father is rooted in this time. The narrator portrays her father as an immensely moral, generous, loving, and charismatic man, who was highly respected and honored in his community. One of the parishioners describes him as having loved peace and harmony. In order to decipher and construct an image of her father, the narrator relies on the teacher, Limbach, the pastor's old friend and critic. As the teacher observes, the pastor's vocation and the maxims set down by orthodox Protestants, the Pietists, greatly influenced his identity.[25] The pastor's conscience was guided by introspective self-examination and a total commitment to the spiritual well-being of his congregation; his personal investment resembled that of a patriarch's concern for his family. In view of these qualities, the narrator's son wonders, "How did such a superconscience survive the Nazi period without landing in a concentration camp?" (11). Thomas touches on an enigma that compels

---

[25]The Herrenhuter Brotherhood began in the seventeenth century. It founded the Pietist movement, which was based on conscientious, introspective self-examination under the mottoes "Know yourself" and "Look inside yourself! Reflect upon the day in light of God's expectations, not only words and deeds, but also that which produces words and deeds: thoughts, feelings, desires, persuasions." (See Rehmann, *Der Mann auf der Kanzel*, p. 11.)

the narrator to delve deeper into her father's story and the ways he found to sustain his beliefs. His commitment to religious dogma, the Wilhelminian concept of nationalism, and his propensity to yield to authority, the narrator concludes, were the guiding factors in her father's life.

Rehmann introduces a capsule history of the conflicts that arose within the church after Hitler's rise to power in order to illustrate the issues her father faced and the decisions he made in view of his options. One event, a turning point in her father's career, reveals both his coping strategies and the priorities he set for himself. The pastor, the narrator recounts, was utterly destroyed when he discovered dissension within his parish and the secret meetings of the Confessing church (Bekenntniskirche), an underground organization of Christians who renounced the religious ideas and policies of the Nazi party, and who sought to preserve the teachings of the Old and New Testaments. Differences, the pastor believed, could be reconciled through prayer, mutual trust, and heartfelt communication. He interpreted his parishioners' shifting loyalties during the famous church struggle (Kirchenstreit) as a breach of confidence and personal failure.[26] Looking at the structures that affect the pastor's perceptions, Rehmann encounters the failure of high theology both in its neglect of the secular, historical, and political spheres and in the anti-intellectualism it supported.[27]

For the narrator's father, religion functions as a buffer to historical events. Religion offers him possibilities of unconscious retreat without compromising moral superiority due to his focus on the transcendent soul. "Duty helps him to look away," says the teacher, "at least the way in which he understands duty: administering his job, protecting his flock, working in the vineyard, keeping the peace, wrestling for souls" (102). According to Limbach, the pastor intervenes only when he feels that Christian doctrinal

---

[26]The "church debate" (Kirchenstreit) was an expression of Hitler's policies of unification (Gleichschaltung), the purpose of which was the actual uniformizing of all institutions under the theories of National Socialism.

[27]Although as history and many authors have shown, the Catholic church has always been politically articulate and powerful. In Rolf Hochhut's *Der Stellvertreter* (*The Deputy*, 1963), the Catholic church is shown as supportive of Hitler because of his fight against communism, despite its awareness of the persecution of Jews and the existence of concentration camps.

foundations are in jeopardy. He speaks out against the "Glaubensbewegung," a more fanatic form of the politically sanctioned German Christian Movement headed by the Reich bishop Ludwig Müller.[28] Even though this movement introduced the Aryan clause, which called for the expulsion of all "non-Aryan" clergy, the pastor takes issue only with what he perceives as the more serious problem—namely, the intent to rewrite the Christian Scriptures (New Testament) and dispose of the Hebrew Scriptures (Old Testament) altogether. In most cases, the pastor chooses the conservative middle road, guided by his allegiance to authority and the affirmation of church doctrines also sanctioned by the Third Reich. In view of the diversity, and the often leftist or secular orientation, of political tendencies during the Weimar Republic, the pastor expresses relief that this regime promotes Christian ideals: "For fourteen years we demonstrated loyalty to all kinds of governments, red, black, and indifferent, as difficult as it sometimes was for us. Do we want to stab this government—the first one to expressly place itself on the side of positive Christianity—in the back just because of a few initial difficulties?" (125). In hindsight, the pastor's attitudes resonate with tendencies that seem to have prefigured fascism.[29] Certain episodes, for example, demonstrate his anti-Semitism and anti-communism, sentiments that could have allied him with the National Socialist agenda. When the pastor's old opponent questions him about the Aryan clause, the pastor is unaware of its reactivation in 1934. He confirms his opposition to this law but says he understands the government's rejection of Jews because of their supposed monopolies and economic power. Reiterating the pastor's position, the teacher says, "He is, as we all know, an old German

---

[28]For further reference see Ernst Christian Helmreich, *The German Churches under Hitler* (Detroit: Wayne State University Press, 1979). Within the church, there was much resistance toward the German Evangelical Church and particularly the movement of faith (Glaubensbewegung), a much more intense nazification of the church. In reference to the forms of resistance, Helmreich writes that "free synods" were formed; one of the most articulate was the "Free Reformed Synod," which met on 3–4 January 1934. Walter Hofer, ed., *Der Nationalsozialismus Dokument, 1933–1945* (Frankfurt am Main: Fischer, 1982).

[29]In many ways, Edgar Reitz's film *Heimat*, which represents the provinces immediately before, during, and after the Third Reich, serves as an interesting intertext, because he, too, shows the attitudes that shaped this time. Coincidentally, Rehmann's novel *Der Mann auf der Kanzel* also takes place in the Hunsrück, the location of Reitz's film.

nationalist, he makes no secret of that. How is he supposed to forget what the Jewish press did to the emperor [Wilhelm] during and after the war?" (125), when leftists called for the monarch's abdication. The pastor is depicted as a devout monarchist, a nationalist, and a proud veteran of World War I. Loyalty to the monarchy, it seems, deters him from supporting the politics of the Third Reich despite his anti-Semitism. Thus his criticism of the Nazis is not engendered by progressive resistance, but rather derives from a traditional, conservative worldview. Entrenched in systems of absolutism, he balks at the formation of a republic and democracy (a position initially similar to Thomas Mann's at the advent of the Weimar Republic), but he never criticizes the war or questions the authority or principles of the Third Reich.

Attempting to understand her father's worldview, Rehmann points to the way in which he dismissed the contradictions that infused his life and his penchant for selective, unreflected vision. Limbach points out a common strategy inherent in racism—namely, the anonymity of the other set against the recognition of the individual: "In practice it looks like this: He has something against blacks; but the pitch-black deacon from St. Servatius is an 'ideal colleague' and an 'intelligent person.' The Jews poison the people, but the Rabbi Selig from the Aueler Synagogue is 'an incredibly kind-hearted person.' " (103). The teacher also notes that the pastor focuses on "essential" qualities that strip people from the social and historical context and from the very discourses that inform their identities. He perseveringly seeks out the good. Rehmann polemically shows how these worldviews allow for embracing the most contradictory positions. The pastor can even support the Nazis as individuals through his belief of the good in all human beings.

This naively dangerous perspective neither enhances nor sharpens the pastor's vision but places an opaque screen between him and the events that demand attention, particularly from someone with his social standing. For Limbach, the pastor's penchant for relying on the good in everyone is indicative of someone who never needed to learn fear.[30] Necessity does not determine his vision; the

---

[30]The teacher is referring to the Grimm's fairy tale "The Tale of Someone Who Struck Out to Learn Fear" ("Märchen von einem, der auszog, das Fürchten zu lernen").

view from the pulpit and high theology afford him distance. Rehmann presents the grave consequences of her father's "blindness," or, in Christa Wolf's words, his blind spot, in his attempts to defend Germany against what he considers rumors of concentration camps: "Until I have seen one of these concentration camps with my own eyes, I won't believe a word of it." To which the teacher replies: "How can you see if you don't look?" (130). Speaking through the voice of the teacher, which lends a didactic tone to the text, Rehmann addresses the larger context of national amnesia and repression. She explores the ominous possibilities of a breakdown of perception and the denial of events, even when they occur in close range.

Rehmann suggests that the pastor's training in and adherence to absolutist systems of thought explain his perspectives, particularly his belief in obedience and submission. Both the summons in Romans 13 ("Be subject to the authorities that have power over you!"), often quoted by Luther, and the teachings of a divinely ordained hierarchical social order are integral to the pastor's understanding of reality. Moreover, his entire training as a student of the theologian Schlatter is geared toward submitting to the authority of church and state. Rehmann contends that her father's belief in authority enclosed him within conceptual boundaries that he was incapable of transgressing. Uncritical obedience not only prevented him from seeking alternatives—even within the church—but also engendered many blind spots. In *Suchbild*, Christoph Meckel alludes to a similar phenomenon in his father's training: "Authority altered his ability to see" (73).

For Rehmann, perception becomes the key issue in explicating the pastor's role in the Third Reich. His perceptions are strictly organized by the dogmas that structure his knowledge. His wife accuses him of being stubbornly myopic. Her comment highlights the pastor's disposition toward selective awareness (153). He focuses only on those "realities" he chooses to see.

Throughout the narrative, Rehmann represents her father as a victim of a background and training that have ossified his perspective, depriving him of analytical and critical insight. However, her personal assessment lands her in a web of conflicting conclusions that result in a perpetual apologia, despite her thematization of such dangers. The unraveling of her father's biography, as she finds out, does not provide absolute answers about her father's life; instead it serves to define her own views. *Der Mann auf der Kanzel* turns out to be Rehmann's own autobiographical inquiry, challenging her to rethink the past at close range, to find corrective measures, and to gain insight into what Christa Wolf calls the patterns that structure behavior.[31]

Even though the narrator sets out to produce a critical portrait of the father, she duplicates, paradoxically, the psychic structures she attributes to him. Even when she discovers that her father's prejudices swayed his sympathies in a shoot-out between a Nazi and a communist in which the brownshirt is killed, the narrator concludes that dogma guides her father's judgment. Spontaneously, he would most likely believe that the communist incited the fight, the daughter speculates. It is not that he sympathizes with the Nazi, she cautions, but rather that he has a dread of communism. Exonerating her father of any sin or failing beyond impaired perception, she promotes a fatalistic view of his development. She concludes, "He had the vague look of an impractical person who has not learned to examine the visible for its constitution, usability, functionality, correlations" (178). The daughter argues that the pastor is not equipped to interpret the world critically. Ultimately, she empathizes with a lonely man left to flounder in the dark.

In frustration, the daughter blames the teacher, who was more skeptical and politically astute than the pastor, for abandoning him to his myopia. However, the teacher implicates the daughter for not taking personal responsibility and reminds her that she, too, experienced this period as a young adult. She also refrained from challenging her father and eventually turned her back on him. With this insightful response, the daughter shifts her focus to herself and the memories she has denied. The psychic structures she has inherited shape her version of her father's story, including the omissions in her account and testimony. With the teacher's death toward the end of Rehmann's story, the narrator fears investing the past with too many of her own needs based on emotional

---

[31]Gudrun Ensslin, a member of the Baader-Meinhof group, also a pastor's daughter, found her solution in terrorism. Interestingly, her father was a member of the Confessing church. See the film script: Margarethe von Trotta, *Die bleierne Zeit* (*Marianne and Juliane*) (Frankfurt am Main: Fischer, 1981).

attachments. The teacher, she felt, challenged her own perspectives.

Disturbed by the prospect of finishing her version of the pastor's story inconclusively, Rehmann reveals her own relationship to (auto)biographical reconstructions and her desires for closure and to forget or dismiss the past. She concludes that her father, given the structure of his personality, could act no differently. Despite the critical voices of Limbach, the teacher, and her son Thomas, Rehmann's own critical posture dissipates. At the end, the struggle to preserve the memory of her father, revealed in her constant circumnavigation of the consequences of discovery, takes hold in her discussion of the problems confronting the reconstruction of family histories:

> Are you familiar with this: the distance that grows between generations as soon as one tries to tell stories? The change in language that occurs when one tries to bridge that distance? The false tones that these efforts bring about? As though there were something to hide: dark chapters, dirt. . . . Are you familiar with the feeling of disgust aroused by false tones in one's own voice struggling for truth, and the macabre desire to find the dark chapter and the dirt, so that it can be over once and for all: this is the way he was; this is what he did, and now he's dead. (*Der Mann auf der Kanzel*, 15)

In *Der Mann auf der Kanzel*, the narrator grapples with explanations the sincerity of which is in question. Like many authors, Rehmann is faced with supplying answers that inevitably invite more questions. The deeper she delves, the more mistrusting her own words become, particularly when she engages in a convoluted act of excusing her father through a compassionate, conciliatory, and defensive working through of his biography. She frames him in such a way that his actions are comprehensible, if not morally legitimated by his personal history. She is unwilling to alter his image and to rewrite family history.

In contrast to the narrator in Christa Wolf's *Patterns of Childhood*, the daughter in *Der Mann auf der Kanzel* loses sight of the subjective nature of reinvesting the past with a present perspective. The enactment of closure suggests the ability to put the past aside, to close the door, to pull down the shade, and to deny. Again, the daughter reproduces her father's myopia; the characteristics she ascribes to her father become her own. The similarities between father and daughter are poignantly revealed when the narrator reiterates her son's judgment of her: "We have always been able to talk to each other, Thomas and I, even to fight over my 'bourgeois consciousness,' his 'partiality,' my 'deep-seated trust' (which needs to be scrutinized at some point, he thinks). . . . We cannot talk about my father" (11). What the narrator overlooks is that her own qualities reflect precisely the traits she attributes to her father. Her desire for self-reflection predictably breaks off once the topic of discussion involves her father. The inability to deal with her father demonstrates a fundamental identification with his structures of perception. His image mirrors her identity. Although, unlike her brother, who appears to be threatened by any questions directed toward the past, she pursues questions beyond the repertoire of stories that have securely constructed the nest of family memory, yet she ultimately remains inextricably bound within.

Der Mann auf der Kanzel raises questions about the possibility of mourning the German past and the blind spots that inhibit this process. The focus is on the daughter and her work of mourning German history. The dialogue she constructs represents her own desire to reconcile and to repress the voices of the past. In response to the reception of her novel, Rehmann shows that people still take offense at any endeavor to confront the past. For many, Rehmann oversteps her boundaries. She recounts that she has been accused of creating a portrait that is "cold, callous, overly precise, overly critical, lacking understanding. The author's position is arrogant, self-righteous, condescending, unfeminine and *undaughterly.*"[32] Such voices only reflect the continued flight from the past and a desperate need for self-justification.

It is the voice of the protagonist's son which unsettles the narrator's efforts to bury her guilt: "There are so many stories of this kind. They are told in a tone of truth by people whom one likes and respects. Each of them turns and twists a portion of guilt into something humanly understandable, even almost likable" (181). The voice of Thomas, the skeptic, should be heeded in Rehmann's construction of the past if the work of mourning is ever to begin.

---

[32]Rehmann, "Die Väter," 130; my emphasis.

Desire for the Lost Father

The father-daughter relationship has always been an important constellation in literature. In German literature, its most pronounced expression is found in the "bürgerliches Trauerspiel," or bourgeois tragedy, in which daughters like Lessing's Emilia Galotti, Schiller's Luise Miller, and Hebbel's Maria Magdalena display an enduring allegiance to their fathers until a suitor appears and threatens not only the daughter's moral standing, but the father-daughter bond. These literary daughters represent potentially "weak links" in a chain of moral vigilance. They all share the same "flaw": they are female. In order to protect or recover their family's honor—equated with the father's name—they sacrifice themselves and destroy their bodies, the site of transgression and seduction. In demonstrating devotion to the father, these protagonists surrender their lives to "higher" principles established by the male order, thereby securing their moral superiority and the father's with it.

Even though the father-daughter relationship has filled pages of literature and consistently captured the literary imagination, this relationship has become an object of earnest investigation only since the 1980s.[33] In a study of Shakespearean fathers and daughters, Diane Dreher summarizes the problem: "Psychologists are [only now] beginning to understand the deep significance of the father-daughter bond. Much of their research is devoted to mothers and sons, and in a 1979 study, [an] author complains that there is no 'substantive literature on fathers and daughters.' "[34]

Interest in the father-daughter bond has arisen for numerous reasons. For instance, the women's movement and feminist inquiries have contributed to the investigation of the position of the female subject within the family and the formation of female subjectivity. The father, as many researchers and psychologists concur, most surely is an important mediator of female identity in Western nuclear families.[35] Women's representations of the father-daughter

[33]Lynda E. Boose and Betty S. Flowers, eds., *Daughters and Fathers* (Baltimore: Johns Hopkins University Press, 1989), 1.

[34]Diane Elizabeth Dreher, *Domination and Defiance* (Lexington: University of Kentucky Press, 1986), 1.

[35]In sociopsychological terms, the frequency of incest, which has gained public

relationship in literature assist in charting this sparsely mapped terrain. Through autobiographical accounts, stories often neglected and spheres of experience repressed have begun to find unreserved expression. In German literature, there have been few autobiographical confrontations with the father by daughters except for those that fall within the genre. Most renditions belong to the "literature of the fathers."

Paternal identities in German literature are usually enmeshed with representations of the state. Since the father traditionally circulated in the public sphere, he symbolically stood as participant in and agent of morality, history, and politics. In the postwar period, the appearance of the traditional father figure waned with the faltering of German national identity. The increasing repression of Nazism and the horrific crimes committed in its name led to a pervasive absence of the father from literature written between the 1950s and 1970s. The break with the father has much to do with his upbringing during a Wilhelmine era that promoted strict obedience and a regimen of discipline. In the hiatus of discussions concerned with working through the German past and mourning its victims, articles such as "Auf der Suche nach dem verlorenen Vater" (In search of the lost father) began to signal a renewed interest in the father figure.[36] The resuscitation of the father in autobiographical texts undoubtedly reflects a growing preoccupation with historical heritage. It implies a loss or at least a rupture of the relationship between German fathers and their children, a trauma unattended to that has endured for decades. A desire to exhume the lost father in order to explore the continuity of psychohistorical structures informs numerous works of the 1980s.

In Rehmann's (auto)biographical novel, the father doubles in the roles of pastor and parent. It is interesting that the title emphasizes the father's public role as a functionary of the church. Yet, a substratum in the narrative reveals a more oblique investment—

---

attention, as well as provoked examinations of Freud's "seduction theory," has led to questions concerning the dynamics in the relationship between father and daughter. Alice Walker's *The Color Purple* (New York: Washington Square Press, 1982) and Maya Angelou's *I Know Why the Caged Bird Sings* (New York: Bantam, 1970) were among the first works by women to address this issue.

[36]Herbert Glossner, "Auf der Suche nach dem verlorenen Vater," *Deutsches Allgemeines Sonntagsblatt*, 6 April 1980, p. 21.

namely, a desire for the father and sadness over loss—which explains the novel's inconsistent conclusions. Although no outright thematization of gender takes place in Rehmann's autobiographical narrative and no self-reflexive assessment of her position as daughter vis-à-vis her father occurs, events and attitudes are subtly conveyed that specifically shed light on the father-daughter cathexis.

In this novel, the daughter's voice constructs the narrative, but the profile of her own development as a daughter only faintly appears through the biographical confrontation with the father. His biography constitutes her autobiography, where she vanishes while he remains at center stage. Paradoxically, her retreat into the background complies with the Freudian family romance that has greatly neglected the daughter in its narrative. This narrative structure reinstates the relationship that Lynda Boose calls the most "asymmetrically proportioned in terms of gender, age, authority and cultural privilege."[37] Seen traditionally, the daughter epitomizes lack and powerlessness in every aspect of her life; therefore, meaning assigned to daughters is very different from that assigned to sons. For example, a daughter by birth threatens the very fabric of the family through her inability to carry on its name and therefore its tradition. The father's phallus and authority are passed on to the son; the daughter, in Lacanian and Freudian symbology, is left castrated within her own family and must seek the phallus (through bearing a child) outside of her natal family. The family relinquishes continuity and history and surrenders its daughter to find legitimation and a name outside its spheres. In her autobiographical project *Such Sad Tidings*, Elisabeth Plessen confides the stigma accompanying daughterhood. Engaging in an inner monologue, she confesses, "So I was not a celebration, I was a disappointment. The world as son. Preferably (and in all cases) as a series of sons."[38] In contrast to the privileged position of sons within the cultural texts of Western society, daughters have lived in suspension and

[37]Lynda E. Boose, "The Father's House and the Daughter in It: The Structures of Western Culture's Daughter-Father Relationship," in *Daughters and Fathers*, ed. Boose and Flowers, 20.

[38]Elisabeth Plessen, *Such Sad Tidings*, trans. Ruth Hein (New York: Viking Press, 1979), 145. See also Waltraud Anna Mitgutsch's novel *Die Züchtigung* (Munich: Dtv, 1987), in which the narrator, a daughter, describes the punishment she receives for being female.

have been moved along a patrilineage of names. Only recently have daughters, including Rehmann, begun to plot their own narratives and to contribute to the heretofore thin discussion that cordoned them off from the public sphere.

Within the patriarchal script of white Western culture, the father serves as a model, and he projects ideals for his daughter by representing an exciting sphere outside the home. In contrast, the mother is associated with passivity and regression, and her life is defined largely through her husband. Often, that the daughter desires and idealizes the father is a result of his absence. When the narrator retreats into the paradise of childhood, her "unadulterated" memories stray into the realm of the father. Memories of security, acceptance, warmth, and paternal omnipotence mark the beginning of the narrative. The father is described as representing an avenue to the outside world. He stands for autonomy and independence, reinforced by his area of control outside the family and public recognition of his work. In *Der Mann auf der Kanzel*, the narrator recalls walking with her father through his parish: "Admittance into fatherly warmth: to 'go into the community' holding his hand, recognized, greeted, showered with goodwill. . . . 'She is growing up,' the father says, proudly modest. 'She brings us a lot of joy!' " (9).[39] The daughter identifies with the father and feels the pride of association. Through him she gains access to the community and recognition.

In Rehmann's autobiographical exposé, the bond between father and the narrator is expressed in the formula "the two of us," a game played by father and daughter to acknowledge their special affinities and the exclusivity of their rapport. Her attachment poignantly reveals itself in the adult narrator's interpretation of their shared intimacy. In reproducing her past, she idealizes their similarities to the extent that liking the same candies takes on the function of a secular "unio mystica." Rehmann describes an intense spiritual symbiosis between daughter and father manifested in the most banal rituals of their daily life. Moreover, sitting in her father's study and observing his every move, the daughter fully integrates

---

[39]Many of the authors of "Väterliteratur" refer to the sense of security they felt in their father's presence. In *Suchbild*, Meckel writes: "A feeling of security and blind trust, a wonderful certainty in his proximity" (9).

herself into his routine and blends into her father's environment. Like a shadow, she follows him on visits through the parish and experiences his interaction and kindness with awe. As a spectator, she learns to identify with male subjectivity and inevitably takes on the father's perspective on the world. She repeatedly mentions a tacit synchronicity existing between father and daughter which unavoidably results in an internalization of his image and a hypersensitivity toward his needs. The empathy she develops toward him obscures the boundaries between daughter and father. When the father finds no interest in his wife for his war stories, he dejectedly concludes that only men understand this important phase of life. Sensing his defensive isolation, the daughter (stepping in for the mother) devises a game to counter her father's disappointment and at the same time seek approval: "In order to please her father, the child invents a new game: Soldiers" (50). Her emotional life is enmeshed with his; even as a child she works to secure an alliance as though to guarantee the bond and bridge absence.[40] Her supreme willingness to please the father betrays her desire to gain admission into his sphere. "Pleasing others" also belongs to the register of traditional female qualities that advance a psychological asymmetry between the sexes. More broadly, "pleasing others" manifests itself in self-sacrifice and submission (qualities cultivated in Christian theology), often culminating in self-abnegation. Translated into sociopsychological terms, the wish for acceptance in girls within traditional gendered arrangements leads to losing oneself in an identification with the father's perception.

The protagonist's self-awareness as a female derives from the father-daughter relationship, revealing the makings of gender. Already at an early age, the narrator learns to care for her father in a manner approximating traditional female role behavior, which she assesses as a simple role-reversal between parent and child:

> In the game around the chaise longue, the roles are distributed such that the father must lie down and the child must cover him, which he always prevents by catching the blue blanket with his foot and tossing it onto the floor. Finally he lets himself be tucked in and goes

[40]Jessica Benjamin, *The Bonds of Love: Psychoanalysis, Feminism, and the Problem of Domination* (New York: Pantheon Books, 1988), 115.

to sleep, while the child drags the Lutheran Bible from the table over
to the sofa. She lies down with the Bible. Sleeping is not required,
just silence. (22)

Her conditioning as a daughter runs along a multiplicity of axes,
one of which is learning to be silent. For the pastor, an orthodox
Protestant, the notion of "woman" is strongly informed by religion
and, especially by the epistles of Paul. The pastor asserts in a
dispute with the vicar's wife that women should above all be silent.
"But when women do open their mouths, then something soft
should come out, praising, approving, encouraging." He jokingly
yet conspiratorially calls upon the daughter to hand over an umbrella to shield him against women's speech, since "zealous women
inevitably spray saliva" (149). Her learning to be silent and invisible
is only mentioned at those times the daughter is in the presence
of the father: when he works in his study or when he visits parishioners, she is expected to wait in the corner of the room. Spatially marginalized, she remains an observer. Although their
relationship during her childhood is depicted as generally playful,
it is underpinned by a strong sense of the daughter's obedience
to, accommodation of, and understanding of her father. Significantly, the daughter is positioned to adapt to his needs, to learn
complacency, and to respect his authority. She is taught to respect
the thresholds and borders of her father's desires—a prerequisite
for gaining entrance into his sphere.

A child's self-awareness and the relationship between parent and
child are partly defined by the types of discourses that a family
permits and encourages and those they minimize or prohibit. In
the pastor's home, sexuality ranks with money, politics, and crime
as subjects that are emphatically taboo. The avoidance of these
topics imbues them with negativity or leads to a denial of their
existence altogether. It is not surprising that a tension besets the
pastor's relationship with his daughter once she linguistically asserts her gendered identity and announces that she no longer
wishes to be referred to as a child (in German marked by the neuter
pronoun "es") but rather as *she*. The father promptly retains a zone
of comfort by continuing to regard his daughter as a child and,
more important, by voicing his relief at her displays of so-called
tomboyishness: "she would have made a good boy" (135).

Their relationship later undergoes remarkable changes with the daughter's physical maturation, which implicitly brings with it a process of separation from the father. Referring to the child in the third person, which she sustains throughout the narrative and which reflects both her pronounced distance from herself and her inability to fully claim herself as child, the narrator recalls that "there is something about her growing up that he doesn't like, which is never named, not even hinted at or circumscribed, just this cool ray of dissatisfaction, always on the same silenced spot, which obviously cannot be loved, neither by him, nor by God. Which therefore should not exist" (135). The daughter's sexuality arouses the patriarch's anxiety, even though she continuously represses sexual curiosity. The father's unspoken disapproval and withdrawal of attention signal to the daughter that a maturing girl cannot be loved and suggest that the female body represents sin and even family shame. The daughter fears a break in the intimate bond with the father; she fears expulsion from her father's sphere and from his grace. The daughter's sexual development (which one critic reads as culturally threatening to "pollute the internal dynamics within the family space" by forcing its redefinition) is denied by the father, who refuses to acknowledge puberty, which, he contends, he never noticed when he was growing up.[41] The narrator speculates that the loss of childhood innocence threatens the pastor—it stands for the banishment from paradise and the possibility of evil, which he seems to have repressed in himself. The narrator wonders whether "a great and wise man like the father could be afraid of an adolescent" (138). As the daughter matures, the unity between father and daughter deteriorates, despite their nostalgic, albeit awkward, attempts to preserve its rituals: "When the father and child run into each other in the house, they sometimes stop and say: 'Do you remember—the two of us!?' like before, but it doesn't sound like that anymore" (136). A sense of loss accompanies their exchange, adumbrating the daughter's rejection as a sexual being.

Female sexuality interferes with the father-daughter relationship, just as the eighteenth-century "bourgeois tragedy" and other cultural texts and fictions teach. The erasure or containment of female

---

[41]Boose, "The Father's House and the Daughter," 35.

sexuality in order to sustain the father-daughter bond occurs through the daughter's self-sacrificial death in earlier fictions. In *Der Mann auf der Kanzel*, the father asks: "I wonder if we will reach that point again—the two of us" (136). The daughter dismisses his question, turning her thoughts to a missed rendezvous, as though replacing the father with another love object. The bond as it was is irretrievable, in part because the mature female body has wedged its way between father and daughter.

As the daughter moves away from the family into school and compulsory youth organizations, she grows estranged from her father. Awareness of his dwindling power, exacerbated by sickness, leaves her with a sense of abandonment. He no longer provides the security she once knew. Still, both father and daughter attempt to maintain their habitual rapport, indicating a relationship that has not survived changes and a fear of destabilizing the fragile harmony that neither is willing to unsettle, let alone challenge. The narrator plays the dutiful daughter, creating an ever-growing schism between gesture and desire. She avoids her father, afraid to confront his emotional needs and risk a redefinition of their relationship, as she is forced to do years later through her autobiographical exploration. Their steps are no longer synchronized. Contrary to the opening scenes of the novel, their walk at the end is haunted by an inner dissonance: "They flee while they closely walk next to each other, in arduous unison setting one foot in front of the other, their thoughts rushing past each other to form images that each one keeps within, and in the abandoned space in between only fright remains" (169). Stifled communication, tactics of avoidance, and a lack of honesty point to a growing barrier between father and daughter as the boundaries she had once learned to respect divide them now.

At the end, the autobiographer describes a wasteland between the two of them that she never satisfactorily crosses due to the fear of confronting and confirming what no longer exists. A stagnant relationship that defies the dynamic of history and process can only be proclaimed dead. The daughter's guilt and remorse appear to be over the lost possibility of engaging in a dialogue with her father and missing the opportunity for intimacy. The narrator regretfully concludes: "Instead of obligingly bowing one's head and letting the words fall in and somehow go to pieces, along with other unrecognized undertones and signals, a dialogue between people could have ensued. As it was, it remains despite the obliging answers a lost monologue, a call into emptiness" (170). The daughter does not hear her father's wishes, nor does she understand his fear during what turns out to be their last walk.

Many postwar authors admit to not really knowing their parents; in fact, they describe themselves as living on the periphery of the adult world as observers who lack the breadth of information to interpret their parents' lives. In the case of Rehmann's contemporaries, whose parents lived through World War II as adults and who as children witnessed their parents' daily life, a larger gap must be bridged because of their own implication in this period in Germany's history. A sense of guilt pervades the end of the narrative as the father is left without support, to confront his death as well as his life choices alone.

The incongruity between a child's knowledge of the father's public life and his or her emotional attachment to the father can make the gap between generations abysmal, depending on the extent of the father's involvement in the policies and politics of the Third Reich. For Rehmann, attempting to conflate two seemingly incompatible father images, the public and the private, leads to divergent readings of her father's biography. She wavers, assigning him historical guilt, on the one hand, and exonerating him, on the other. In many ways, the protagonist's behavior reflects Christa Wolf's observation of her generation's relationship to their parents. In an interview, Wolf astutely differentiates between her own generation and what she calls the third and fourth that follow:

> We who were young then were held for too long in father-son, mother-daughter relationships that made it hard for us to become mature. I believe that many of my generation never really recovered from that. They maintained the older, confining but also more comfortable bonds, instead of again reexamining the relationship in the process of their own maturation, to reformulate it from within, with a new understanding for the contradictions and conflicts of the older generation, for their mistakes, for the reasons for their failure on

certain points. It always takes two to make monuments and statues out of living people.[42]

Even though the daughter outgrows the father, she does not take leave of him. She has grown up amid patriarchs who have left indelible marks on her development. The teacher reminds the narrator of the child who sat silent in her father's study—a room filled with the aura of many fathers. He remarks upon her difficulty in leaving this secure setting of omnipotence and authority:

> Her father had three fathers: the biological one, the father in heaven, and the old emperor and king of Prussia. They were all gathered in this room, and between them, tiny, the child that you were. She stood behind her father on a footstool at the window, three or four years old, supposedly a lively child, but here she was as quiet as a mouse. "She's not a bother," the father praised, "one hardly notices that she is here." When I saw her so silent and self-content looking down at the street, I thought that it must be hard, almost impossible for such a child to leave this room overflowing with fatherliness. (16–17)

The teacher alludes to the difficulty of emotionally severing oneself from such a powerful influence. The autobiographer has internalized an adherence to authority, which Christa Wolf identifies as a primary structure passed on to succeeding generations in Germany. Rehmann at first counters the teacher's conjecture: " 'I'm an adult,' I said. 'The room no longer exists.' " He ominously responds: "Are you so sure?" (17).

The author's autobiographical inquiry begins by reentering this paternal sphere after many years to describe the very room she sets out to deny. Its place at the beginning and end of the narrative suggests its profound hold on her, as well as her disguised desire to reenter the father's realm where she experienced security through union. The mother and the narrator's two daughters all but vanish from the paternal script Rehmann reinstates. They are repressed, like the author's own voice, within the paternal lineage

---

[42]Christa Wolf, "Unerledigte Widersprüche," in *Im Dialog* (Luchterhand: Darmstadt, 1990), 30.

she plots. Only the son is willing to advance the narrative. Thomas, the biblical doubter, puts his finger on the difficulty of choosing a subject so existentially intertwined with personal identity. He represents Rehmann's self-reflective voice in the form of a third person aware of the perils inherent in her undertaking and of her personal guilt in avoiding her father. Instead of heeding the warning, she creates a monument of the father and a mausoleum for her memories. The narrator has inherited her father's selective vision. In the end, she remains caught within the room of fathers, too fearful to cross the threshold she was taught to respect.

4

Helma Sanders-Brahms's
Germany, Pale Mother

This motherhood is the fantasy that is nurtured by the adult,
man or woman, of a lost territory.
> Julia Kristeva, "Stabat Mater"

The past falls into ruin and vanishes only in appearance.
> Maurice Halbwachs, *On Collective Memory*

A Cinematic Triptych

What is it like to be a child of parents who lived through World
War II? How do their experiences intersect with the formation of
one's own identity and influence the profiles of one's own life?
Questions like these have given rise to personal explorations in
which writers and filmmakers set out to become the ethnogra-
phers of their own lives. Filmmakers such as Jeanine Meerapfel
(*Malou*, 1981), Jutta Brückner (*Years of Hunger*, 1980), and Marianne
Rosenbaum (*Peppermint Peace*, 1982), took part in this investigation
that dominated the early 1980s. In *Deutschland, bleiche Mutter*
(*Germany, Pale Mother*), which premiered at the Berlin Film Festival
in 1980, Helma Sanders-Brahms traces her life as a child during
World War II and the postwar years of reconstruction.[1] In exploring her own subjectivity, she focuses on her parents' lives
and the collision between their private dreams and the politics
of the Third Reich.

Personal histories deal primarily with the private realm. When
childhood is restaged, the home often becomes the site of nostalgic
reminiscences, eliciting a sense of security. In *Berliner Kindheit*, according to Burkhardt Lindner, Walter Benjamin "re-writes the topography of childhood" as a poetics of rooms, the spatial trans-

---

[1]Helma Sanders-Brahms, *Deutschland, bleiche Mutter: Film-Erzählung* (Hamburg:
Rowohlt, 1980). All quotes designated by page numbers are taken from this edition;
the translations are mine.

lation of intimacy and interiority.[2] Secure within the walls of memory, Elias Canetti, in his autobiographical novel *The Tongue Set Free*, sentimentally recalls his childhood as a time that set him on his course as a writer. Unlike a number of autobiographical renditions of childhood in German literature before the 1960s, many contemporary autobiographical representations portray the home and family as the ground of oppression and discontent. In *A Sorrow beyond Dreams*, for example, Peter Handke speculates on the restrictive conditions of Austrian society and the limited possibilities for women as factors that drove the narrator's mother to commit suicide. *Why Is There Salt in the Sea?* by Brigitte Schwaiger, another Austrian, expresses disillusionment with marriage and family in a cynical account of the middle-class conventions that stifle individual development.[3] Seen by many authors as an ideological construct supported by nineteenth-century beliefs, the intimate realm of marriage and family today evokes troubled responses.

For Sanders-Brahms, the home, as synecdoche for family, stands for confinement, death, and the intrusion of the father, of the "fatherland." Sanders-Brahms introduces the house as a construct of ideology and marks three phases in her tableau of the past: entry into the domestic sphere; a period of homelessness standing for paternal absence and a pure psychological symbiosis with the mother; and the reconstruction of the house. The filmmaker introduces these three phases to delineate her autobiographical beginnings.

Moreover, the film functions as a triptych, a form symbolically reinforced by a three-paneled mirror appearing at various times throughout the film. Traditionally serving as an altarpiece, the triptych was used as a visual narrative depicting religious scenes or figures that transmitted Christian values through a sequence of images. The montage of scenes could be seen as an early precursor to moving pictures. In the twentieth century, the triptych has often been used to depict the rejection and unmasking of bourgeois ide-

[2]Burkhardt Lindner, "The Archaeology of the Recent Past," *New German Critique* 39 (1986): 26.

[3]In several works written after the 1970s, the home has become the target of critical confrontation. See especially works by Thomas Bernhard, Elfriede Jelinek, Waltraud Anna Mitgutsch, and Gabriele Wohmann.

ology and the interests concealed in the name of religion. As in *Germany, Pale Mother*, the tripartite division magnifies the tension among the ideals promoted by Christianity, its sanctification of marriage and family, and the translation of Christian ideals into concrete sociohistorical contexts. Like the Expressionist painters Max Beckmann and Otto Dix, and later the artist Francis Bacon, Sanders-Brahms polemically reproduces a religiously imbued form of representation and subverts it within its own framework. She shows how her parents' lives and hopes were shaped by ideals promoted for ideological reasons that were exploited in fascist Germany.

Traditionally, too, the middle panel of a triptych contains the central event. The disruption of the nuclear family during World War II is presented as the most significant phase of the autobiographer's development. It is flanked by representations of an intact family triad, first as an institution, biblically legitimated as the seat of happiness and harmony, then, as a "Lost Paradise." Because of the irreparability of the ruptured myth, and more important, the sudden dissolution of the exclusive bond between mother and daughter, this paradise is irretrievable. In each segment, the house metonymically represents the sphere of woman's oppression.

When one looks closely at *Germany, Pale Mother* as a cinematic triptych, one sees that the first segment establishes the relationship of the couple Hans and Lene, played by the actors Ernst Jacobi and Eva Mattes. The layers of fictional subtexts that inform their love story are woven throughout the narrative. Their dreams and expectations are largely defined by fictions that, in Bill Nichols's words, "contribute to our sense of who we are and our everyday engagement with the world around us."[4] As cultural models, these fictions shape perceptions and assign meaning to experiences.[5] When the bride Lene enters her new home for the first time, she

---

[4]Bill Nichols, *Ideology and the Image: Social Representation in the Cinema and Other Media* (Bloomington: Indiana University Press, 1981), 3.

[5]See Jean Jacques Rousseau, *The Confessions*, trans. J. M. Cohen (Middlesex, England: Penguin Books, 1953), 21. In *The Confessions*, Rousseau dates the beginning of his self-consciousness from his first encounter with literature: "I knew nothing of myself till I was five or six. I do not know how I learnt to read. I only remember my first books and their effect upon me; it is from my earliest reading that I date the unbroken consciousness of my own existence."

concurs with a neighbor's comparison of her wedding day to a film: "Mrs. Meierholt from next door said that it's just like a film." Hans affirms: "It's really like in a film" (36).

The mediated "reality" organizes meaning and serves as her reference point, forming a subtext in the first part of the film that affirms the couple's innocence. In order to verify the reality of her story and new environment, Lene walks around the room touching various objects. The pricking of her finger on a needle in the bedroom alludes to the fairy tale "Sleeping Beauty," and its prophecy of misfortune is conveyed by Hans's putting Lene's finger to his lips as though drawing the life out of her. Later, the reflection of Hans and Lene together in the three-paneled mirror visually consummates their unity in an idealized existence as unsuspecting, even blameless, participants in the fictions that inform their lives. In a voice-over, the filmmaker as daughter describes her mother and the type of life for which she was prepared: "And my mother, brought up to be a serious, loving, and innocent girl, who entered marriage with honesty and tenderness" (10). Yet Hans and Lene's lives take an abrupt turn when Hans receives his draft notice. A jump cut into a triste, claustrophobic image of the private sphere, filtered in brown tones instead of the lighter tones of the preceding scene, visually reinforces the violent transition. Hitler's blaring radio voice and the Nazi greeting penetrate the idyll as the politics of the public sphere and their consequences literally shatter the home.[6]

The transition to the middle section of the triptych is marked by the destruction of the house. One panel of the mirror protrudes from the rubble to reflect Lene's changed identity. Looking into the damaged mirror, she comments, "And that was once me" (58). Now outside the constraint of an established order, she begins a new life. Sanders-Brahms romantically emphasizes the release of Lene's hidden strengths as she emerges from her former silence. The autobiographical focus also changes significantly with the introduction of the child, Anna, the filmmaker's persona, played in part by Sanders-Brahms's own daughter. A time of idealized symbiosis between mother and daughter is exhibited, their exclusive

---

[6]Sanders-Brahms's use of the radio throughout her film is reminiscent of Rainer Werner Fassbinder's in illustrating the interdependence of public and private.

"That was our house . . . and that was once me."

Eva Mattes in *Germany, Pale Mother*

mutual dependency intensified by the lack of other caretakers in the child's life. For Anna, the exterior circumstances inhibit any possibility of separation, nurturing a stronger than usual attachment to Lene. The filmmaker's remembrance of this exclusive commitment translates into Lene and Anna's walk to Berlin, ebulliently characterized as an adventure in which they roam through war-torn Germany like the German poet Joseph von Eichendorff's romantic Taugenichts character: "To Berlin on foot. On high heels, with high spirits. The vagabond Lene and I" (113). The wide-open spaces impart a sense of freedom in a world suspiciously outside of history, outside of time and context.

Reproducing a child's subjective, emotional perspective in order to explicate her own personal history and development during this time, Sanders-Brahms casts the image of mother and daughter with

a naive comment: "You became loyal after the house was destroyed. That's when we really did well, once everything was
gone" (113). The daughter's perspective not only controls the narrative, but the reproduction of subjective memory for the most part
shapes Sanders-Brahms's project. She goes so far as to cast the
older-looking Ernst Jacobi in the role of her father, since, as she
admits: "You were as young as she was, my father. But in my
memory, your face is always as old as when you returned from
the war to which they sent you" (112). The discordance between
sentiment and the historical background caused by the child's myopic perspective has provoked much critical concern.[7] The filmmaker, however, commits only partially to this singular perspective
that appears theoretically justifiable only within the framework of
an autobiographical project motivated by the desire to reassemble
a segment of time past. One advantage in immersing oneself in
subjective memory, as Helen Fehervary suggests, is the possibility
of rendering alternative histories. By this, I mean the providing of
additional information to expand historical understanding, particularly of a time that continuously escapes representation. In an
interview, Fehervary explores the relationship to history many
women have pursued: "The relationship between history and so-
called subjective processes is not a matter of grasping the truth in
history as some objective entity, but in finding the truth of experience. Evidently, this kind of experiential immediacy has to do
with women's own history and self-consciousness."[8] The reconstruction of history guided by a subjective inquiry or "subjective
authenticity," to use Christa Wolf's term, coincides with many
feminist efforts of the 1970s that were faced with little, if any,
documentation of women's activities.

But Sanders-Brahms also guards against the use of the child's
perspective as sole mediator. Interspliced documentary footage re-

[7]The fascination with exploring a child's vision of the world is not new. In
Amarcord, Fellini thematizes the spatially distorted view of an eight-year-old. In
Günter Grass's *Die Blechtrommel* (*The Tin Drum*), which Volker Schlöndorff adapted
for film, the world is seen through the child Oskar's eyes.

[8]Helen Fehervary, Claudia Lenssen, and Judith Mayne, "From Hitler to Hepburn:
A Discussion of Women's Film Production and Reception," *New German Critique*
24–25 (1982): 176.

lativizes Anna's viewpoint and emphasizes the subjective processing of experience. When Anna and Lene bathe after arriving
in Berlin, the voice-over conspicuously reenacts Anna's feelings:
"This is the way Lene and I loved each other in the bathtub and
flew over rooftops like witches" (113). A documentary aerial view
of Berlin destroyed by bombs juxtaposes the child's perspective
and undermines the sentiment produced by the voice-over. The
same sobering strategy appears in an earlier scene when Lene,
carrying Anna on her shoulders, talks to a homeless boy, depicted
in documentary footage. He has been searching for his parents for
more than a month. Besides calling attention to Anna's privileged
position of security, the combination of documentary footage with
"fiction" or autobiographical remembrance reminds the viewer
that history, like any written text, is a process of reconstruction.
A number of contemporary German filmmakers, such as Helke
Sander, Jutta Brückner, and Alexander Kluge, have used this strategy to dissolve the borders between fact and fiction, between subjectivity and objectivity, and to question traditional boundaries.

Even though the traumas of wartime often become a secondary
experience in autobiographical recollections of childhood, since the
child does not take issue with the broader meaning of war, the
historical context inevitably influences the autobiographer's understanding of her or his life. Drawing on Helga Schütz's novel
Mädchenrätsel (Girls' riddles), Werner Brettschneider addresses the
ways in which children process their experiences of war: "The
children's kingdom remains sovereign amidst the ruins. What
grown-ups do lies on the fringes, only perceived insofar as it
touches the children's world; it is taken in, reflected, and transformed into [the child's] manner of experiencing."[9] His description
applies to Sanders-Brahms's autobiographical rendering of this
time period. The effects of war unavoidably influence and provide
reference points for the child's formative years, even though she

---

[9]Werner Brettschneider, *Kindheitsmuster: Kindheit als Thema autobiographischer Dichtung* (Berlin: Erich Schmidt Verlag, 1982), 25. Brettschneider's observation is best
illustrated by Marianne Rosenbaum's autobiographical film *Peppermint Peace* (1982),
in which the war and postwar years are filtered through a child's eyes. The limitations of her interpretive powers and her lack of knowledge lead to a convoluted
piecing together of information.

processes them in relation to her own immediate needs. Because of the war, Anna becomes the focal point of Lene's life during Hans's absence. In many ways, she even serves as his substitute.[10]

In *Germany, Pale Mother*, the father-daughter relationship is actually rooted in the father's pervasive absence. Unlike the father in Rehmann's novel, the father in Sanders-Brahms's film remains a stranger who threatens the daughter's exclusive right to the mother and who later causes the violent separation of mother and daughter. Reconstructing her feelings as a child, the narrator comments: "What was my father supposed to do with me? I was jealous of him and he of me" (113). Oral histories recently compiled reveal that estrangement between fathers and their children was not uncommon after World War II. For Anna, Hans belongs to a gender signifying danger and destruction. The rape of her mother by American soldiers at the war's end and the Grimm's fairy tale of the robber bridegroom, which Anna's mother recites while they travel through stark landscapes of war-torn Germany, inform her concept of men. But rather than indict the father as a figure of patriarchy, Sanders-Brahms sympathetically and equitably portrays the influences that ravage his life, beginning with her father's induction into a war he did not support. These events shape the narrator's biography as well.[11]

The third segment of the cinematic triptych represents the postwar restoration of the home and nuclear family. The private sphere becomes a displaced battlefield. The matte blue tonalities of the house's interior suggest a dismal and tense climate, in contrast to the clear, crisp colors of the landscapes during the war. The private

[10]Eva Hiller, "Mütter und Töchter," *Frauen und Film* 24 (1980): 30. The relationship between mother and daughter, according to Hiller, is intensified through the absence of the father: "Anna is conceived with the explicit intention that she become both a memory of and a substitute for the absent father. From the start she does not belong to herself, but rather is a fetish. From the time of birth on one sees mostly images of mother and daughter together. The outwardly imposed necessity of being together appears to pose no problem. The child never wants to leave the mother's warmth, and Lene tightly holds onto her daughter. Both of them seem to guarantee security for each other and an independence from the rest of the world. Everything outside is suspiciously tested and rejected."

[11]*Germany, Pale Mother* is primarily Lene's story. In her fifty-two-minute documentary film *My Father, Hermann S.* (1986), Sanders-Brahms explores various episodes of her father's life during the war. Accompanying him to the sites at which he fought in France, she listens while he retraces his past.

sphere is horrifyingly transformed from a site of desire and hope to one of death and disillusionment at the end. A foreboding voice-over intones: "Lene, what should we have expected of peace? At first after the war, cleaning up was still fun. But the rocks that we hammered were used to build houses that were worse than before. Lene, if only we had known that" (113). And then: "That was the return of the living rooms. The war inside began when there was peace outside" (113). Documentary footage of the famed "Trümmerfrauen" ("women of the rubbble") ironically dramatizes women rebuilding the sites of their own demise.[12]

The first scene marking reentry into the home demonstrates the attempt to retrieve the past by reasserting traditional roles. Lene appears fragmented; the camera focuses on her hands, metonymically signifying servitude as she carries a tray of coffee, while Anna fastidiously practices her handwriting. Engaged in separate activities, the family members appear disconnected from one another rather than harmoniously united. Lene and Anna, distant and isolated, are confined within their own frames of film in sharp contrast to their prior physical proximity. When Hans commands Anna to write neatly, he reveals his desire to return to a prewar order as well as the misconception that the readjustment of the outer world contains inner chaos.

Sanders-Brahms explores the encroachment of the war and its aftershocks on her life. She shows how prewar illusions of home, marriage, and family cannot survive in the postwar era, since an emotionally devastating vacuum accompanies the loss of innocence. Both Hans and Lene needed to reconcile experiences of war and reassess the expectations derived from their earlier preparation for life. Among the concepts that demanded an altered understanding is the notion of the private sphere as a timeless, reliable refuge. In her focus on Lene, Sanders-Brahms looks at the destructiveness of culturally determined schisms between life spheres. The characterization of the private sphere as static discredited and even silenced vast realms of experience. Lene's war ordeals contradict Hans's image of the home front: "You have it good here at home. You can still dance. You can't even imagine what is happening on

---

[12]Sibylle Meyer and Eva Schulze, *"Wie wir das alles geschafft haben"—alleinstehende Frauen berichten über ihr Leben nach 1945* (Munich: Beck, 1984).

the front" (67). His misrepresentation heightens the sense of estrangement of a husband and a wife already isolated by their disparate circumstances, long separation, and the horrors of war. No ideology helps Hans and Lene link historical events to personal fates to interpret or mourn the collective and personal war experience. They reassemble their lives, repressing the historical continuity, without coming to terms with their immediate pasts.

Sanders-Brahms shows the generation of silence and its devastating effects, such as the misreading and the denial of symptoms; for instance, Hans mistakes Lene's distance for a sign of infidelity and her psychosomatic paralysis for an orthodontic malady.[13] Old models of interpretation prove inadequate for the comprehension of the postwar psychology; they only obscure reasons for Lene's behavior, which eventuates in a distortion of her face. The prescribed treatment, extracting her teeth, further disempowers and leads to her withdrawal. Hans and Lene's disillusionment with resuming life as before finds no productive outlet, and their unarticulated war experiences make it impossible to return to a relationship of reciprocity and understanding. Unlike the former Nazi, Ulrich, Hans and Lene are unable to bury their problems in the frenzy of Erhardt's economic miracle of the 1950s. Their love story is irredeemable. Alexander Kluge, whose filmic montages

[13]One reason *Germany, Pale Mother* was so controversial was the filmmaker's explicit portrayal of the private sphere, which threatens the fabric of society, questions the authority of that realm, and therefore, in some minds, should remain a private matter. Certainly, many generations were taught not to discuss family problems outside of the home. This attitude toward the private sphere and especially toward the recent German past, which some would rather have erased from popular memory, naturally influenced the reception of Sanders-Brahms's film. Some critics even created a psychogram of the various reactions to the film in order to address the sense of threat that confrontations with the personal realm produce. See Olav Münzberg "Schaudern vor der bleichen Mutter," *Medium* 10, no. 7 (1980): 34–37. Münzberg's sociopsychological analysis of the reviews of *Germany, Pale Mother* suggests that the film, by breaking cultural taboos, arouses unresolved anxieties. Not surprisingly, reception of the film was much more positive outside the Federal Republic, where spectators were conceivably less emotionally involved. In an interview with Renate Fischetti, Sanders-Brahms discusses her film's popularity in France, where it played for one and a half years in one movie theater. It also won first prize at the 1980 Women's Film Festival in Sceaux. See Renate Fischetti, *Das neue Kino: Acht Porträts von deutschen Regisseurinnen* (Dülmen-Hiddingsel: Tende, 1992) 145; interview with Helma Sanders-Brahms in *Die Kunst ist weiblich*, ed. Gabriele Presber (Munich: Knauer, 1988), 280–309.

highlight the collision between private lives and history, capsulizes this problem as follows:

> What is a love story when measured against compulsory military service? Imagine two lovers in August of 1939. They just got to know one another. And a love story ensues, just like Fontane would describe the beginnings of a love story. And then the first of September 1939 comes along and he is drafted. And he may be able to take leave three times, if he's lucky. Once he even had four days off. It's too short to love each other and too long to start doing something together. He returns from a Soviet prisoner-of-war camp in 1953, and now this couple is supposed to dutifully continue the love affair that began in August of 1939 and "was only briefly interrupted for a few years." This is an example of history's relationship to the history of people's relationships; and we of course only have experience with the latter.[14]

Germany, Pale Mother, like many feminist projects, looks at the inevitable interdependence of the private and public spheres and the consequences of misconceiving, and even repressing, the interchange between them. "I want to have my peace and quiet. And the brunette. Just live, do you understand? The Führer can't have anything against that" (30). This sentence echoes ominously throughout the film. The final sequence and the knowledge of two failed lives serve as an epitaphic response to the impossibility of pulling down the blind to escape history, as Lene does at the beginning of the film when she sees Rahel Bernstein dragged away by the Gestapo, or when she goes into the ransacked Jewish-owned store to look for embroidery thread.

Sanders-Brahms addresses her parents' lives and provides them with the forum they lacked. In her film script, the filmmaker explains: "And I believe that my parents are also looking for someone to tell them about their own history. Not by moralizing, not in the sense of: it had to turn out that way, but rather in a way that makes them recognize it and think about it one more time, instead of continuing to repress it" (10). Sanders-Brahms does not revert to the accusatory tone of the student movement of the late 1960s,

[14]Alexander Kluge, "Das Politische als Intensität alltäglicher Gefühle," *Freibeuter* 1 (1979): 57.

but instead she compassionately investigates the conditions that touched her parents' lives. *Germany, Pale Mother* exemplifies the new orientation toward parents that became a trademark of the 1980s in the Federal Republic. The change resulted from the need of a generation of historical orphans born between 1940 and 1945 to deal with themselves and Germany's recent past. Even though she speaks to her parents, Sanders-Brahms focuses, as does any autobiographical project, on her own story. She works through her parents' pasts and sets the stage for a confrontation with her own legacy: "It's true, and I believe them when they say they didn't want all this to happen. They didn't prevent it, either. We reproach them, but with what justification? How are we any better, except that we have the advantage of being the next generation . . . I have decided to tell my parents' story, because I know them, because it affects me" (11). The question remains whether Sanders-Brahms possesses the same psychic structures as her parents, or whether she is able to work through a history that is apt to be repeated.

The Cinematic Epistolary

There has been little discussion of film and female authorship since women have taken their place as filmmakers. As Judith Mayne observes, "Theoretical discussions of female authorship in the cinema have been surprisingly sparse."[15] Without any tradition of female cinematic authorship, women filmmakers must reformulate their relationship to the cinematic apparatus, especially when establishing strategies to secure an "I" and to "inflect the noun *authorship* in a way significant enough to challenge or displace its patriarchal and proprietary implications."[16] Even less discussion can be accounted for in terms of women filmmakers and autobiographical representation.

Germany, Pale Mother exists on the cusp between alternative cinema and narrative, or dominant, cinema in relation to some of the fundamental questions raised by feminist or avant-garde film the-

[15] Judith Mayne, *The Woman at the Keyhole* (Bloomington: Indiana University Press, 1990), 90.
[16] Ibid., 95.

ories. One of the central questions is the positioning of the spectator within the film, or, as Claire Johnston puts it, "what kind of reader the film text constructs."[17] If the need to maintain the transparency of enunciation is axiomatic in autobiographical representations, then it is necessary to investigate the various strategies of film viewing that deter or promote knowledge of "who or what is speaking."

In "Story/Discourse: Notes on Two Kinds of Voyeurism" (1975/ 76), film theorist Christian Metz relies on a binary structure to reconstitute the film text as an utterance. He distinguishes between two types of cinematic enunciation: story and discourse. Story typifies the structure of narrative cinema as a complete and hermetically closed form "that obliterates all traces of enunciation" with a narrative that purports to tell everything, and "based on a refusal to admit that anything is lacking or that anything has to be sought for."[18] "Histoire" or "story," Metz continues, is a "story from nowhere, that nobody tells, but which, nevertheless, somebody receives (otherwise it would not exist)."[19] The story cannot exist without a spectator inscribed in the fiction.

The camera subsequently simulates the viewer's perspective, which corresponds to the perspective of a character, creating an illusionary and manipulated identification with the imaginary. One of the most conventional means of promoting visual identification is the shot/countershot, which visually "sutures" the viewer into the film's enunciation by assimilating the viewer's perspective with that of the fictional character. Seduced into the narrative, the viewer becomes complicit with the narrative and, according to some film theories, silently affirms the "truth content" of the classical narrative structure. The sequence of events takes on a semblance of inevitability so that meaning and a certain type of logic become naturalized. The uncritical viewer succumbs to the reading of the

[17]Claire Johnston, "Toward a Feminist Film Practice: Some Theses," in *Movies and Methods* II, ed. Bill Nichols (Berkeley: University of California Press, 1985), 316.

[18]Christian Metz, "Story/Discourse: Notes on Two Kinds of Voyeurism," in *Movies and Methods* II, ed. Bill Nichols (Berkeley: University of California Press, 1985), 544. Metz's argument, based on the concept of a binary opposition, poses theoretical problems in terms of the spectator he constructs. Yet, his observations are helpful in understanding the text as enunciation. His analysis is especially productive for understanding autobiographical practices in filmmaking.

[19]Ibid., 548.

world through the ideology promoted by the narrative that controls the cinematic apparatus. Mas'ud Zavarzadeh explains: "The framing ideology places the spectator in a position of intelligibility from which she understands the ideologically available . . . meaning of the film to be its 'real meaning'."[20] A mass audience that engages in a potentially heterogeneous viewing experience is given a single perspective. The possibility of an autobiographical mode—a response rooted in different individual experiences—dissipates.[21]

In contrast to the structures that characterize "story," in Metz's view, "discourse" profiles the source of enunciation and initiates a dialogue between "I," the initiator of the speech act, and "you," its recipient. The subjective perspective is secured through the first-person pronoun and the interaction between speaker and addressee. In other words, the viewer is not manipulated to identify with a particular viewpoint. The discursive quality of *Germany, Pale Mother* is established with the voice-over, a disembodied female voice (Sanders-Brahms's own voice) that comments on the images. Unlike filmmakers in a number of other contemporary feminist films, Sanders-Brahms uses the voice-over sparingly, produces only sporadic moments of distance, and does not self-reflexively take issue with the ways in which she produces a historical narrative. Whereas for Christa Wolf in *Patterns of Childhood*, memory is itself problematic, Anton Kaes has noted that "in Sanders-Brahms's film, the actual process of historical reconstruction does not seem to pose a problem; memory and narration run parallel."[22] When the voice off-camera, the voice of memory, is implemented, however, the dialogue extends beyond the parameters of the diegesis and, more important, asserts both an exteriority and interiority. The viewer becomes involved with the experiences portrayed.

[20]Mas'ud Zavarzadeh, *Seeing Film Politically* (Albany: State University of New York Press, 1991), 19.

[21]There has been much discussion on the relationship between spectator and film in film criticism. For a comprehensive and searching (even autobiographical at times) discussion of the various profiles of the spectator in film criticism, see *Camera Obscura* 20–21 (1989), the issue on "Spectatrix." It is not my intention to reinstall a monolithic spectator who bears no traces of gender, race, class, or ethnicity or to deny the possibility of different forms of interaction. My aim is to distinguish filmmaking processes that traditionally suppress the enunciation and do not engage in self-reflexivity from those that do.

[22]Anton Kaes, *From Hitler to Heimat: The Return of History as Film* (Cambridge: Harvard University Press, 1989), 146.

In *Germany, Pale Mother*, the primacy of the filmmaker's perspective through the inscription of the author within the text is
secured at the outset, when she identifies her parents and establishes herself as the narrator of Hans and Lene's story. Although
the seams of the film are not clearly exposed—as in, for example,
Laura Mulvey's experimental feminist film *Riddles of the Sphinx*
(1977), which immediately acknowledges the source of enunciation
by the intertitle "Laura speaks"—in *Germany, Pale Mother* the voice-
over cuts between the filmic image and the viewer, who is often
challenged to reassess the visual information and fill in the gaps.
The narrator is the author as well as the speaking subject; she
reconstructs and narrates her mother's past. The commentary interprets the images and establishes the autobiographical viewpoint
in relation to the image. When Hans and Lene embrace as new-
lyweds, for instance, the commentary interrupts the intimacy conveyed in the image and robs it of its innocence and romance. A
third person wedges her way between them, establishing a space
comfortably occupied by the child, and one that the adult desires
to reconfigure: "I cannot imagine your embrace. I cannot imagine
how your skin and yours touch each other. You are my parents.
I am between you. I never married. I learned better of it from you"
(12). The voice-over not only distances the viewer but also directs
attention toward the narrator as the subject of speech.

Through the voice-over, the filmmaker controls the gaze from
outside the diegesis and forcefully brings the past into relation with
the present. A dialogue between past and present, between the
filmmaker as child and as adult and between daughter and mother
is established. Sanders-Brahms introduces herself as "I," the speaking subject, who, as Kaja Silverman notes, "refers to the existential
person engaged in discourse, and the subject of speech."[23] Sanders-
Brahms introduces Lene as "you" in the form of a visual letter—
a letter of desire. Through her use of the first-person pronoun, the
narrator activates her own subjectivity and allies herself with a
tradition of letter writing, a literary form rooted in female self-
expression. Desire for the lost mother orchestrates the "reading"
of the filmmaker's epistolary cinema.

[23]Kaja Silverman, *The Acoustic Mirror: The Female Voice in Psychoanalysis and Cinema*
(Bloomington: Indiana University Press, 1988), 200.

In *Women's Pictures: Feminism and Cinema*, Annette Kuhn differentiates between deconstructive cinema or countercinema, and cinema constituted by a female voice. The difference, she avers, lies in the techniques employed to challenge the signifying practices of narrative cinema. In early deconstructive films by Helke Sander, Claudia Alemann, Ulrike Ottinger, and Valie Export, Kuhn says that cinema sets out to "break down and challenge the forms of pleasure privileged by dominant texts"; whereas cinema structured around the female voice attempts to create new forms of pleasure.[24] Pleasure, for example, may be derived from the textual organization and new forms of identification and subjectivity diverging from traditional dominant narrative patterns. A nonlinear format differs from mainstream representation, as does the introduction of an authorial female voice. Since it is generally associated with diegetic interiority and denied an active role in discourse, the female voice as agent of the narrative deviates markedly from the classical paradigm.

Even though Sanders-Brahms does not highlight the fiction-making process, like many deconstructive feminist filmmakers do, she implicitly resists various structures of narrative cinema in the way she develops her film's autobiographical properties. This does not hold true for her later films, such as *Flügel und Fessel* (*The Future of Emily*, 1984) and *Laputa* (1986), which pursue traditional narrative patterns and lapse further into awkward melodrama than does *Germany, Pale Mother*, the melodramatic effects of which at times function subversively.[25]

As already mentioned, the voice-over plays a key role in pro-

---

[24]Annette Kuhn, *Women's Pictures: Feminism and Cinema* (London: Routledge and Kegana, 1982), 168.

[25]For a discussion of melodrama in Sanders-Brahms's film, see Ellen E. Seiter, "Women's History, Women's Melodrama: *Deutschland, bleiche Mutter*," *German Quarterly* 59, no. 4 (1986). Even though discussions of melodrama do not fall within the scope of my analysis, many critics have analyzed the melodramatic effects of *Germany, Pale Mother*. In *Politics of the Self: Feminism and the Postmodern in West German Literature and Film* (Princeton: Princeton University Press, 1991), Richard McCormick gives an excellent analysis of Sanders-Brahms's subversive implementation of melodrama and its politicizing function through Brechtian techniques of distanciation. For further feminist readings of melodrama, see Christine Gledhill, "The Melodramatic Field: An Investigation," *Home Is Where The Heart Is: Studies in Melodrama and the Woman's Film*, ed. Christine Gledhill (London: British Film Institute, 1987), 5–39.

ducing the autobiographical mode in *Germany, Pale Mother*. The filmmaker's commentary demonstrates discursive power and authorial subjectivity while engaging in the work of memory. Yet the authorial perspective is not confined to the voice-over: it appears within recurring images that reveal various sites of desire and emotional investment; it appears in the camera work and even in the cut. The camera-eye in *Germany, Pale Mother* visually explores its subjects, creating the effect that someone is looking in from outside. The camera explores space and evokes an autobiographical curiosity as the detached camera perspective emphasizes the process of looking or watching. In some scenes—as when Lene enters her new home for the first time—the camera even simulates a wandering eye, optically caressing the images. While Lene slowly walks through the rooms, the camera-eye glides down her bridal gown, watches her footsteps, and then follows her and Hans. Because the perspective is not diegetically established, it suggests an observer, someone outside the frame both temporally and spatially. The hand-held camera also self-reflexively alludes to an exterior presence. As Hans Blumenberg notes, these episodes are invitations to look.[26] Yet the act of looking has been highly codified in mainstream cinema. The gaze, traditionally enjoyed by the male, has seldom been the privilege of the female. By calling attention to the process of looking and a field of vision, secured by the female voice, Sanders-Brahms counters classical paradigms with an alternative aesthetic.

That the filmmaker rarely uses the technique of cutting also suggests a subjective commentary and relation to the image. Especially at the film's beginning and center, unusually long, uncut sequences suggest visual pleasure and a meditative mode or dreamlike quality. Blumenberg observes, "From the very first image on, Helma Sanders privileges a planned sequence, the representation of an event without cutting, with long, often complicated angles that explore scenes of action, establishing relationships between characters."[27] The editing resembles the turning of album pages and a

---

[26] Hans C. Blumenberg, "Ein Brief an Lene," Review of *Germany, Pale Mother* by Helma Sanders-Brahms, *Die Zeit*, 10 October 1980, p. 54.

[27] Ibid., 54. The next lines of Blumenberg's critique reveal the prejudices that still shroud women's artistic productions. Blumenberg uses stereotypical imagery that

lingering fascination. The fast cuts in the film, usually associated with Hans, emulate the tension that builds in the private sphere and the sense of intrusion. The shot/reverse shot registers aggression as the rift between Hans and Lene grows. The visual severance of emotional space is emblematic of the couple's development. Besides the subjective camera and editing, the author outside the text merges at times with the diegesis. The image of the child, for instance, mirrors the author within the text.

Much harder to discern is the "libidinal coherence" that Kaja Silverman cites as "the desire that circulates [in the text], more or less perceptibly."[28] Silverman argues that authorial desire can be detected at the nodal points to which an author continuously returns. Authorial desire can be read in the relationship established by an image, a landscape, or a sound. What the camera lens sees becomes a synecdoche for the first-person pronoun or agent, disclosing subjective predisposition and divulging sites of desire. In *Germany, Pale Mother*, desire is directed toward the mother's face, from the camera's first bonding with Lene's image to its fixing on Lene at the end. She is the site to which the filmmaker repeatedly returns.

Even after Lene's suicide attempt at the film's end, the narrator reassures herself of her mother's presence: "It took a long time for Lene to open the door, and I sometimes think that she is still behind it, and I am still outside and that she will never again come out to me, and I have to be grown up and alone. But she is still here. Lene is still here" (114). The cinematic letter ends in a postscript; Lene's inaccessibility compels the filmmaker to surrender the intimate second-person form of address and refer to the mother in the more distanced third person. The narrator evaluates her present relationship to Lene and assures herself of Lene's continued presence. The insistent reiteration of the word *da* (here) conjures up Freud's notes on his grandson playing with a wooden reel in a game of disappearance and return.[29] Freud interprets the "fort/da" game as a symbolic strategy of overcoming the pain of separation

---

identifies woman with nature and posits a "feminine aesthetic" to describe the film: "Smooth, organic movements determine the first part of the film."

[28]Silverman, *The Acoustic Mirror*, 212.

[29]Sigmund Freud, *Beyond the Pleasure Principle*, trans. James Strachey (New York: Norton, 1961), 8–11.

from the mother. With *Germany, Pale Mother*, Sanders-Brahms attempts to stage the mother's return and to conjure up an image to fill the emptiness caused by her absence, but Lene's distant look betrays a separation that can hardly be bridged.

Desire for the Lost Mother

The textualization of the modern self includes documenting the polyphony of voices that contribute to its construction. In uncovering a plurality of social, gendered subjects who share a common historical and cultural context, the investigation of the self inevitably leads to a confrontation with ideology, the coalescing force that binds culture and family.

The Nazi flag hauntingly present in the opening scenes of *Germany, Pale Mother* places every move and emotion in relation to the politics of the Third Reich. An extreme close-up of the flag covered with flies visually suggests the infestation of Germany by National Socialism, which cannot be contained within the borders of the frame and reaches well beyond the borders of one generation's life. The establishing shot of the flag as a reflection intimates that the filmmaker can only situate herself in this historical context conceptually at first. As we find out, she begins to explore the family history antecedent to her birth with the time her parents first meet. In a voice-over, the narrator comments on her beginning relationship to Germany's past: "I cannot remember anything anymore about the time before my life. I am not responsible for the things that happened before I was born. I did not exist then. I began when my father saw my mother for the first time" (112). In placing herself into a past before her birth, Sanders-Brahms, born too late to share complicity in the crimes of Nazism, claims a part in German history. Engaged in mourning, she recognizes her historical inheritance and the profound influences it had on the patterns of her childhood and adult life.

One questions the parameters of Sanders-Brahms's autobiographical representation because she so curiously includes scenes that she neither witnessed nor remembers. What legitimately constitutes autobiographical representation? And what knowledge contributes to the repertoire of the self? Sanders-Brahms extends

Lene and I went to the end of the earth—that was in Pomerania—and that's where everything came to a sudden halt. We did and so did the war.

Helma Sanders-Brahms in *Germany Pale Mother*

the borders of the self beyond firsthand experience and presents the self as an extension of other selves, as a weaving of stories. She defines herself through a lineage of selves in the construction of her beginnings. The narrating subject becomes a composition of narrative strands that precede and succeed the awareness of an "I." The traditional boundaries of autobiographical representation are provocatively dissolved to show that the self has no point of origin and that it conceives itself through language.

The mother-daughter relationship is central to the film's psychic structuring, as it is also the center of the cinematic triptych. An undisturbed symbiotic relationship of daughter and mother during a time of strong identification and security is reconstructed. The mother's body is in continous contact with the child Anna, the narrator's persona, throughout the central portion of the film, emphasizing an enclosure that obscures ego boundaries. Scenes of Anna's birth and infancy and later on her bath shared with Lene evoke a dream of a primordial unity between mother and daughter. The close-up of Lene with the infant in her arms, resembling the Madonna, a maternal image repeated in a photography Hans carries, represents an intimate realm inhabited exclusively by mother and daughter. The "Christian Maternal" and the historical mother are conflated in this icon of maternal love, a deterrent to death, as Julia Kristeva suggests in "Stabat Mater."[30] Anna cries for her mother's attention when Hans returns from the front on a two-day leave and displaces the daughter. While Lene cuddles the child, the voice-over of the adult looking back remarks: "That's what I wanted. That is exactly what I wanted. But not him, whom I didn't know" (*Germany, Pale Mother*, 113). With the father's return at the end of the war, the bond between daughter and mother is abruptly severed. A wasteland progressively grows between Anna and her mother as Lene retreats into a severe depression from her role as nurturer and provider. For the daughter, the traumatic loss of the mother effects relocating the mother as object of desire and fantasy to the film itself. In recovering Lene's image and, particularly, her voice, Sanders-Brahms engages in an important step in the exploration of female subjectivity.

At the outset of *Germany, Pale Mother*, the autobiographer establishes the genesis of her language. As her mother sits crying on the riverbank after being harassed by Nazi youths, the filmmaker comments in a voice-over: "My mother. I learned to be silent, you said. From you, I learned to speak. Mother tongue [Muttersprache]" (112). The camera dissolves the distance between the daughter's voice and the mother's image by zooming in on Lene. As it closes in, image and voice bond to establish an aural and visual unification of mother and daughter. The desire to merge with the mother constitutes the main theme of *Germany, Pale Mother*.

In *The Acoustic Mirror*, Silverman brilliantly analyzes the relationship of the infant to the maternal voice and the cultural fantasy of infantile envelopment and security. "No matter how it is conceptualized," she observes, "the image of the infant contained

---

[30]Julia Kristeva, "Stabat Mater," in *The Julia Kristeva Reader*, ed. Toril Moi (New York: Columbia University Press, 1986), 160–86.

within the sonorous envelope of the mother's voice is a fantasy of origins—a fantasy about precultural sexuality, about the entry into language, and about the inauguration of subjectivity."[31] The cinematic apparatus, she claims, reproduces the fantasy or memory of the maternal voice, and, depending on the psychic predisposition toward that voice, it produces either a feeling of pleasure (unity and plenitude) or a feeling of entrapment and danger (paranoia and castration). Film potentially re-creates the original sense of psychic pleasure, or else works through anxiety or pain, in which case the maternal voice is punished. In traditional Western families, the mother's voice is a primary infant experience that plays a crucial role in the subject's formation. It lives on in the unconscious, repressed by a language that in recent years has been referred to in Lacanian terms as the Symbolic. Furthermore, psychoanalysis has disavowed the female subject's erotic investment in the mother. Most cultural texts have instead projected female desire onto the father in the oedipal conflict, devaluing, forgetting, and denying the maternal voice. Acknowledgment of the lost mother-daughter bond has opened a new space for exploring female subjectivity in Anglo-European culture. The (auto)biographical reconstruction of the mother in *Germany, Pale Mother* resuscitates the maternal voice while staging its deprivation and loss.

The middle panel of the triptych especially resonates with the maternal voice which envelops the daughter. The filmmaker reinstates Lene's verbal authority and assigns power to the voice rather than stripping it of discursive potency. Time and again, Lene is shown speaking to Anna, holding and carrying her, dancing, singing, and playing.

In a twenty-minute, almost uninterrupted recitation of one of Grimm's tales, "Der Räuberbräutigam" ("The Robber Bridegroom"), the daughter is completely enveloped in the maternal voice. The daughter is joined in unity and harmony to the mother (in what Kristeva calls a "choric" enclosure), as Lene names the world for the child. In "The Robber Bridegroom," an old woman warns a girl against her murderous fiancé. Hidden behind the oven, the girl watches in horror as he and his companions bring another girl to the robbers' house, mutilate her body and prepare

[31]Silverman, *The Acoustic Mirror*, 74.

to cannibalize her.[32] The fairy tale conveys the message of survival and illustrates women conspiring to ward off their own destruction in a male world. Fairy tales, as the child psychologist Bruno Bettelheim suggests, help children deal with their anxieties by compartmentalizing experience and by producing clear-cut responses to and due punishment for transgressive behavior. They provide reservoirs of images on which the child can project herself or himself to allay fears and to confirm a belief that justice prevails. Revealing patterns of victimization and retaliation or transgression and punishment, many fairy tales serve as didactic paradigms, or reference points for interpreting experience.[33] Children are taught how to comport themselves in order either to avoid the fate of unfortunate protagonists or to win rewards similar to those of happy protagonists.

In the fairy-tale sequence, the maternal voice transmits cultural information reminiscent of oral traditions and forms of storytelling which pass from generation to generation, from mothers to daughters. During this sequence, the daughter, rocked by the jostling train and held by the voice, silently listens as though internalizing the images the mother's voice produces.

Besides structurally enclosing the daughter, the fairy tale in *Germany, Pale Mother* mirrors Lene's experience as well as Germany's. Metaphorically, marriage signifies woman's death. And the "murderer's house" through which mother and daughter roam signifies Germany and the house of Germany, the pale mother whose sons have defiled her, as in Brecht's poem. Working within the complex of powerful contrasts, Sanders-Brahms draws stereotypical parallels between male and female realms of experience. Although she does not indict her father, she shows that male culture clearly per-

---

[32]Maria Tatar, *The Hard Facts of the Grimms' Fairy Tales* (Princeton: Princeton University Press, 1987), 5. See also Ruth B. Bottigheimer, *Grimms' Bad Girls and Bold Boys* (New Haven: Yale University Press, 1987). For an excellent close reading of the fairy tale, see Barbara Hyams, "Is the Apolitical Woman at Peace? A Reading of the Fairy Tale in *Germany, Pale Mother*," *Wide Angle* 10, no. 3 (1988) 41–51.

[33]Bruno Bettelheim, *The Uses of Enchantment* (New York: Alfred A. Knopf, 1976). Bottigheimer points out, however, that Bettelheim assumes "many of the Grimm's fairy tales express Christian values. But 'important and fascinating' as he finds 'these religious aspects of fairy stories,' they occur, apparently paradoxically, in connection with brutality, threat, and extortion, a fact Bettelheim either overlooks or chooses to ignore" (144).

petrates death. In an interview with Renate Möhrmann, Sanders-Brahms explains the allegorical function of the fairy tale:

> I suddenly saw incredible parallels to Lene's development there. How she built up an increasing horror of men while in flight with the child. I saw the deep psychic fears women have of men. Just like in a fairy tale. The man dismembers and cuts up the woman, and her heart bursts. But at the same time, this fairy tale describes German history as well. That is very strange. And German mothers told their children this very fairy tale.[34]

A reciprocity among image, sound, and text is established as Lene and Anna enter the ruins of an abandoned factory. The camera lingers on two smokestacks that evoke the furnaces of concentration camps, while Lene repeats the tale's ominous refrain, "Go back, go back, young bride," a warning that rings throughout the film.

From the start, Sanders-Brahms sets up a dialectical relation between the absence and the presence of a female voice. Lene passes from silence, her image voiceless (indicating her function within male culture), to speech, and then back again to silence.[35] Watching Lene as she walks along the riverbank, Hans and Ulrich conclude: "A German woman. A real German woman" (28). She doesn't scream when attacked; she remains silent. Silence, a sign of the mother's oppression within patriarchal culture, divides her from her daughter. With the end of the war, Lene is again rendered speechless as the "Muttersprache" recedes into a dead silence. The mother's voice disappears as traditional family culture and patriarchal society at large strip it away. Lene's paralysis exteriorizes her disempowerment as does the extraction of her teeth—a further form of mutilation and stifling. Reduced to weeping and cries of

---

[34]Helma Sanders-Brahms, "Gespräch mit Helma Sanders-Brahms," in *Die Frau mit der Kamera*, ed. Renate Möhrmann (Munich: Hanser, 1980), 155.

[35]For an insightful discussion of female silence in the opening scene of *Germany, Pale Mother*, see Angelika Bammer, "Through a Daughter's Eyes: Helma Sanders-Brahms's *Germany, Pale Mother*," *New German Critique* 36 (1985): 91–109. See also E. Ann Kaplan, "The Search for the Mother/Land in Sanders-Brahms's *Germany, Pale Mother*," in *German Film and Literature*, ed. Eric Rentschler (New York: Methuen, 1987), 289–304.

anguish, she finally loses her voice altogether. After a hindered suicide attempt, Lene looks vacantly into the room and withdraws.

Sanders-Brahms re-creates the trauma of that loss. Metaphorically, the child is forced out of the *chora* and aligned with the realm of the father. Yet, as the narrating "I" in *Germany, Pale Mother* contends, the struggle for the mother does not take place outside of language but within it. The daughter's language or "psychic reality" stems from the mother, her body *and* her stories, which place the mother inside and outside of the chora. The father imposes another spatial enclosure—within which "Muttersprache" exists and resists—the "fatherland," a geopolitical enclosure marked by culture and history. While both culture and history repress or sublimate the maternal voice, both are shaped by the chora. "The chora," Silverman writes, "remains one of the permanent scenes of subjectivity, not so much superseded as covered over and denied by succeeding spatial developments."[36]

However, an interesting exchange takes place in Sanders-Brahms's film. Through the use of the voice-over, the "sonorous envelope" that earlier enclosed the daughter now encloses the mother. The enclosure regenerates the space with the mother so that the daughter can identify and gain entrance anew. The daughter is represented by "pure" voice, while the image of the mother fills the interior of the film. The positions reverse, indicating a nonregressive movement. The daughter remains on the exterior after separation but rejoins the mother to understand herself. The use of the female voice-over challenges cinematic traditions of female speechlessness as well. Since woman's voice in mainstream cinema is generally allied with a female image, Sanders-Brahms's use of the disembodied voice, which never finds a corresponding image, subverts the norm her mother represents. At the same time, she speaks for Lene, as well as to her. The auctorial voice, usually reserved for the male and often seen as exemplary of male subjectivity in film language, is claimed by a woman.

Sanders-Brahms's language, then, is not rooted in the victimization and devaluation of the mother, but in her mother as a figure of strength and independence, and in "positive" memories of the maternal voice. As the filmmaker sees it, a sense of security and

---

[36]Silverman, *The Acoustic Mirror*, 105.

independence was ostensibly imparted to the daughter and to a generation of women whose mothers lived through this period of German history. In the preface of the film script, Sanders-Brahms writes, "It is no wonder that women like Gesine Strempel, Helke Sander, Margarethe von Trotta . . . are all rubble children, children of these mothers. Women who live without men, as they learned it from their mothers in the first years of life" (26). According to the narrator, her identity is anchored in a time when she and her mother resided outside of any community, outside of social constraints, in flight. In the absence of the father or "the Law," "Muttersprache" both literally and figuratively found unrestrained expression. In many ways, "Muttersprache" stands for "activating the fantasmatic scene, which corresponds to maternal desire, one which the symbolic does at best to cordon off and render inactive by denying it representational support," as Silverman writes.[37] *Germany, Pale Mother* reclaims the mother and, with her, the language the filmmaker views as her inheritance.

In contrast to the confrontational literary representations of the mother-daughter relationship prominent during the 1970s, the image of Lene idealizes devotion and self-sacrifice while the filmmaker commiserates with her sufferings. Although the film reflects the daughter's emotional longings and Lene as the object of the daughter's desire, Sanders-Brahms at times slips into mythologizing the mother. Ellen Seiter correctly perceives one of the problems in abstracting the mother from material relationships. She points out that *Germany, Pale Mother* "illustrates the problem with all forms of feminism which mythologize the mother. The emphasis on the psychological self-sufficiency of the mother and daughter relationship results in the detachment of women from social, economic and political relationships—those relationships that define the very meaning of motherhood."[38] Like many critics, Seiter seems more provoked by the central "movement" of the film than by its framing segments, which intersect motherhood and politics or the public sphere.

The synchronicity of disparate narrative strands—one strand

---

[37]Silverman, *The Acoustic Mirror*, 124.

[38]Seiter, "Women's History," 572. See also Caroline Neubaur, "Wenn Du noch eine Mutter hast," *Freibeuter* 4 (1980): 168–69.

structured by the desire for the mother, the other by the representation of World War II as a "positive" history—poses numerous problems. A dangerously distorted cinematography of wartime occurs because of the concentration on the mother-daughter relationship. Furthermore, pairing the loss of and mourning for the maternal voice with the experiences of Lene as an allegory of Germany has politically skewed consequences. For instance, in one scene a radio broadcast transmitting the voices of German soldiers singing "Silent Night" in unison at different fronts throughout Europe—a historically unprecedented occurrence—is interrupted by an air raid alarm. Lene, whose Madonna-like pose is reinforced by aligning her image with the sound track of the Christmas song, runs out of the house to protect herself and her infant from destruction. She becomes the victim, the "pale mother" whose sons, as Bertolt Brecht wrote in his 1933 poem of that title, defile and shame her, and whose house becomes the site of lies and death. The mother passively takes the blame for the crimes of her sons. She ambivalently stands as victim and accused, since she must hide the truth. By using Brecht's poem, read by his daughter Hanne Hiob, as a preface, Sanders-Brahms implies that a personal history stands for the history of a nation. If Lene is equated with Brecht's fictional figure, then Germany coterminously stands for the victim, the mother, who is committed to protecting her murderous sons.[39]

In addition, this equivalence elides the question of the role of women as perpetrators of National Socialism.[40] By rendering Lene's life allegorically, Sanders-Brahms not only diffuses women's historical role in the Third Reich but simultaneously draws an ir-

---

[39]See Anton Kaes's discussion of Sanders-Brahms's use of Brecht's poem to introduce her autobiographical film in *From Hitler to Heimat*, pp. 147–48.

[40]Beginning in the 1980s studies have concentrated on the role women played during the Third Reich, showing many women's intensive involvement in and strong support of the dominant politics of that period. These books seem to be a reaction to the view of women's innocent and marginalized relationship to history and their victimization (à la Sanders-Brahms) extensively implied in the early years of second wave feminism. See Claudia Koonz, *Mothers in the Fatherland: Women, the Family, and Nazi Politics* (New York: St. Martin's Press, 1987); Linda Gordon, "Nazi Feminists," review of *Mothers in the Fatherland*, by Claudia Koonz, *Feminist Review* 27 (1987): 97–105; Helga Schubert, *Judasfrauen: Zehn Fallgeschichten weiblicher Denunziation im Dritten Reich* (Frankfurt am Main: Luchterhand, 1989). See also Martina I. Kischke, "Ein gehorsamer Geist in einem gesunden Körper," review of *Frausein im Dritten Reich*, by Rita Thalmann, *Frankfurter Rundschau*, 12 January 1985.

responsible analogy between Germany and Lene. Many critics have cited the contradictions and polemical ambiguities in the portrayal of Lene as both victim and conformist as the film's principal weakness.[41] When Lene attempts to obtain embroidery thread from a vacant shop once belonging to Jews, her personal interests interfere with any potential moral indignation or remorse. However, understanding German history in terms of personal history is not misguided unless this personal history is viewed as emblematic of a nation. Because Sanders-Brahms does tend to conflate personal and national history, *Germany, Pale Mother* indeed becomes a highly disconcerting version of the nation's story.

Despite these shortcomings, *Germany, Pale Mother* contributes importantly to our understanding the necessity of recognizing the function of the maternal voice in the development of an individual female subject and female subjectivity in general. Even though several critics rightly conclude that Sanders-Brahms's film is primarily the story of a mother-daughter relationship, few have understood the significant role Lene plays in the articulation of female subjectivity. Doris Krininger and Claudia Cippitelli, for example, state: "The events of the war, which in this film are essentially limited to demonstrating the absence of men, serve as a foil for the performance of female self-consciousness, defined by an uninterrupted mother-daughter symbiosis. . . . The scene of action becomes interchangeable, it is above all one of freedom, regardless of whether mother and daughter walk between corpses or fragrant spring flowers."[42] Yet, what these critics do not see is that precisely the interruption (and not the continuation) of the mother-daughter relationship catalyzes the narrative. The war and its extreme circumstances (and not a walk through a garden of spring flowers) intensify the bond, heightening the trauma of separation. The female narrator takes a step to overcome the melancholy that, as Silverman postulates, constitutes normative female subjectivity af-

[41]For a critique of Sanders-Brahms's coupling of autobiography and German history, see also Wolfram Schütte, "Mütter, Töchter, Krieg und Terror," *Frankfurter Rundschau*, 25 February 1980; Peter Hornung, "Von Räubern und Menschen," *Saarbrücker Zeitung*, 7 November 1980; Christian Bauer, "Auf der Suche nach verlorenen Müttern," *Süddeutsche Zeitung*, 3 January 1981.

[42]Doris Krininger and Claudia Cippitelli, "Distanz, nicht Distanzierung," *Medium* 11 (1981): 46.

fected by the denial and devaluation of the mother (the original love object) and the corresponding internalization of her image as inferior object of identification. Instead of negating the image of the mother, the narrator elevates the position of the mother and embraces this bond, recognizing its importance in the process of defining herself.

History and Experience

Germany, Pale Mother represents an uncommon perspective of history because of its autobiographical emphasis and focus on women's experiences. By looking at the effects of war on the private sphere, the filmmaker delivers an approach absent in traditional renderings of history and repressed in much the same way that the maternal voice is repressed. According to Bodo von Borries, this perspective has become part of the historical repertoire only since 1975, and even then, it remains peripheral.[43] The history of disenfranchised people is still treated as an exception. New discoveries and the reevaluation of criteria determining historical significance call for history to be rewritten and new judgments solicited.

By addressing Lene's experiences and those of her contemporaries in the light of the narrow range of possibilities they possessed, Sanders-Brahms simultaneously opens two strata of repressed histories: women's history and Germany's history during the Third Reich and the postwar years. In the first instance, the filmmaker takes part in what Adrienne Rich has called a process of "re-visioning," of reading history against the grain. In her essay collection *On Lies, Secrets, and Silence*, Rich calls for opening up the "master narratives" to new perspectives and underrepresented voices in order to engage in the dissolution of a unifying point of

[43]Bodo von Borries, "Forschung und Lernen an Frauengeschichte—Versuch einer Zwischenbilanz," in *Frauen in der Geschichte* VI, ed. Annette Kuhn et al. (Düsseldorf: Schwann, 1985), 49. He states, "Even if one possessed a personal interest and an analytical curiosity, one could not learn about or research women's history because of the lack of models and materials." Borries's contention applies largely to earlier histories, even though he reflects a sentiment shared by a number of feminist scholars who are faced with the sparse documentation of women's lives.

view on history.[44] Inundated with images of combat, destruction, and concepts of victory and defeat, the "old texts," reinforced by mainstream cinema, have dominated and determined historical memory. Yet personal memories often run counter to the commercial images that vie to replace them and to homogenize history in support of the hegemony. In order to prevent a linear understanding of history based on exclusion, personal histories must be preserved.

Excavating her own history in order to produce a counterhistory as well as to secure her personal history, Sanders-Brahms writes, in the accompanying film script: "I did not like war films and all their pyrotechnics. [They] may have reflected how generals imagine war, when they plan it as a huge game of robbers and desecrators with fatal consequences for a few million people: this is the way war would actually have to be, the way pyrotechnics make it. But based on my memory, I knew that it wasn't like that" (118). Her memories are drawn from the private sphere and the history of daily life. Sanders-Brahms refers to her autobiographical narrative as the representation of "the positive history of Germany during fascism, World War II, and afterwards. The history of women, who kept life going while the men were used for killing" (25). Women's roles during this time bear significance for Sanders-Brahms's own development as a feminist. She sets forth another facet of history—the story of survival—which at times is rather simplistically juxtaposed with that of destruction. In blatant stylizations of essentialized gender polarities (life and death, woman and man), the filmmaker reinforces stereotypical dualities reminiscent of the Verständigungsliteratur of the 1970s. Within the paradigms established here, women are symbolically equated with life-giving processes, while men function as the bearers of death. (In two scenes Hans kills two women who look like Lene.) Hence, the birthing scene, intercut with scenes of a bomber, reduces sexual difference to culturally contrived formulas. At times, Germany, Pale Mother moves from trivial to insightful readings of personal experience. Rather than constructing woman as a self-sacrificing victim or martyr and consequently creating a skewed, reactionary view

---

[44]Adrienne Rich, "When We Dead Awaken: Writing as Re-vision," On Lies, Secrets, and Silence (New York: W. W. Norton, 1979), 35.

of Germany as victim, a more profound understanding of divergent gendered and individual experiences and their determination by social institutions and practices is necessary.

Because women's voices have been underrepresented in historical discourse, the possibilities of women coming to terms with their own roles in the political miasma of World War II and thereafter have been very limited. Autobiographical recollections serve as a first step in initiating a dialogue among women, as well as in providing images in which women can finally begin to recognize themselves and their roles in history. One's understanding of one's own position within the Third Reich, as Ellen Seiter observes, is essential to any process of understanding and mourning: "The attempt to reconcile personal experience with objective historical accounts is of particular importance in dealing with fascism, where individual repression has been seen as one of the enabling conditions of its success as a mass political movement."[45] The more women begin to generate their own texts, the more they may feel compelled to ask questions about their own roles in history and to see themselves as part of the historical process.[46] Film, as a public event, has widely contributed to the circulation of images and the amplification of voices by providing the public forum necessary to reconstruct memory. Helke Sander's film *BeFreier und Befreite* (Liberator and liberated, 1991), for example, attempts to excavate stories of massive rape during World War II and its immediate aftermath which many women have long feared disclosing. In interviews, the victims of rape and the children of the victims relate the profound impact this event has had on their lives, despite its concealment.[47]

Since the 1970s, many feminist historians have sought to situate women within the historical process, however conflicting the narrative outcome may be. Yet, the recovery of information is not an

[45]Seiter, "Women's History," 573.

[46]Again, see Bodo von Borries for a further discussion of the significant interconnection between historical consciousness and self-consciousness.

[47]For further discussion of Helke Sander's film, see Viola Roggenkamp, "Warum haben die Frauen geschwiegen?" *Die Zeit*, 2 October 1992, p. 40. It is also interesting to note that Sanders-Brahms includes a scene in which Lene is raped by American soldiers. In the longer version of *Germany, Pale Mother*, which received hefty criticism, Sanders-Brahms also dealt with the experience of rape by Russian soldiers.

easy task, since female speech and behavior for centuries have been generally denigrated, denied, or deemed irrational and unpredictable.[48] The repression of women's histories may be rooted in the repression of the maternal voice. For this reason, Sanders-Brahms appeals to the imaginary, as does film, in order to seduce the viewer into a position of belief. Just as the young woman in the fairy tale "The Robber Bridegroom" veils her story by recounting a "dream" and then produces the dead girl's finger as tangible evidence of her story's "truth content," so, too, does the filmmaker employ the imaginary realm as proof of her mother's story and of many women's similar stories. At the same time, Sanders-Brahms speaks to her own daughter, Anna, to whom the film is dedicated, of her personal and historical inheritance. Through Anna, she continues the dialogue with the past.[49]

[48]Susan Brownmiller, *Femininity* (New York: Fawcett Columbine, 1984), 207.

[49]Sanders-Brahms, "Gespräch mit Helma Sanders-Brahms," 152. In this interview, Sanders-Brahms relates one of her motives for making the film: "The relationship between a mother and a daughter is certainly a relationship between the present and the past and history in its actual form. I strongly experienced that as I was about to have a child. . . . To write history, not from the male perspective, nor from that of soldiers, . . . but from the perspective of a child. That became tremendously important to me because I wanted to leave the film for my daughter as a kind of work of memory—as a bequeathment. Everything that I can give my daughter in terms of education is in this film." For a discussion of the three fictional surfaces, see Irene Heidelberger-Leonard, "Brecht, Grimm, Sanders-Brahms—Drei Variationen zum selben Thema: *Deutschland, bleiche Mutter,*" *Etudes Germaniques* 39 (1984): 51–55.

5

Jutta Brückner's
Years of Hunger

I want to go into the boundless, to return to myself.
Else Lasker-Schüler, *Weltflucht*

A Language of Difference

Winning wide acclaim at the Berlin film festival in 1980, *Hungerjahre in einem reichen Land* (*Years of Hunger*) was among the many "women's films" that populated that year's film landscape.[1] In these films, as in much literature published by women at the time, the mother-daughter relationship was a predominant theme. Jutta Brückner focuses on this relationship in probing the factors that shaped her as a young woman. Her attention turns to the repression of the female body and the emergence of a self-destructive, self-hating female subjectivity, which she insists goes far beyond one individual case. Her autobiographical portrait is an expression of what Brückner describes as "a trend particularly developed in women, most of whom have suffered under their biographies in a very silent and incomprehensible way."[2] Staging her life between the ages of 13 and 16 by means of a self-reflexive dialogue, the filmmaker portrays the crisis-ridden turning point in the maturation of a female adolescent, her initiation into gendered identity. Her experiences as a child of the "golden fifties," from 1953 to 1956, are set in a time of economic prosperity, historical amnesia, and repression. The title *Years of Hunger* refers to a spiritual hunger in the midst of material plenty.

[1]*Hungerjahre in einem reichen Land* (*Years of Hunger*), directed by Jutta Brückner, Basis-Film, 1980. The critics' response to Brückner's film was far more positive than the response to Sanders-Brahms's film *Germany, Pale Mother*, owing to Brückner's more rigorous, materialist confrontation with German history.

[2]Jutta Brückner, "Frau zur Freiheit, interview with Kurt Habernoll," *Der Abend*, 23 February 1980, p. 46.

In *Years of Hunger*, Brückner reinterprets from a feminist perspective the crucial years that mark puberty. Among the many issues addressed in the early phases of feminism were the discriminative criteria implemented to establish normative behavior. Well known now are the biases directing psychological studies that designated men's experiences as the norm while casting women into the inauspicious role of the second sex, as Simone de Beauvoir called it, the deviant "other."[3] Since these structures and misinformed attitudes, functioning as cultural mirrors, inevitably influenced women's perceptions of themselves, the early feminist agenda called for rigorous scrutiny of traditional epistemologies. Subsequently, "deficiency," descriptive of and synonymous with "woman," was exposed as the lack of female perspectives; it was a deficiency rather of representations of female experiences in male-centered inquiries. A reorientation within these discursive fields called for a focus on female experiences to produce new understandings of women's lives.[4] In order to develop a new language with which to speak about female subjectivity and to discover the body, feminists insisted on a proliferation of women's stories. These often programmatic and tendentious stories optimistically conformed to a feminist desire for rebirth. Autobiographical treatments of women's lives were to be the foundation for future explorations.

In the early phases of feminist filmmaking, women involved in this venture had to oppose structures that have denied them language or promoted their linguistic oppression.[5] Brückner equips herself with a language based on personal knowledge and interpretations of her own experiences as a girl and as a woman outside linguistically sanctioned discourses. By shifting her past into a new light and applying a feminist language to her own experience, as

---

[3]Carol Gilligan, *In a Different Voice: Psychological Theory and Women's Development* (Cambridge: Harvard University Press, 1982), 14.

[4]Many feminists in the academy today are calling for a personalization of criticism, in other words, for critics to situate themselves in their writing. As a result, the autobiographical mode has become more common in academic writing. See Nancy Miller, *Getting Personal: Feminist Occasions and Other Autobiographical Acts* (New York: Routledge, 1991).

[5]Elizabeth Grosz, "Philosophy, Subjectivity, and the Body: Kristeva and Irigaray," in *Feminist Challenges: Social and Political Theory*, ed. Carole Pateman and Elizabeth Grosz (Boston: Northeastern University Press, 1986).

many women of her time tried to do, she invites traditionally unexplored perspectives to emerge. The confrontation with her own biography addresses a long-standing need for different models of interpretation.

For women, the desire to represent themselves or to assign meaning involves a conceptual quest that demands an ongoing pursuit of alternative signification processes. The feminist project calls for experimenting with a new poetics to avoid recycling traditional scripts that inhibit female subjectivities. In *This Sex Which Is Not One*, Luce Irigaray begins her concluding text, "When Our Lips Speak Together," with a recognition of women's specific relationship to language, referring here to the psychological structuring of knowledge. Women, she argues, like any oppressed group, must struggle to speak differently in order to challenge the texts that have disadvantaged them. "If we keep on speaking the same language together, we're going to reproduce the same history. Begin the same old stories all over again. Don't you think so?"[6]

For Brückner, film facilitates the creation of new syntaxes. Besides its ability to produce a public forum, film, through its images, Brückner believes, partakes directly of the internal experiential world and allows for forms of expression that evade language. Language fails to express visual memory, as the situation of the dreamteller who flounders in translating images into words demonstrates. Similarly, "the description of a photograph is literally impossible," Roland Barthes asserts, owing to its nonlinearity and openness to multiple interpretations of the visual.[7] Brückner comments on the significance of film in expressing the unspeakable: "Film for me offers the sole medium in which we can explore our collective labor of mourning for the cultural paralyzing of our bodies, our eyes, and our time-space relations. The goal: recuperating the means to reconstruct symbolically. . . . I mean recuperating our [women's] capacity to look."[8] Brückner suggests that film can convey as yet unspoken knowledge, since the images need not sur-

[6]Luce Irigaray, *This Sex Which Is Not One*, trans. Catherine Porter with Carolyn Burke (Ithaca: Cornell University Press, 1985), 205.

[7]Roland Barthes, *Image/Music/Text*, trans. Stephen Heath (New York: Hill and Wang, 1977), 18.

[8]Jutta Brückner, interview, "Recognizing Collective Gestures," with Marc Silberman, *Jump Cut* 27 (1982): 46.

render- to linear structures. The images are open to a multiplicity of meanings and associations. Furthermore, through a feminist countercinema, the libidinal economy that structures dominant cinema is challenged, and strategies of looking are newly explored.

Autobiography, the most self-reflexive of literary and cinematic forms, has proven a vital arena in which to confront normative social practices and develop alternative ways of seeing. In feminist autobiographies, the autobiographer traverses a textual space beginning with the construction of her subjectivity and moves toward its open-ended deconstruction. Marguerite Duras calls it emerging from darkness, leaving the Freudian "dark continent" behind and metaphorically initiating a rebirth—a motif that often shapes autobiographies strongly influenced by the prescriptive agendas of the women's movement, and criticized as such.[9] In *Years of Hunger*, the beginning sequence of each year is introduced by water, the river Styx, the river that separates the underworld and death from life.[10]

For Brückner, woman, whose body and voice have been repressed for centuries, begins to leave the site of death when she becomes alert to her location within the configurations of social practices that have named her. Motivated by a desire to come to terms with her life, to develop a personal interest in herself (a new passion, as she calls it), the narrator reveals in a voice-over her unprecedented engagement in self-discovery: "to destroy the cowardliness, to call things by their names, to feel a passion for myself, to be curious about myself, to get on with myself, to ask myself, to listen to, and answer myself."[11]

Consciously creating a new relationship to herself, the autobiographer partakes in self-analysis and reconstruction. She probes the social configurations that have informed her development as well as the intersubjective relations that have shaped her identity. As in most feminist films, autobiography functions as a subversive

---

[9]Marguerite Duras, "From an Interview," in *New French Feminisms*, ed. Elaine Marks and Isabelle de Courtivron (New York: Schocken, 1981), 174.

[10]Explicating her own film at a seminar in West Berlin's Pädagogische Hochschule in 1986, Brückner discussed this imagery at length, identifying it as representing death.

[11]Because no film script of *Years of Hunger* is available, all quotes are taken directly from the film distributed by West Glen in New York. All translations are my own.

form of enunciation particularly when the female "I" critically constructs a past self from the distance of the present. In many cases, the autobiographical script resists the traditional catalogue of expectations and stereotypes of female desire and development. When asked whether her films are autobiographical, Brückner replies:

> All my films are autobiographical. Autobiographical motivations counter the false generalizations into which we have been molded for years. . . . We women tend to notice them more because our individuality simply cannot be contained within these generalizations. We must not just constitute images out of the small banalities of life, to do that is only false realism. Rather, we must find new forms to narrate private life, to recognize collective gestures in the most banal ones. I am trying to disrupt the habitual ways we see people.[12]

Admitting to the autobiographical content of her films, Brückner sets the self-referential parameter for the films that precede and include *Years of Hunger*. In 1976, she filmed *Ein ganz und gar verwahrlostes Mädchen* (A thoroughly neglected girl), the biography of a woman whose identity is enmeshed in romantic scenes of marriage and desperate wishes of acceptance. In *Tue recht und scheue niemand* (Do right and fear no one, 1975), she explores her mother's biography and the demands placed on a woman who becomes a wife and mother.[13] Yet autobiography, Brückner notes, as a reproduction of the "way it was," a story or "histoire" in the Metzian sense, does not suffice. She believes that each autobiography should be discursively dissected, illuminated, and newly interpreted; autobiography should self-reflexively initiate a dialogue with the present. In addition, Brückner's film innovatively intermingles fact and fiction, fantasy and reality, self and others, working from a theoretical framework that promotes new insights. "To

[12]Brückner, "Recognizing," 46.
[13]See Renate Fischetti, *Das neue Kino—Acht Porträts von deutschen Regisseurinnen* (Dülmen-Hiddingsel: Tende, 1992), 184–210. In an interview, Brückner reveals that her mother was reevaluating her own identity when she reluctantly agreed to participate in the film. Brückner believes that the project became therapeutic for her mother, a result that reinforced Brückner's desire to make psychoanalytical films, films that open channels of memory.

call things by their names" is the underlying challenge of Brückner's project.

The importance of naming echoes throughout many feminist
projects and critiques. In "The Crisis of Naming in Feminist Cinema," Ruby Rich discusses the need for a new set of terms to define
a poetics of feminist filmmaking, in order to free female productions
from what she alludes to as a predisposed male subjectivity.
Among the register of expressions she introduces, Rich speaks of
a "cinema of correspondence" to describe countercinematic structures in films by women, in contrast to "modernist cinema" represented by male filmmakers such as Jean-Luc Godard and
Alexander Kluge: "The cinema of correspondence then, would be
those investigating correspondences, i.e. between emotion and objectivity, narrative and deconstruction, art and ideology. What distinguishes such films of correspondence from formally similar films
by male avant-garde filmmakers is their inclusion of the author
within the text."[14] On one level, "correspondence" pertains to the
tradition of letter writing, a form of enunciation popularized in the
seventeenth and eighteenth centuries which allowed women a free,
highly subjective form of artistic expression. Women became subjects of their own epistolary narrations, and they enjoyed unrestrained articulation, at least in relation to their positions in the
social and cultural order. Letter writing had not been accepted as
an art form; it resided outside the literary establishment and the
public sphere. It was associated with the intimate realm traditionally occupied by women. Recognizing letter writing as a vital outlet
for female artistic production, Rich symbolically appropriates this
tradition for film, at least in name, in order to create a specific
lineage. Since autobiography in many ways resembles letter writing, Rich's designation "cinema of correspondence" aptly char-
acterizes films that are structured by the autobiographical impulse.
In *Years of Hunger*, the textualization of a female subject is the
ultimate aim.

Moreover, in Brückner's film, as in Sanders-Brahms's *Germany,
Pale Mother*, correspondence implies a discursive mode secured by
the use of a voice-over spoken by the filmmaker, making the source

[14]Ruby Rich, "The Crisis of Naming in Feminist Cinema," *Jump Cut* 19 (1979): 9–
12.

of enunciation, or "who is speaking," clear. As in a letter, the address is directed toward an addressee. In part, the filmmaker self-reflectingly plays both these roles. The materialization of her thought—the translation of thought into film—also presumes another addressee, the spectator. Brückner avoids absorbing the viewer by such manipulative mechanics of mainstream cinema as suturing, a process by which the spectator assumes the perspective of various characters and is "sewn into" the film. Instead, she engages the viewer in dialogue and encourages an active participation in the act of interpretation by ensuring a distance between image and spectator. With women constituting the primary audience, *Years of Hunger* invites identification with and reflection on moments in the film that resemble ones in their own lives. Brückner relies on techniques of discursive filmmaking, securing an I/you relationship, to mediate her own past.

Within the framework of feminist filmmaking, however, her film falls into the category of "discourse" (a dialogue), rather than "story." The inclusion of the narrator, the female voice within the text (the subjective, autobiographical "I"), the interchange between the self as the intersection of various social and historical discourses, the representation of intersubjective relationships such as that between mother and daughter, the interspersion of documentary footage to highlight the interdependence of public and private realms, and the invitation to identify with the protagonist by comparing one's own story to the events represented and to engage in a dialogue—all qualify *Years of Hunger* as a "cinema of correspondence."

Remembering Oneself

As in *Germany, Pale Mother*, the autobiographical form in *Years of Hunger* is sustained through Brückner's own voice off camera. This voice-over presents an inner dialogue and signals the subjective relationship between voice and image. Owing to the dominance of the female voice-over at the beginning, strengthened by the disembodied speaker, the visual representation becomes anchored in the verbal sign. The "I" is introduced at the outset of the film, signaling the single perspective fundamental to the autobiographical project. The first person pronoun becomes the reference point for the ensuing repository of images that compose the filmmaker's past. By saying "I," the filmmaker uses the self-conscious narrative form to claim the image and establish the adolescent Ursula as a representation of herself. As in literature, the first-person pronoun represents the subjective mode, in which the speaker leaves his or her mark on the utterance. My usage of the term *subjectivity* here is based on the statements of Emile Benveniste. He describes subjectivity as "the capacity of the speaker to posit himself (herself) as 'subject,' " the ability to say "I."[15] According to Benveniste, "the psychic unit that transcends the totality of the actual experience is assembled (by the I) and that makes the permanence of consciousness."[16] The filmmaker as authorial voice appears within the narrative as she remembers and interprets the story of her life.

Brückner places herself as a female subject at the heart of her narrative. Unlike the narrator in Alexander Kluge's modernist film *The Part-Time Work of a Domestic Slave* (1973), in which "a distanced olympian viewpoint telescopically watches and judges the protagonist's actions" (as Rich notes), the narrator in Brückner's "cinema of correspondence" moves through the various moments of Ursula's life, empathetically reassessing the events that have informed her identity.[17] The narrator is compassionate and introspective, identifying with the protagonist and self-reflectively recounting her life: "I could no longer manage. I felt superfluous." The commentary that accompanies Ursula's emotional crisis does not indicate a sovereign position.[18] At no time does the narrative voice-over betray the authoritarian or patronizing disposition heard in documentary films, in which the source remains an obscure, unidentified voice from nowhere, disseminating supposedly objective information. In addition, Brückner avoids manipulating the spectator into identifying with the disembodied voice by minimizing

[15]Emile Benveniste, *Problems in General Linguistics*, trans. M. E. Meek (Coral Gables: University of Miami Press, 1971), 219.

[16]Ibid., 220.

[17]Ruby Rich, "She Says, He Says: The Power of the Narrator in Modernist Film Politics," *Discourse* 6 (1983): 37–38.

[18]Heide Schlüpmann and Karola Gramann, "*Hungerjahre*," *medienPraktisch*, ed. Gemeinschaft der Evangelischen Publizistik (1983): 19–23.

its intervention. The voice-over reminds the viewer of who is speaking, yet undermines any complicity that might reduce the range of interpretation. Whereas in Kluge's film the male voice-over controls commentary on the female protagonist's actions, in Brückner's film a woman comments on a woman's story.

The congruence of the three interconnected voices of autobiographical narration—narrator, author, and protagonist—is implied at the beginning of Brückner's film by the alternation of the narrator's and the protagonist's voice-overs. Both reveal interiority, one in the form of an expository monologue divulging a personal revelation, and the other as a passage from fiction—a fantasy that Ursula, played by Britta Pohland, quietly reads to herself. In the first voice-over, the adult narrator admits to being a fugitive from her own past. The voice-over that follows speaks of adventure: "When he went out into the world, he was supposed to find a lot of wonderful things." By paralleling these statements, the filmmaker embarks on the adventure that was once forbidden her as a young woman. The adventure entails the exploration of new surfaces unlike those depicted in the fictional passage marked by "he." During the 1950s, as Brückner shows, women were often relegated to the private sphere as wives and mothers, while men were allowed to ride off to play what Karl May, a popular German author of the nineteenth century, called "the wild Kurdistan."[19] In retrieving and reconstructing selected moments of the past, the narrator does not use the masculine pronoun, since it entails self-deceit and a disavowal of female subjectivity. Instead, the filmmaker reflects on her own experiences, self-consciously writing and filming as a woman who aspires to possess herself as a subject of narration.

Coming to terms with a burdened and painful past requires distance, a stance outside the events. Even though identification between the off-camera narrator and the visual protagonist is clearly highlighted, Brückner distances the autobiographical past by calling herself Ursula Scheuner. Besides effecting the necessary detachment for a critical evaluation of her life, this difference between the filmmaker's own name and the name of her persona

---

[19]Jutta Brückner, "Vom Pathos des Leibes oder: Der revolutionäre Exorzismus," *Ästhetik und Kommunikation*: 57/58 (1985): 56.

implies a tenuous emotional distance. As much as Ursula embodies a part of the present narrator, she also represents what the narrator has repressed. Christa Wolf similarly reveals her emotional ambivalence toward the child in *Patterns of Childhood*. Both Brückner and Wolf use the third person to mark a temporal and emotional distance as well as to signal the inability to "authentically" reconstruct the emotional life of the child. The disparity between past and present is further reinforced by the diegetic absence of the present-tense narrator.

Recognizing this fissure within the subject is a momentous act of contemporary autobiographical writing or filming, since it acknowledges that memory cannot purely recapture past events or evoke past sentiments as they actually existed. The present perspective invariably intervenes, not to mention the unconscious processes that displace and distort memories. New variables also constantly challenge the subject to reinterpret herself, to reassess her development. The autobiographical "I" inevitably joins in an expression of self-invention. Furthermore, it is not only the fallibility and imaginative deceptions of memory that confound authentic reproduction. The properties of language and the collaborative nature of filming produce a schism between the person writing and the created persona.[20] Even though the autobiographical enterprise demands representations that refer to verifiable "realities," acknowledging the split between autobiographer and autobiographical subject is perhaps the most sincere approach to autobiographical writing and filmmaking. What once was accepted as a reliable, authentic reproduction of selfhood is considered today an act of discursive interpretation. The filmmaker's voice off-camera marks two levels of time: the past and the present. The present clearly frames the narrative, since the filmmaker's voice is the first and last heard. Here, "the first person," as Jean Starobinski notes, "embodies both the present reflection and the multiplicity of past states."[21]

The film functions essentially as a product of reflection, of sub-

---

[20]See Paul de Man, "Autobiography as De-facement," *Modern Language Notes* 95,5 (1979): 919–30.

[21]Jean Starobinski, "The Style of Autobiography," in *Autobiography: Essays Theoretical and Critical*, ed. James Olney (Princeton: Princeton University Press, 1972), 73–83.

jective memory. Besides its allusion to death, the establishing shot of a lake, with water as the source of reflection and reflection as the speculum of identity, also signals that the process of memory organizes the narrative. This same shot demarcates the beginning of each year represented—1953, 1954, 1955, and 1956. Memory is not a verbatim reproduction of prior perception. It constantly reinterprets the past. "Remembering is itself a creative act," Roy Pascal observes in *Design and Truth in Autobiography*.[22] After spending years fleeing from herself and trying to forget, Brückner returns to the past that has psychically crippled her. Recognizing the need for a retrospective confrontation, she tests the repressed images (in film, the manifestations of the unconscious) that lie buried, yet not forgotten.

Her autobiographical inquiry begins at the age of thirty, recognizing much as Christa Wolf recognized, that the past, like a shadow, disappears only tentatively and that it manifests itself in unconscious ways. Brückner introduces her filmic memoir by saying:

> But I had repressed myself from my memories. I always found new goals, so that I would always have to look ahead. If I got too close to myself, I escaped into a frantic work pace or a paralyzing illness. I was already thirty years old when I noticed that the past was not going to let go of me. I was living with a petrified heart that was still thirteen years old. And I forced myself to remember.

Through film, Brückner analytically works through an imprisoning past that she has repeated neurotically.

Brückner refers to her film as "a daughter's subjective work of mourning," a work of mourning that implies grief over the loss of a loved one, possibly the daughter herself. Mourning and melancholia are similar emotional states, except that, as Freud notes: "The fall in self-esteem is absent in grief."[23] The lack of self-esteem, a symptom of melancholia, is also characteristic of female subjectivity, and as Silverman suggests in the *Acoustic Mirror*, is inherent

[22]Roy Pascal, *Design and Truth in Autobiography* (Cambridge: Harvard University Press, 1960), 182–83.

[23]Sigmund Freud, "Mourning and Melancholia," *General Psychological Theory* (New York: Macmillan, 1963), 165.

in the protagonist's status as daughter. By restaging the past, the narrator discovers a means of addressing the repressed adolescent. Film provides her with an "analytic space of freedom," a form of self-therapy.[24] According to Brückner, autobiographical filming enables her to articulate her experiences of sexuality and shame: "The more I think about it, I notice that the realm in which I am able to experience sexuality and shame is not the word but rather the image. The most synthetic of all art forms, film is the space in which the representative and symbolic birth of a female person can take place through the reconstruction of her history."[25]

In many ways, writing or filming personal histories resembles the writing of a materialist history. Once again we are reminded of Walter Benjamin's "Theses on the Philosophy of History," in which Benjamin expresses the need for understanding history as it intersects with the present. The construction of the past relies on a dynamic interchange between past and present. In an attempt to understand the aetiology of her feelings, the narrator filters her experiences through a specific discursive grid, which contours the patterns that emerge. In *Years of Hunger*, almost every image programmatically responds to feminist concerns. The film is a reply to the question: What was it like for a young woman to grow up in West Germany in the 1950s? Her personal history is a distillation of key moments, or what Roland Barthes calls "biophemes," that mainly display the processes engendering a female subject traumatized by self-negation and denial.

Even though Brückner privileges a nonlinear format, the series of episodes depicting Ursula's private story are rigidly structured, though not sequentially, to illustrate the development of her neurosis. Most autobiographers tend to assemble past events causally, since their ordering facilitates interpreting, however tenuously, the complex network of occurrences that construct a subject—except in cases of radical autobiographical representations in which the "subject" is unrecognizably dispersed, merely an effect of language and reflection, as Barthes calls it in *Roland Barthes by Roland Barthes*. For the sake of coherence and unity, the reconstruction of the past

[24]Richard King, "Memory and Phantasy," *Modern Language Notes* 98.5 (1983): 1197–1213.
[25]Jutta Brückner, "Vom Erinnern, Vergessen, dem Leib und der Wut. Ein Kultur-Film-Projekt," *Frauen und Film* 35 (1983): 47.

entails mapping out events, with key experiences serving as markers. The events constitute miniature personal legends that structure the past and provide an orientation for self-analysis and interpretation. Even though these legends exist only as simulacra of "the way it was," coextensive with a referent in experience, they serve primarily to fix a text of the self, a personal mythology.

Through montage, Brückner reifies the processes of memory in her autobiographical representation. A visual montage, used to construct, contradict, and draw associations filmically, simulates a stream of consciousness. The use of montage highlights the piecing together of the past self like a mosaic or puzzle. Brückner explains her approach:

> This film is an attempt at a psychoanalytic cinematic form. The problem concerning me is the relationship between the individual and society, a central issue of the women's movement that also implies the question of film content. As to the form, I try to work in newsreels and photos and with sound structures that introduce anonymous consciousness as anonymous voices. Someone remembers experiences from the past but not in the linearity of a narrative sequence. The images are disparate and uncoordinated, juxtaposed just as memory progresses by leaps and associations. I don't like to reproduce reality as if history were simply a costume party. I am trying to suggest the complexity of a whole period, of the fifties, by letting it speak for itself.[26]

The Intersection of Histories

The variety of public and private voices in *Years of Hunger* reflects the heteroglossia of voices that compose a personal history.[27] The past self is presented as an intertextual network, with still photographs, documentary footage, biographical inserts, radio announcements, slogans, private thoughts, fantasies, and fictions providing a variety of discursive strands. Consequently, the traditional linear narrative that conveniently condenses the complex-

---

[26]Brückner, "Recognizing," 47.

[27]I am borrowing M. M. Bakhtin's neologism introduced in *The Dialogic Imagination: Four Essays*, trans. Caryl Emerson and Michael Holquist (Austin: University of Texas Press, 1981), to refer to the multiplicity of voices whose meanings are rooted in a particular sociohistorical context.

ity of the modern world into a binary formula is abandoned to accentuate the synchronicity of multiple voices that make up a time period and intersect in one body. By providing these various textual coordinates, the filmmaker highlights the miasma of contradictions in her life. She constructs and deconstructs events, focusing on the unresolved tensions of postwar Germany of the 1950s. For example, Ursula's teacher works for an organization that promotes Catholic and Jewish cooperation, yet she sings a Nazi song she learned while in the League of German Girls (Bund deutscher Mädchen, BDM). This sequence is intercut with still photographs of girls in their BDM uniforms projecting a sense of community and happiness and, more significantly, the formation of an emotional structure that continues unreflected throughout the life of the adult.

Brückner charts her development across multiple textual layers. Through her personal view, the myth of the "golden fifties," with its dreams of Chippendale furniture, kidney tables, and rubber plants, becomes flawed and fades. *Years of Hunger* functions in counterpoint to the nostalgic, postmodern revival of the 1950s that pervaded the early 1980s.[28] The fifties are reproduced in the film as a time stricken with social, sexual, and political repression in the name of stability. Wanting to forget the war years and the politics of the Third Reich and to build a promising future, the population embraced the hope tenuously offered by Konrad Adenauer's conservative government. "Order" sealed off memories of wartime. In literature, the 1950s are similarly criticized in such autobiographical works as Peter O. Chotjewitz's *Dreißigjähriger Frieden* (Thirty years of peace), Angelika Mechtel's *Wir sind arm, wir sind reich* (We are poor, we are rich) and Jürgen Theobaldy's *Sonntags Kino* (Sunday's movies).

German society's continued adoption of strict ideological structures resulted in the predilection for a conservative morality leading to the repression of women and sexuality. The de-eroticized representations of women in film and the stereotypic gender differences promoted in advertisements attest to the technologies of

---

[28]See Bernd Neumann, " 'Als ob das Zeitgenössische leer wäre . . . ': Über die Anwesenheit der 50er Jahre in der Gegenwartsliteratur," *Zeitschrift für Literaturwissenschaft und Linguistik* 9 (1979): 82–95.

repression that drove women out of the labor force into the private sphere.[29] In *Years of Hunger*, Brückner analyzes the relation between social repression and the female body. But first her portrait of the time.

The claustrophobic atmosphere and the stifling silence that haunted the 1950s were displaced by the Federal Republic's era of economic prosperity. The unprecedented availability of consumer goods, along with the desire to forget, anesthetized the population. Consumption served to placate the senses and temporarily fill the emotional vacuum.[30] Chocolate was the substitute for confrontation. Ursula receives sweets to allay her melancholia. When she learns of her father's illicit affair, he gives her cake as a peace offering to ease his guilt. It is not surprising that Ursula unconsolably surfeits herself to compensate for the inner emptiness.

Consumption was Germany's means of avoiding the past. A table overflowing with groceries and the family polishing the new car are both signs of recovery in Brückner's film. But appearances deceive. The autobiographical glimpse behind glossy pictures shows that the "economic miracle" had no exchange value on the emotional market. The loss of a positive identity, for the individual as well as the nation, resulted in a psychological abyss.[31] Ursula's growing isolation is visually portrayed by the partitions that stand between her and the outside. The diffusion of her image behind a windowpane, moreover, suggests the progressive dissolution of

[29]Heide Schlüpmann, "Deutsche Liebespaare," *Frauen und Film* 35 (1983): 12–23. This issue deals exclusively with film in the 1950s. Also see *Rendez-vous unterm Nierentisch*, a compilation of 1950s advertisements shown first at the Berlin film festival, in 1986.

[30]Günter Grass, "Geschenkte Freiheit: Versagen, Schuld, vertane Chancen," *Die Zeit*, 10 May 1985, p. 20. In a speech given on 8 May 1985 commemorating Germany's capitulation, Grass addressed the deceptive transfiguration of the 1950s in contemporary popular culture, which to a large extent reveals today's misrepresentation and misconception of that time: "The private sphere, the comfortable niche, the neo-neo-Biedermeier is groomed as well. Yet, this decade was anything but comfortable, and only fashionable stupidity leads to the retrospective swooning over the false fifties. . . . The decade of falsifications and illusions. The decade of reconstruction without a foundation. The era of master charlatans among them statesmen. The years of hard actualities: rearmament in tandem with the desire to escape reality."

[31]Horst Ehmke, "Was ist des Deutschen Vaterland?" in *Stichworte zur "Geistigen Situation der Zeit*," ed. Jürgen Habermas (Frankfurt am Main: Suhrkamp, 1979); *Niemandsland* 1 (1987).

"What's the matter? Did you get a bad grade?"
    "I just feel sad sometimes . . . for no reason, just like that."
    "Here, but don't eat it [a chocolate bar] all at once."
                    Sylvia Ulrich and Britta Pohland in *Years of Hunger*

her self-image. Brückner's personal story coincides with that of a nation that Alexander and Margarete Mitscherlich diagnose as experiencing a blow to its narcissism.[32]

A long period of political restoration accompanied finance minister Ludwig Erhard's program to rebuild Germany and guarantee economic prosperity. Both Adenauer's reinstatement of the oblig-

---

[32]Alexander Mitscherlich and Margarete Mitscherlich, *The Inability to Mourn: Principles of Collective Behavior*, trans. Beverley R. Placzek (New York: Grove Press, 1975). The Mitscherlichs contended that many German citizens strongly identified with Hitler. Hitler's death and the end of the Third Reich signified a loss that needed to be mourned. However, as the title implies, coming to terms with the past did not take place. Instead, the past was repressed and, as Heide Schlüpmann argues, de-realized in film. Ursula's story parallels Germany's insofar as her narcissistic needs find no outlet. They are continuously thwarted.

atory military service, allegedly to protect the Federal Republic against Communism, and the prohibition against the Communist party (Kommunistische Partei Deutschlands, KPD) in 1956 are but two examples of the events that Brückner includes. Cold War policies, as she shows, fundamentally determined the political climate. Her use of black-and-white film reinforces the severe polarities cultivated at the time. The blatant battle of ideologies is further highlighted by the inclusion of documentary footage of the workers' uprising in East Berlin on 17 June 1953, reported by Adenauer and an official East German news commentator. The overlapping voice-overs emphasize the simultaneity of opposing political referents: the East announces that Western agitators induced the workers to strike in order to undermine the Socialist state, while the West contends that the strike expressed the discontent of the proletariat and the failure of socialism. By presenting these diametrically opposed interpretations of events, the notion of truthful reporting recedes. The premise of objectivity is undermined altogether as it becomes clear that perceptions of "reality" are based on prevailing interests, cultures, and ideologies. Thus the addressee is constantly engaged in a process of negotiating meaning. Similarly, the autobiographical project and the subjective rendition of personal history are legitimated when the concept of objectivity is descredited.

In the Federal Republic of Germany, the pursuit of social stability and order at all costs was fueled by anxiety about the possibility of another war. When Ursula asks what freedom is, her mother's response demonstrates a personalization of history: "When we are doing well, and when we don't have to be afraid." Until the late 1960s, the private sphere provided a refuge for a nation that was disoriented, bereft, defeated, and guilty; the guilt, for atrocities inflicted upon millions, was often unacknowledged. Since the family was ostensibly the only institution to emerge intact from World War II, it was strongly promoted by the government. The establishment of the first "Familienministerium" in 1953, with the Protestant minister Franz-Josef Wuermeling as its spokesperson, reflects the continuity of certain values carried over from National Socialism.

The conservatism of government policy toward the family extended into the legislative branch, acutely polarizing gender roles.

In acts such as Amendment 1356 of the nation's constitution (Bür-gerliches Gesetzbuch, BGB), women were reminded of their pri-mary obligation to the private sphere: "Women are entitled to employment, if work does not conflict with the obligations of mar-riage and family."[33] Unless her financial contribution proved in-dispensable, the ideal woman devoted herself exclusively to home and family. Such laws betray a desperate desire to reinstate the father, who traditionally functions as a symbolic embodiment of the state.

Asked why she chose to thematize the 1950s, Brückner replied:

> Above all because I experienced them as a time in which everything got swept under the carpet; no problems were openly discussed. It was a time of unbelievable schizophrenia, especially for women. They were needed for reconstruction, but worked with a bad conscience for neglecting their children. There was a court judgment in those days that entitled women to employment only if they did not neglect their duties as housewives, mothers and wives.[34]

Brückner shows how gender roles translate into daily life. In *Years of Hunger*, the conflict between family and job escalates when Frau Scheuner expresses desire to work outside the home to increase the family's buying power. Her husband balks at the idea, finding it an insult to his image as provider. Her sister warns against raising a latchkey child, to which her mother adds: "Watch Ursel. She has adventure on her mind." The tension between Frau Scheuner's wishes and "maternal guilt" is not fully explored, since the daugh-ter's perception of the mother-daughter relationship constitutes the autobiographical focus.

Brückner radically emphasizes the interrelationship of the subject and the historical context, between past and present. In doing so, she dissolves the traditional public/private dichotomy, a separation

---

[33]Ingrid Langer, "Die Mohrinnen hatten ihre Schuldigkeit getan . . . Staatlich-moralische Aufrüstung der Familie," in *Die fünfziger Jahre*, ed. Dieter Bänsch (Tüb-ingen: Günter Narr, 1985), 108–30. Langer states: "In substance the judges ruled that both parties must contribute to taking care of the family according to their strengths, . . . the man through employment outside of the home as financial pro-vider, and the woman through managing the household and caring for the chil-dren."

[34]Brückner, "Frau zur Freiheit," 46.

staunchly upheld during the 1950s. Alluding to Alexander Kluge's film *The Patriot*, whose protagonist Gabi Teichert, a history teacher, literally digs through layers of German soil in search of a nonofficial history, Brückner calls her autobiographical project an excavation with goals similar to Gabi's. "Gabi Teichert delves deep down into German history; we, too, delve deep into ourselves and find German history even in the way we delve."[35] Brückner's undertaking derives from the acute need felt by the generation of those born during the war to shatter the shell of postwar silence and confront their nation's past. Born in 1941, Brückner took part in the student movement of the late 1960s as well as the feminist movement; these discourses lent her an interpretive apparatus with which to pierce the silence that enveloped a whole nation as well as her own history. The title *Years of Hunger* appears on screen for the first time when Ursula asks why the previous renters, an unmarried couple, were evicted. Her mother, refusing to respond at first, answers: "One shouldn't always want to know everything." Any knowledge that may unsettle the status quo, much like the horrific events of the Nazi period, remains denied and unmourned.

The Body and the Maternal Voice

In presenting the polyphony of voices, Brückner delves beneath the fragile surface "realities" that were cautiously guarded during the 1950s to explore the voices that informed her identity. As in most autobiographical renderings, the voices most audible come from the private sphere. They compose the subject cubistically, much in the manner Hélène Cixous suggests when she writes: "The composition of the subject, the fact that I am a composition of persons, whether recognizable or not, of my mother, my daughter, your mother . . . and many others, of my father, and every time I speak, the question 'Who is speaking?' is again triggered."[36] The autobiographical self is composed of intersubjective voices. The most prominent voice in Ursula's life is her mother's, which, unlike

---

[35]Jutta Brückner, "Hoffnung auf ein selbst-bewußtes Leben," *Frankfurter Rundschau*, 26 August 1980.

[36]Taken from Hélène Cixous, *Weiblichkeit in der Schrift* (Berlin: Merve, 1980), 29.

the idealized maternal voice in *Germany, Pale Mother*, Brückner reconstitutes as oppressive. Internalization of the mother and submission to her regime in *Years of Hunger* initiate a negative experience of gender and female sexuality.

As much research on mother-daughter relationships since the 1970s points out, many of the attitudes women develop toward themselves as sexual beings are transmitted to daughters by mothers. Partly, this is because the mother's proximity as primary caretaker in traditional Western families predisposes her to name the world for the child and to lay the groundwork for female subjectivity; moreover, because mother and daughter have the same gender, the mother responds differently to the female child than to the male child. Girls are less encouraged to separate from the mother, and their profound emotional bond to the mother is never surrendered.[37] In *Years of Hunger*, a fatal continuum of female powerlessness and a negative self-image associated with normative female subjectivity are perpetuated. Owing to the devaluation of the maternal body and restrictive social practices, the continuum proceeds from mother to daughter. The proclivity of some generations to resist this inheritance takes the form mostly of a struggle against the internalized image of insufficiency and denigration.

Brückner contrasts two mother-daughter relationships spanning three generations of women. The regressive, unfettered bond between Frau Scheuner and her mother juxtaposed with endless confrontations between Ursula and her own mother indicate the daughter's need to escape the maternal realm and its confinement.[38] Comparing her own body and her mother's body in the mirror, Ursula asserts the difference between them. The daughter's relationship to her own body, however, oscillates between a positive and negative mirror image. The more Ursula is forced to surrender to her mother's anxieties about sexuality and to the imperatives her mother imposes on her body, the more marred the mirror-image becomes. Ursula complains to her paternal grand-

---

[37]Gilligan, *In a Different Voice*, 7–8.

[38]For a discussion of the changing image of women in the 1950s, see Barbara Sichtermann, "Über Schönheit, Demokratie und Tod," *Ästhetik und Kommunikation* 7 (1981): 13–25; *Perlon Zeit: Wie die Frauen ihr Wirtschaftswunder erlebten*, ed. Elefanten Press (Berlin: Elefanten Press, 1985); Christiane Gibiec, "Der Rückzug in die Idylle," *Frankfurter Rundschau*, 2 March 1985, p. 5.

"We don't look at all alike."

Britta Pohland in *Years of Hunger*

mother: "She doesn't like me. She can't expect that I turn out to be exactly like her."

Even though identification with the mother ultimately signifies self-denial, the line demarcating mother and daughter is difficult to discern, as Barbara Franck shows in *Ich schau in den Spiegel und sehe meine Mutter* (I look into the mirror and see my mother, 1980), a series of interviews with daughters. The information transmitted from one generation of women to the next inevitably prepares the daughter to act out the same roles into which the mother has been socialized.[39] The mother, in this instance, however, is not portrayed as an ontological essence, but as a purely psychological event (or the site of desire); this portrayal places Brückner's narrative in

[39]Christiane Olivier, *Jocasta's Children: The Imprint of the Mother* (New York: Routledge, 1989).

opposition to many theoretical discourses surrounding the mother fantasy. Instead, Brückner contextualizes the mother's existence by providing the sociohistorical relations from which she has derived her meaning. The mother represents the repressive agent in the daughter's development.

Of equal importance is the daughter's relationship to the father, whom she idealizes as a heroic wartime resister. Film critics seldom discuss the significant role he plays in the oedipal triad, which Brückner seems to reinscribe. He is first shown as a source of identification outside the maternal sphere in the family romance, a point of desire and authority. When Ursula intercepts a letter from her father's lover and discovers his marital "infidelity," she experiences a profound breach of trust and loss. The effect of paternal transgression on the daughter's psychological development, rarely addressed, constitutes a turning point in the film. The stranger claims that Ursula's father never loved her mother, which Ursula projects onto herself, eliciting a sense of rejection. Not only is family unity jeopardized, but both mother and daughter are betrayed.

The trauma of abandonment appears insurmountable throughout the film. The father becomes a marginal figure aggressively faulted for his armchair politics and co-optation. Ursula challenges him: "Every day you talk about being against rearmament and against banning the German Communist Party, against the way that old Nazis regained their positions. But what do you do about it? Nothing!" In reality, the accusations express her own sense of desertion and betrayal. The trauma of loss results in depression and insatiable food binges. Her window reflection diffuses as she is left to duplicate the mother, a personification of deficiency, unworthy of her husband's love: "I'll always be good in school," Ursula stresses, "and study well and never leave you." With the symbolic loss of the father (Ursula touches his pajamas on the clothesline as though mourning his absence), the daughter is left to identify with her mother, the person no longer desired. After watching a scene of "lovemaking" between her mother and father through the keyhole, Ursula flees from the sight and sounds of her mother's subjugation. Melancholia pervades the rest of Ursula's biography as her initiation into a negative relation to her own body continues, culminating in self-punishment.

Of the influences Brückner discusses in her filmic memoir, the most powerful are those directed at the female body. The meaning attached to women's bodies and the messages Ursula receives as a female adolescent about her sexuality and gender choreograph her identity. A voice-over at the beginning, the romantic description of a male's exotic adventure to the Ivory Coast, contrasted with Ursula's curious question about a veil, implies the traditional orientation of her socialization. As a girl, she is metaphorically veiled, concealed, and sequestered. The reduction of women to their reproductive function is magnified, moreover, by the absence of both birth control and the possibility of abortion. For Ursula's mother, protecting her daughter from an unwanted pregnancy calls for rigorously guarding the body from possible transgressions. Just the thought of an illegitimate child provokes deep anxieties: "I'll kill you, child. I couldn't bear my only daughter throwing herself away." More specifically, though, these warnings and moral imperatives ascribe to the female body an intrinsically negative value, and they rob sexuality of pleasure. The mother, who says that *someone* must bear children, suggests that women must accept their sexuality with resignation. Sex, for her, represents an unwelcome and troublesome obligation: "It's not fair that we're made this way. We should be able to rip out our ovaries. A life filled with fear of getting pregnant again."

Contempt for her own body predisposes Ursula's mother to be contemptuous of Ursula's incipient sexuality and makes her both the primary agent of her daughter's stifled conditioning and the most powerful agent in opposing her sexuality. The mother effaces the sensual female body as she tucks her daughter into bed, tightly pulling the sheet over her, as though putting her into a straitjacket. As an afterthought, she takes Ursula's hands out from under the sheet to prevent her from self-discovery. As a representation of the suppression of female sexuality, *Years of Hunger* stands as a modern rendition of the nineteenth-century "bürgerliches Trauerspiel" (bourgeois tragedy) without its prescriptive moral transgression. Instead, the sullen morality of the petit bourgeoisie and the mother's oppressive surveillance over her daughter's body together effect the deformation of a young woman.

Other attitudes toward sexuality which shape Ursula's understanding of her identity and gender are conveyed through gestures.

Brückner explores what Teresa de Lauretis calls "the experience of gender, the meaning effects and self-representations produced in the subject by the sociocultural practices, discourses and institutions devoted to the production of women."[40] The mother's inhibition is displayed when she conceals her breasts from Ursula, who suddenly enters the bathroom, or when she struggles to don her nightgown beneath her clothes in the dark—a gesture that Ursula later repeats. When Ursula's parents make love, her mother, passive and utilized for her husband's gratification, remains silent and detached. Ursula learns to associate heterosexual intercourse with violence, as intimated by the recurring vision of her mother lying naked in the grass, signifying the victimization of the female body. The haunting shadow of a man with a hat who approaches her—an allusion to the murderer in Fritz Lang's film *M*—and the accompanying voice-over of a children's rhyme reinforce the image of sexual violation. Ursula's identification with the role of women as objects and victims becomes evident during her first sexual encounter, which appears as rape.[41]

Brückner's portrayal of the most intimate spheres of female experience not only challenges the aesthetics of narrative cinema but also calls for a recognition of the gestures that deny female sexuality. The rare cinematic presentation of menstruation is a traumatic turning point in Ursula's life, primarily because of the cultural meaning attached to it. Ursula interprets bleeding as a sign of illness, a disturbance of her relationship to her own healthy female body. Her initial fear of a physical dysfunction is reinforced by the conflicting fragments of information she receives. Her mother's assurance that "it is nice to be a woman" is paradoxically accompanied by a number of restrictions: she can no longer play with boys or bathe when she has her period. Moreover, the sanitary napkin held with straps impairs freedom of movement. A shameful

[40]Teresa de Lauretis, *Technologies of Gender: Essays on Theory, Film, and Fiction* (Bloomington: Indiana University Press, 1987), 19.

[41]Since the man Ursula meets is Algerian, this scene is problematic in itself because it runs the danger of confirming stereotypes. This scene may be read in two ways. First, Ursula is only able to have her first sexual experience with someone who lives in a form of exile as well. Or, second, female sexual oppression and objectification surpasses national boundaries.

silence further demeans the natural function of the female body when her father is told that Ursula has a stomachache from eating too much cake, while she desperately hugs him in an attempt to seek refuge from womanhood. Women's discomfort in speaking about their sexuality is exemplified by Ursula's grandmother's advice to use the cryptic designation "d.u." to describe her condition, even though none of the women actually know what the term means.[42]

Both the exclusion of female subjectivities from the public sphere and the absence of a language to describe women's experiences both contribute to the shame surrounding the female body. The absence of an adequate language to represent female sexuality was widely discussed in the 1970s. Faced with the impossibility of describing the female body without reverting to the "virgin" language of clinicians or "vamp" language of pimps, Verena Stefan begins her feminist work *Shedding* [*Häutungen*, 1976) by addressing this linguistic deficiency.[43] Brückner faced problems when she chose to challenge a cultural taboo by showing a used sanitary napkin. Her male camera operator refused to film the scene; when he finally acceded, he closed his eyes to withdraw the gaze.

The dominant scopic economy, based predominantly on male pleasure, as many film theorists have argued, denies aspects of female experiences. When women view their own lives, however, these areas of knowledge can hardly be suppressed. They influence female subjectivity, as much as do the images of glamour that serve as models for female identification mediated through the male gaze. Brückner intercuts documentary footage of a fashion show at which women are staged in bathing suits, as commodified spectacles. She includes close-ups in which the female body is programmatically

[42]A version of this chapter appears as "Repressing Female Sexuality: On Jutta Brückner's Film *Years of Hunger*," in *Gender and German Cinema: Feminist Interventions*, ed. Sandra Frieden et al. (Providence, R.I.: Berg, 1993), 241–52. I would like to thank the editors for finding out that d.u. stands for "dienstuntauglich," a military term that translates as "unfit for duty." This designation is a prime example of how the male realm of experience is drawn upon to describe women's experiences.

[43]The great need to acquaint women with their own bodies explains the success of such publications as *Our Bodies, Our Selves*, first published in 1973 by the Boston Women's Collective, and Shere Hite's *Sexual Honesty: By Women for Women*, 1974. Both quickly became best-sellers.

dissected and fetishized for male visual enjoyment. A voice-over of a ribald song accompanied by laughter undercuts the visual panorama by pushing the scene in the direction of burlesque.

Such traditional images of femininity were revived in the 1950s; they constructed female subjectivity and delineated female experience. After the war, as shown in *Germany, Pale Mother*, women were called upon to relinquish their function in the public sphere. In front of the mirror with crossed legs, a French beret, and a cigarette, pulling down her knee socks to study her legs, Ursula works on constructing herself, presumably to be looked at. Her image is reflected in two mirrors that visually fragment and dichotomize her body. One mirror reflects her head, and the other, markedly larger, her body. She reenacts this pose when a young man approaches her. When she timidly pulls up her shirt in a previous scene to look at her breasts in the mirror, her inner voice, designated by a voice-over, repeats a sexually offensive rhyme. Paradoxically, she resists the inclination to look and sticks out her tongue at the reflected image; her developing body becomes her barrier to the outside world. Interestingly, in these scenes she assumes the position of two kinds of spectators: one simulates the male gaze and becomes aligned with male subjectivity, and the other becomes aligned with a female subjectivity riddled with insecurity and a sense of inadequacy.[44] The association of her body

[44]Laura Mulvey, "Visual Pleasure and Narrative Cinema," *Movies and Methods: An Anthology*, ed. Bill Nichols (Berkeley: University of California Press, 1985: 303–15. In this classic feminist essay, Mulvey discusses the projection of male "fantasies and obsessions" onto "the silent image of woman." Yet, feminist film theory's treatment of spectatorship has undergone a number of conceptual changes. One could trace a lineage beginning with Christian Metz who posited a monolithic spectator. Then Mulvey, who attempted to situate a historical female subject, created a monolithic female spectator. With time, additional differences were taken into account which distinguished spectators in terms of race, ethnicity, class, and history. Since even a basic list of references would be too extensive, I will cite only a few: Claire Johnston, ed., *Notes on Women's Cinema* (London: SEFT, 1974); Annette Kuhn, *Women's Pictures: Feminism and Cinema* (London: Routledge & Kegan Paul, 1982); E. Ann Kaplan, *Women and Film: Both Sides of the Camera* (New York: Methuen, 1983) and *Motherhood and Representation: The Mother in Popular Culture and Melodrama* (New York: Routledge: 1992); Teresa de Lauretis, *Alice Doesn't: Feminism, Semiotics, Cinema* (Bloomington: Indiana University Press, 1984); Mary Ann Doane, *The Desire to Desire: The Woman's Film of the 1940s* (Bloomington: Indiana University Press, 1987); and Constance Penley, ed., *Feminism and Film Theory* (New York: Routledge, 1988).

and the lewd rhyme signals the internalization of outer voices that denigrate her own sexuality.

Under maternal surveillance, the daughter has no possibility of forming a positive self-image. The mother shields the daughter to the extent that she prevents the daughter from any social interaction. Ursula is torn by her inner desire to become a "normal girl" and by the outer bourgeois asceticism personified by her mother. The images of "normality" remain in the imaginary. Still photographs of the school dance, which she is not allowed to attend, cannot be animated by personal memories. They are juxtaposed to a shot of Ursula sitting in her room, filling the inner void by eating. The incongruities between desire and possibility drive her into self-destructive isolation. The female body, the cause of her hardship, constitutes the point at which these two moments collide. The narrator recounts the attempts to efface herself; Ursula is shown cutting herself in order to destroy a body stunted by maternal control: "Stunted, destroy the coldness, break through the shell." Elfriede Jelinek's novel *The Piano Teacher* (*Die Klavierspielerin*) similarly produces a female protagonist who uses razor blades to revive her body, which has atrophied under the mother's overbearing direction. In both instances, mutilating the body connotes punishing female sexuality and performing the cultural imperatives that view the female body as deficient or even evil. According to Brückner, the body is the inevitable point at which various sociohistorical textual coordinates converge: "The soul and the body and the body and the world are then always the materialization of inside and outside and the body in its central position is both simultaneously: the place where the invisible soul is able to make itself visible and the visible world can be inscribed in the invisible."[45] The body, directly involved in both the political and personal spheres, becomes the surface of Brückner's textual exploration.[46] Hence, the story of the female body comprises the "bio" of her autobiography.

The effort to de-privatize individual experience and the body by restoring them to their sociohistorical context pervades Brückner's

[45]Brückner, "Vom Pathos des Leibes oder: Der revolutionäre Exorzismus," 59.

[46]See *The Female Body in Western Culture: Contemporary Perspectives*, ed. Susan Rubin Suleiman (Cambridge: Harvard University Press, 1985); Christina von Braun, *Nicht Ich/Ich Nicht: Logik, Lüge, Libido* (Frankfurt: Neue Kritik, 1985).

autobiographical project. Through the use of documentary footage of explosive historical moments of the 1950s, she polemically places the individual within a political framework. References to the workers' uprising in East Berlin and the Algerian revolution against French colonizers expand the contextual meaning of oppression and spatially disperse the narrative. Documentary footage is placed strategically to politicize the personal realm. As Brückner argues in her article "Vom Pathos des Leibes oder: Der revolutionäre Exorzismus" (On the pathos of the body; or, revolutionary exorcism), the inclusion of documentary footage provides the possibility of connecting personal oppression with political resistance to a bourgeois ideology that restricts individual opportunities through its naturalization of dichotomies. She draws an explicit parallel between the colonization of the female body and social or political colonization of nations by political systems and discourses. The image of Ursula cutting herself in the classroom, for instance, is juxtaposed to the date "1789"—the year of the French Revolution—on the blackboard. In view of such historical referents, self-destruction is misdirected energy. Such sequences activate a dialectical process between personal and sociopolitical occurrences and demonstrate the necessity of opening up the interpretive spectrum of autobiographical self-exploration. In a voice-over, the adult narrator asks, "How could one live inside and outside at the same time?" An image of an atomic explosion, indicative of suffering and destruction, appears to express the neglected link between private and public.

Like many recent autobiographies that accede to a prescriptive feminist telos, *Years of Hunger* chronicles a process as well as a psychological rebirth. A rebirth, however, presumes a death, and the adult narrator condemns the image of her youth to its symbolic death. An epitaphic voice-over declares: "Whoever wants to accomplish something has to execute something—herself." At the end, the portrait of a female adolescent, reassembled and remembered throughout the film, is seized, in the form of a snapshot, and burned. Ursula Scheuner's burning portrait evinces the autobiographer's exorcism of a self-image and a part of the past. By releasing long-repressed memories and restaging the key moments of her life in their historical context, Brückner programmatically completes the first step of mourning by working through and destroying the old self-image.

Yet the relationship with the mother, whose inability to decipher her daughter's needs all along remains only partially dealt with. Even Ursula's suicide attempt, in which she ingests food and pills to fill the inner emptiness, meets with misrecognition: The film ends ominously with a voice-over of Frau Scheuner questioning: "But why didn't you say anything, child? You have everything. Everything you need, don't you? I mean, what's missing?" The ending suggests that coming to terms with oneself involves going beyond the mother: the mother's disembodied, "pure" voice is no longer anchored to her body. Her voice has become a part of the daughter's psychic structure. Even though the narrative moves toward recovery, this feminist agenda allows for too facile a resolution. The mother's voice, as Brückner shows is not reconciled; the fire is hardly extinguished.

Self-exploration, in feminist terms, is an ongoing project. As most literary and filmic autobiographies by women show, the process of extricating female identities from a long tradition of normative representations and conditions has taken many critical turns since the early 1970s. The renaming and restaging of personal histories raise questions about the female self that these autobiographers create but also about the new possibilities such explorations provide. *Years of Hunger* is an example of such an adventure, which, Brückner might say, was born of necessity.

Conclusion:
Topographies of the Self

We know that in his work Proust did not describe a life as
it actually was, but a life as it was remembered by the one
who had lived it. And yet even this statement is imprecise
and far too crude. For the important thing for the remembering author is not what he experienced, but the weaving
of his memory, the Penelope work of recollection. Or should
one call it, rather a Penelope work of forgetting?

Walter Benjamin, *Illuminations*

And identity is funny being yourself is funny as you are never
yourself to yourself except as you remember yourself and
then of course you do not believe yourself. That is really the
trouble with an autobiography you do not of course you do
not believe yourself why should you, you know so well so
very well that it is not yourself, it could not be yourself
because you cannot remember right and if you do remember
right it does not sound right because it is not right. You are
of course never yourself.

Gertrude Stein, *Everybody's Autobiography*

Walter Benjamin's reference to the process of weaving in Proust's
reconstruction of the past best describes the work of memory and
the multiple strands that are brought together to produce the narratives of life. The patterns woven, however, always vary, depending on the questions and events that trigger remembrance.
Rarely treated as absolute and authentic representations of the past,
contemporary autobiographies restage the past. As the site of remembering, in terms of recollecting and connecting, autobiographies join past and present, with the past acting as the foil against
which the present is interpreted. The past is not separate from the
present, and, as Christa Wolf maintains, "it is not even past." The
process of bridging temporalities implicit in the autobiographical
enterprise thus dislocates the ideological notions of discontinuity
and of seeing the past isolated and severed from the present. A
new relevance to historical understanding emerges in many recent

autobiographies written in Germany; a link between history and subjective processes is revitalized. History, consequently, is no longer read as "out there"; instead, it is seen as an integral part of the personal realm, as the autobiographers I have discussed demonstrate.[1]

The autobiographies written in Germany in the 1970s and 1980s largely respond to the widespread preoccupation with excavating Germany's history and working through the intersection of history and daily life. They attempt to permeate the "fortifications" (to borrow Christa Wolf's metaphor) that surround memories of Germany's fascist past, traces of which, as many of the autobiographers found out, live on in the present.

These narratives are boundary breaking. As we have seen, they consistently challenge the boundaries conventionally set between narrative and document, between subjectivity and objectivity, between the private sphere and the public sphere, in addition to the divisions commonly set between autobiography and biography expression. The authors destabilize deep-rooted dichotomies in favor of exploring the multiple layers of discourse. The acknowledgment of the interdependence of categories rather than the insistence on their separation has allowed for broader interpretive and critical considerations within the study of autobiography and within life itself. Furthermore, the traditional barriers placed between subjective processes and official renderings of events, between history and genre as well as between literature and film, are overcome through the magnification of their interchanges. As a result, doors have been unbarred and dialogic processes along multiple axes initiated. In the context of the dismantling of the wall between East Germany and West Germany, traversing borders gains a new significance and acuity.

The two literary texts and the two cinematic texts examined here share a preoccupation with the working through of trauma and loss, which turns these texts into acts of mourning. The autobiographers attempt to bring to a cognitive level the patterns of behavior that the protagonists have internalized as children, since, as Wolf and Brückner recognize, these patterns, ideas, and beliefs do not

---

[1]The illustration of the interdependence of the personal and private realms is also one of the guiding projects of New German Cinema.

merely exhaust themselves over time, but are continuously reproduced. Moreover, "one does not relinquish patterns of behavior,
ideas, or fantasies," Eric Santner points out, "simply because one
is told they are wrong, immoral, or even self-destructive. To relinquish something requires a labor of mourning, and mourning requires a space in which its elegiac procedures can unfold."[2]
Autobiography provides a significant space for engaging in such
a labor of mourning through the remembrance and reconstruction
of moments of loss.

Many contemporary autobiographical texts produced by women
in Germany reflect a need to question and work through experiences of a traumatized gendered and national identity. At first, the
experiential literature produced under the auspices of the women's
movement and the second wave of feminism vigorously questioned
dominant culture in an attempt to expose the conditions that restricted women. Women writers and filmmakers drew exclusive
borders around themselves as a form of resistance in order to take
possession of their bodies and voices. This literature marked a
celebratory "shedding" of cultural practices that narrowly defined
(and confined) gendered subjectivities.' Yet to attribute to the "feminine" positive new values and by extension to essentialize the
"feminine," as many of these texts did, tended to reconfirm and
solidify the same traditional paradigms of binary oppositions. Concentration on mothering, female experience, and women-defined
spaces only recirculated the tendencies that conflated sex and gender and elided differences among women through the text's fixation
on biological similarity. The popularity of this form of expression
in its dogmatic version soon exhausted itself as new theoretical
orientations developed. The female self was no longer reductively
placed in a linear relationship to the male but was represented in
the diversity of her social, historical, and psychological configurations. Next to gender, other socializing factors such as race, class,
ethnicity, and historical particularity came under scrutiny.

The autobiographies presented here focused primarily on the
family as it is shaped by historical experience and as the primary
agent of socialization and subject-formation. The construction of

[2]Eric L. Santner, *Stranded Objects: Mourning, Memory, and Film in Postwar Germany*
(Ithaca: Cornell University Press, 1990), 151.

their personal histories allowed these female writers and filmmakers to look closely at interpersonal, or intersubjective, relationships. The mother-daughter relationship, characterized by either stifling proximity or abandonment, appeared as the most prominent topic of confrontation, with the father-daughter relationship following close behind. Whereas Jutta Brückner's protagonist strives to free herself from maternal control in order to renegotiate an identity, the adult in Helma Sanders-Brahms's film expresses her desire for renewed bonding with the lost mother. In Christa Wolf's narrative the sense of abandonment which circulates throughout her autobiographical inquiry is compounded by the loss of her mother at the time of writing. All three representations reflect facets of women's efforts to grapple with the mother's role in identity formation.

Sparked first by the student movement, then by cinematic representations of the past, and later by the historians' controversial debate, interest in questions of German national identity and history mounted in the early 1980s. A number of autobiographies that focused on the fathers emphasized less the conditions that shaped the daughter's gendered development than the effect of growing up during the Third Reich and the influence of paternal experiences on the child's life.[3] Ruth Rehmann's work particularly stands out, exemplifying the unconscious resistance toward confronting the past and the inextricable intertwining of personal identity and national identity. Her work is perhaps most important, however, for its failure to recognize the psychic structures the narrator perpetuates. She exculpates the father and maintains his authority.

The autobiographical portraits under discussion mark the first steps in an open-ended process of remembering designed to reconfigure identity and the understanding of history. Wolf's *Patterns of Childhood*, for instance, ends with the narrator speculating on an "awakening" that enables her to surrender herself to the "unspeakable" that consciousness resists. Still, the narrator expresses uncertainty and questions her own ability to merge subconscious

---

[3]In regard to cinematic representations, public debate of German history was rekindled by Hollywood's television series "Holocaust," aired in Germany in 1979. Filmmaker Edgar Reitz responded with *Heimat*, his sixteen-hour film made for television in 1984. New German cinema, moreover, has been obsessed with German history and the need to initiate the labor of mourning that history.

and conscious processes in a stable "I." She ends the narrative with the confession "I don't know." Disavowing the ability to create a unified subject, the traditional "cogito ergo sum," she uses the first-person pronoun to introduce doubt and negate the process of complete knowing. She thereby alludes to process and the constant struggle in dealing with self-reflection. The narrator in Rehmann's *Der Mann auf der Kanzel* awkwardly warns against a rewriting of history which dismisses historical culpability and painstakingly attempts to explain psychic structures that allow for conformity. When Ursula Scheuner burns her portrait in Brückner's *Years of Hunger*, she signals a turning point that implies a release from the image she once was. The exposure and destruction of the static image that was buried in Ursula's subconscious allows for a more dynamic processing of her own history. In Sanders-Brahms's *Germany, Pale Mother*, the daughter's interpretation of the past serves as a starting point for personal and public reflection. The film reveals a powerful need to enter into dialogue with the lost mother as well as the desire to embrace the past.

Most autobiographical texts by women in the 1970s and 1980s in Germany are either driven by crisis or guided by the outgrowth of new epistemological orientations. Rather than conform to a priori structures, the texts reflect a rigorous confrontation with the polyvocal inflections and multiple axes that constitute the diverse modes of identity and which define self-consciousness. By this I mean that they explore the various voices, private and institutional, which contribute to the composition of the self and which influence the choices one makes. These autobiographers filter, process and reinvest information in order to map the topography of the self. The autobiographical productions by Wolf, Rehmann, Brückner, and Sanders-Brahms uncover (discover) a number of discourses and practices that shape their authors' identities. No longer conceived of as a fixed, dehistoricized essence, or unity, the self constructed in these contemporary texts is constituted by a sum of experiences, which include abandonment, sexual repression, desire for recognition, and crises of identity formed by social practices and historical context.

Yet modernists like Gertrude Stein already argued that the mere concept of the modern self defies any boundaries. Identity is constantly being shifted and renegotiated; it is alterable, dynamic, and in flux. This understanding of selfhood allows for reevaluating and changing the positions assigned to women. It leaves spaces open for the exploration of different subjectivities, which, according to Teresa de Lauretis are constituted by "one's personal, subjective engagement in the practices, discourses, and institutions that lend significance (value, meaning, and affect) to the events of the world."[4] Knowledge informed by a perspective, is not objective but rather invested with the autobiographer's social, political, and personal interests.

Theoretical attempts to explicate autobiographical expression and postulate its function, value, possibilities, and even its end have fomented much debate.[5] Despite their different approaches, contemporary critics agree that autobiography has abdicated its function as the storehouse of truth. Instead, autobiography is widely regarded as the site of self-invention and self-enactment. It is the site of constructing a self in order to reflect on personal history. It is an interplay of imagination, desire, and memory. For the authors mentioned here, the defining element is their growing up during the Third Reich or the postwar period in Germany. The redefinition or recasting of autobiography thus has invited a reexamination of the premises of selfhood.

Since the contemporary autobiography (much like the postmodern novel) calls into question the factors that constitute subjectivity, history, and even reference, it also challenges the concepts of authority, and uniqueness, a challenge that accelerated during the 1960s with the student movement and feminism. The white male has traditionally been identified with the universal self in Western culture, and autobiography has been his story. Now, women's texts have the radical potential to challenge this perceptual monopoly. Yet, only self-reflectively written works by women challenge the

---

[4]Teresa de Lauretis, *Alice Doesn't: Feminism, Semiotics, Cinema* (Bloomington: Indiana University Press, 1984), 159.

[5]Ironically, the end of autobiography may be a consequence not only of conceptual and interpretive revolutions in philosophy but also of pure practicality. More and more lawsuits for libel are being brought against authors. For instance, the filming of Sylvia Plath's novel *The Bell Jar* drew protest from a woman who saw herself portrayed and implicated in acts in which she allegedly never took part. See Richard Lacayo, "Of Whom the Bell Told," *Time*, 9 February 1987, p. 26.

exclusions and the premises of a male-authored subjectivity. Otherwise, women who adopt the traditional structure of autobiographical writing inevitably partake in self-effacement, since the
structures sustained by the traditional format are entrenched in
male/bourgeois subjectivity, which excludes heterogeneous expressions of desire and agency. Sidonie Smith goes so far as to charge
that women who do not break with the traditions of autobiography
do not write autobiographies, they only submit to the scripts that
have been imposed on their lives. Conventional autobiography,
Smith writes, only "serves as one of those generic contracts that
reproduces the patrilineage and its ideologies of gender," whether
written by men or women.[6]

The autobiographical enterprise practiced by many contemporary German women writers and filmmakers, exemplified by Wolf,
Rehmann, Sanders-Brahms, and Brückner, reveals a search that
crosses frontiers. The interplay between society, history, and the
individual constitutes the most compelling focal point of their work.
By piecing together, juxtaposing, and realigning literary and cinematic images, the autobiographical narrator in each of these texts,
in an existential interpretive process, assigns her own meaning to
the significant moments in her life. As she doubles herself through
mimesis, the narrated "I" moves through mirrored corridors of the
past which admittedly distort owing to the gap between past and
present, to the operations of language, and to the deceptions of
memory. Such distortions are hardly a liability; on the contrary,
they are necessary for conceptualizing and reevaluating.

The autobiographer consequently restages moments of the past
in order to denaturalize or estrange the gestures that have confined
her perspective. The possibility of looking in these mirrors of the
past in a process of self-reflection allows for new models of identity
to emerge. For Wolf and Brückner, the introduction of a third
person persona purposely heightens and acknowledges the distance needed for self-analysis. Rehmann's third person is the father, although she fails to recognize his mirroring function. And

[6]Sidonie Smith, *A Poetics of Women's Autobiography: Marginality and the Fictions of
Self-Representation* (Bloomington: Indiana University Press, 1987), 44. For an example
of a woman's autobiography that reinvents the traditional borders of this genre,
see Leni Riefenstahl, *Memoiren* (Munich: Albrecht Knaus, 1987).

for Sanders-Brahms, the projection of memory onto the child and Lene permits self-evaluation.

The deluge of "experiential literature" as well as of autobiographical prose shows that writing stands in opposition to the silence that historically marked most women's lives. These texts manifest the desire to explore one's own life, to take control by claiming images, producing new sensibilities, and assigning meaning. In Ingeborg Bachmann's unfinished novel *Der Fall Franza* (The case of Franza), the gravity of making sense of one's own experience by writing is alluded to when the narrator, who has been psychically "killed" with the pen of her psychiatrist husband, states: "The living should describe the living." Bachmann represents how authorship as traditionally practiced throughout Western culture colonizes and destroys the voices and bodies of the Other, much like Walter Benjamin warns in his writings on history. The Other is inscribed with the expectations and desires of the dominant culture through descriptive and prescriptive operations. In autobiography, the "living" participate in the writing and interpreting of their own lives. Moreover, they engage in an exploration of the conventions that fabricate subjectivity and identity through the interaction of national identity, historical specificity, and normative expectations placed on gender. As a result, autobiographical writing can become an invaluable arena of dissent, since repressed voices and unconscious processes find articulation there. The significance of this task can be measured against the silence from which women's autobiographies emerged and the new perspectives these women writers have brought to bear. Perhaps this is the underlying utopic moment in these works.

In many respects it can be said that autobiographical texts by women implicitly promote a political agenda. First, they represent experiences and remembrances that go against the tide of collective narratives (metanarratives) overwhelmingly marked by the hegemonic structures of Western culture. Second, they secure a position within the historical process by making women's self-conscious autobiographical writing a form of historiography that writes against absence and exclusion, opening the historical text to diverse voices and rendering historical documentation inclusive. Autobiographical texts often "brush history against the grain," as Walter

Benjamin puts it.[7] Finally, personal histories provide access to subjective knowledge, revealing the psychic structures that underpin and shape history. The comprehension of these structures, one of the most compelling reasons for the autobiographical narratives discussed here, has become vital in view of Germany's past. Women filmmakers and writers of autobiography, such as the four women cited here, have taken important steps in excavating these structures by closely looking at their parents' lives as well as at the behavior and perceptions that have been internalized and perpetuated through generations.

In my readings, I have attempted to emphasize the discursive quality of these autobiographies and suggested that the dialogue extends beyond the textual surface. All the references to correspondence, dialogue, speaking, and mediating suggest that communication and inquiry, which play a part in recasting autobiography, are the overriding motives of the narratives discussed in this book. These "oral histories" illuminate the history of daily life and become the mirrors for the next generation's reflection. At the same time, the inscription of an addressee who most often belongs to a younger generation suggests a connection and an exchange between the past, the present, and the future. In addition to opening up diverse epistemological realms, the dialogical connections among these various temporalities give personal histories a profound significance, especially if we are to "Live in the Present. Learn from the Past. Look to the Future," as Susan Rubin Suleiman exhorts.[8]

Through writing autobiographies, many women have participated in mapping their own lives, investigating and interpreting their experiences in the sense of Walter Benjamin's description of remembering. Many women autobiographers defy the narratives that have directed, judged, and repressed the diversity of expression, subjectivity, and desire, and as Sanders-Brahms shows, they challenge historiography's exclusions. The investigation of auto-

[7]Walter Benjamin, *Illuminations: Essays and Reflections*, trans. Harry Zohn (New York: Schocken, 1978), 257.

[8]Susan Rubin Suleiman, "Feminism and Postmodernism," in *Zeitgeist in Babel: The Postmodernist Controversy*, ed. Ingeborg Hoesterey (Bloomington: Indiana University Press, 1991), 125. In this article Suleiman quotes from a poster showing Delacroix's "Liberty Leading the People."

biographical and biographical works by women in Germany is still a relatively new undertaking in literary and film studies. Thus, the thresholds women will cross when they become the agents of their own desires still remain a matter of curiosity. On the basis of the autobiographies discussed here, there is much left to be discovered. With the end of the wall between East and West and the subsequent redrawing of geopolitical boundaries, many new questions will surface in Germany. I suspect that in response to these questions autobiographies will change and map new topographies of the self.

Bibliography/Filmography

Primary Sources

Brückner, Jutta, dir. *Hungerjahre in einem reichen Land* [*Years of Hunger*]. Basis, 1979. 108 min. U.S. distributor: West Glen Films, New York.

Rehmann, Ruth. *Der Mann auf der Kanzel: Fragen an einen Vater* [The man in the pulpit: Questions for a father]. Munich: Deutscher Taschenbuch Verlag, 1981.

Sanders-Brahms, Helma, dir. *Deutschland, bleiche Mutter* [*Germany, Pale Mother*]. Basis, 1979. 125 min. U.S. distributor: West Glen Films, New York.

——. *Deutschland, bleiche Mutter: Film-Erzählung*. Hamburg: Rowohlt, 1980.

Wolf, Christa. *Kindheitsmuster*. Darmstadt: Luchterhand, 1976. *Patterns of Childhood* (formerly *A Model Childhood*). Translated by Ursule Molinaro and Hedwig Rappolt. New York: Farrar, Straus and Giroux, 1980.

Secondary Sources

Adelson, Leslie. "Subjectivity Reconsidered: Botho Strauss and Contemporary West German Prose." *New German Critique* 30 (1983): 3–59.

Adorno, Theodor W. *Minima Moralia: Reflexionen aus dem beschädigten Leben*. Frankfurt am Main: Suhrkamp, 1951.

——. "Was bedeutet: Aufarbeitung der Vergangenheit?" *Eingriffe: Neun kritische Modelle*. Frankfurt am Main: Suhrkamp, 1963.

Alcoff, Linda. "Cultural Feminism versus Post-Structuralism: The Identity Crisis in Feminist Theory." *Signs: Journal of Women in Culture and Society* 13 (1988): 405–36.

Altbach, Edith Hoshino. "The New German Women's Movement." *Signs: Journal of Women and Culture in Society* 9.3 (1984): 454–69.

——, ed. and trans. *German Feminism: Readings in Politics and Literature*. Albany: State University of New York Press, 1984.

André, Michael. "Vom Leben und Tod." Review of *Deutschland, bleiche Mutter*, dir. by Helma Sanders-Brahms. *Rheinische Post*, 6 December 1980.

Anselm, Sigrun, et al., eds. *Theorien weiblicher Subjektivität*. Frankfurt: Verlag Neue Kritik, 1985.

Ästhetik und Kommunikation 57/58 (1985).

Bachmann, Ingeborg. *Malina*. Translated by Philip Boehm. New York: Holmes and Meier, 1990.

——. *Die Wahrheit ist dem Menschen zumutbar*. Munich: Piper, 1981.

Badinter, Elisabeth. *Motherlove: Myth and Reality*. New York: Macmillan, 1981.

Bail, Gabriele. *Weibliche Identität: Ingeborg Bachmanns "Malina."* Göttingen: Edition Herodot, 1984.

Bammer, Angelika. "Through a Daughter's Eyes: Helma Sanders-Brahms's *Germany, Pale Mother*." *New German Critique* 36 (1985): 91–109.

Bar-On, Dan. *Legacy of Silence: Encounters with Children of the Third Reich*. Cambridge: Harvard University Press, 1989.

Barthes, Roland. "The Death of the Author." In *Image-Music-Text*. Translated by Stephen Heath. New York: Hill and Wang, 1977.

——. *The Pleasure of the Text*. Translated by Richard Miller. New York, Hill and Wang, 1975.

——. *Roland Barthes by Roland Barthes*. Translated by Richard Howard. New York: Hill and Wang, 1977.

Bauer, Christian. "Auf der Suche nach verlorenen Müttern." *Süddeutsche Zeitung*, 3 January 1981.

Baumgart, Reinhard. "Dem Leben hinterhergeschrieben." *Die Zeit*, 5 October 1984, p. 72.

Beck, Evelyn Torton, and Biddy Martin. "Westdeutsche Frauenliteratur der siebziger Jahre." In *Deutsche Literatur in der Bundesrepublik seit 1965*, edited by P. M. Lützeler and Egon Schwarz, 135–49. Königstein/TS: Athenäum, 1980.

Becker-Cantarino, Barbara. "Leben als Text." In *Frauen, Literatur, Geschichte: Schreibende Frauen vom Mittelalter bis zur Gegenwart*, edited by Hiltrud Gnüg and Renate Möhrmann. Stuttgart: Metzler, 1985.

Beicken, Peter. " 'Neue Subjektivität': Zur Prosa der siebziger Jahre." In *Deutsche Literatur in der Bundesrepublik seit 1965*, edited by P. M. Lützeler and Egon Schwarz, 164–81. Königstein/TS: Athenäum, 1980.

Belenky, Mary Field, et al., eds. *Women's Ways of Knowing: The Development of Self, Voice, and Mind*. New York: Basic Books, 1986.

Benjamin, Walter. *Berliner Kindheit*. Frankfurt am Main: Suhrkamp, 1950.

——. *Illuminations: Essays and Reflections*. Translated by Harry Zohn. New York: Schocken, 1978.

——. *Das Passagen-Werk*. Edited by Rolf Tiedemann. 2 vols. Frankfurt am Main: Suhrkamp, 1982.

——. "Theses on the Philosophy of History." In *Illuminations*, translated by Harry Zohn, 253–64. New York: Schocken, 1978.

Benstock, Shari, ed. *The Private Self: Theory and Practice of Women's Auto-biographical Writings.* Chapel Hill: University of North Carolina Press, 1988.

Benveniste, Emile. *Problems in General Linguistics.* Translated by M. E. Meek. Coral Gables: University of Miami Press, 1971.

Berger, John. *Ways of Seeing.* London: British Broadcasting Corp., 1972.

Blöcker, Günther. "Auf der Suche nach dem Vater." *Merkur* 25 (1974): 397.

Bloom, Lynn Z. "Heritages: Discussions of Mother-Daughter Relationships in Women's Autobiographies." In *The Lost Tradition: Mothers and Daughters in Literature,* edited by Cathy N. Davidson and E. M. Broner, 291–302. New York: Ungar, 1980.

———. "Promises Fulfilled: Positive Images of Women in Twentieth-Century Autobiography." In *Feminist Criticism: Essays on Theory, Poetry and Prose,* edited by Cheryl Brown and Karen Olson, 324–38. Metuchen, N.J.: Scarecrow Press, 1978.

Blumenberg, Hans C. "Ein Brief an Lene." Review of *Germany, Pale Mother* by Helma Sanders-Brahms. *Die Zeit,* 10 October 1980.

Bock, Sigrid. "Christa Wolf: *Kindheitsmuster.*" *Weimarer Beiträge* 23 (1977): 102–30.

Boerner, Peter. *Tagebuch.* Stuttgart: Metzler, 1969.

Böhmer, Ursula. " 'se dire—s'écrire': Frauen, Literatur und Psychoanalyse in den siebziger Jahren in Frankreich." *LiLi* 35 (1979): 60–81.

Boose, Lynda E., and Betty S. Flowers, eds. *Daughters and Fathers.* Baltimore: Johns Hopkins University Press, 1989.

Bordwell, David. *Narration in the Fiction Film.* Madison: University of Wisconsin Press, 1985.

Born, Nicolas, Jürgen Manthey, and Delf Schmidt, eds. *Literaturmagazin* (1978).

———. *Literaturmagazin* (1979).

Borries, Boris von. "Forschung und Lernen an Frauengeschichte—Versuch einer Zwischenbilanz." In *Frauen in der Geschichte* VI, edited by Annette Kuhn et al., 49–91. Düsseldorf: Schwann, 1985.

Bottigheimer, Ruth B. *Grimms' Bad Girls and Bold Boys: The Moral and Social Vision of the Tales.* New Haven: Yale University Press, 1987.

Bovenschen, Silvia. "Is There a Feminine Aesthetic?" In *Feminist Aesthetics,* translated by Beth Weckmüller, edited by Gisela Ecker, 23–50. Boston: Beacon Press, 1986.

Braun, Christina von. *Nicht Ich/Ich Nicht: Logik, Lüge, Libido.* Frankfurt: Neue Kritik, 1985.

Breitling, Gisela. *Die Spuren des Schiffs in den Wellen: Eine autobiographische Suche nach den Frauen in der Kunstgeschichte.* Frankfurt am Main: Fischer, 1986.

Brettschneider, Werner. *Kindheitsmuster: Kindheit als Thema autobiographischer Dichtung.* Berlin: Erich Schmidt, 1982.

Brodzki, Bella, and Celeste Schenck, eds. *Life/Lines: Theorizing Women's Autobiography.* Ithaca: Cornell University Press, 1988.

Bronsen, David. "Autobiographien der siebziger Jahre: Berühmte Schriftsteller befragen ihre Vergangenheit." In *Deutsche Literatur in der Bundesrepublik seit 1965*, edited by P. M. Lützeler and Egon Schwarz, 202–14. Königstein/TS Athenäum, 1980.

Brückner, Jutta. "Conversing Together Finally: Jutta Brückner, Christina Perincioli, and Helga Reidemeister." Interview with Marc Silberman. *Jump Cut* 27 (1982): 47–48.

——. *Ein ganz und gar verwahrlostes Mädchen* [A thoroughly neglected girl]. Unidoc, 1977.

——. "Frau zur Freiheit." With Kurt Habernoll. *Der Abend*, 2 February 1980, p. 46.

——. "Hoffnung auf ein selbst-bewußtes Leben: Filme von Frauen als Spurensuche." *Frankfurter Rundschau*, 26 August 1980.

——. *Laufen lernen* [Learning to run]. Basis-Film, 1980.

——. "Recognizing Collective Gestures." Interview with Marc Silberman. *Jump Cut* 27 (1982): 46–47.

——. "Seh-Verhältnisse: Über Fernsehen, neue Medien und unsere Erfahrung mit dem, was 'wirklich' ist." *Argument* 150 (1985): 229–31.

——. "Sexualität als Arbeit im Pornofilm." *Argument* 141 (1983): 674–84.

——. *Tue recht und scheue niemand* [Do right and fear no one]. Unidoc, 1975.

——. "Vom Erinnern, Vergessen, dem Leib und der Wut. Ein Kultur-Film-Projekt." *Frauen und Film* 35 (1983): 29–47.

——. "Vom Pathos des Leibes oder: Der revolutionäre Exorzismus." *Ästhetik und Kommunikation: Intimität* 57/58 (1985): 55–65.

Bruss, Elizabeth. *Autobiographical Acts: The Changing Situation of a Literary Genre*. Baltimore: Johns Hopkins University Press, 1976.

——. "Eye for I: Making and Unmaking Autobiography in Film." In *Autobiography: Essays Theoretical and Critical*, edited by James Olney, 296–320. Princeton: Princeton University Press, 1980.

Buñuel, Luis. *My Last Sigh*. Translated by Abigail Israel. New York: Alfred Knopf, 1983.

Bürger, Christa. *Tradition und Subjektivität*. Frankfurt am Main: Suhrkamp, 1980.

Buselmeier, Michael. "Nach der Revolte: Die literarische Verarbeitung der Studentenbewegung." In *Literatur und Studentenbewegung: Eine Zwischenbilanz*, edited by Martin Lüdke, 158–85. Opladen: Westdeutscher, 1977.

Camera Obscura 20–21 (1989).

Caughie, John, ed. *Theories of Authorship: A Reader*. New York: Routledge and Kegan Paul, 1981.

Cixous, Hélène. "The Laugh of the Medusa." Translated by Keith Cohen and Paula Cohen. *Signs: Journal of Women in Culture and Society* 4 (1976): 875–94.

——. *Weiblichkeit in der Schrift*. Translated by Eva Duffner. Berlin: Merve, 1980.

Coe, Richard N. *When the Grass Was Taller: Autobiography and the Experience of Childhood*. New Haven: Yale University Press, 1984.

Corrigan, Timothy J. *New German Film: The Displaced Image*. Austin: University of Texas Press, 1983.

Craig, Gordon. "Facing Up to the Nazis." *New York Review of Books*, 36 February 1989, pp. 10–15.

Davidson, Cathy N., and E. M. Broner, eds. *The Lost Tradition: Mothers and Daughters in Literature*. New York: Frederick Ungar Publishing, 1980.

Dehler, Kathleen. "That Need to Tell All: Comparison of Historical and Modern Feminist 'Confessional' Writing." In *Feminist Criticism: Essays on Theory, Poetry, and Prose*, edited by Cheryl L. Brown and Karen Olson, 339–52. Metuchen, N.J.: Scarecrow Press, 1978.

De Lauretis, Teresa. "Aesthetic and Feminist Theory: Rethinking Women's Cinema." *New German Critique* 34 (1985): 154–75.

——. *Alice Doesn't: Feminism, Semiotics, Cinema*. Bloomington: Indiana University Press, 1984.

——. *Technologies of Gender: Essays on Theory, Film, and Fiction*. Bloomington: Indiana University Press, 1987.

——, ed. *Feminist Studies/Critical Studies*. Bloomington: Indiana University Press, 1986.

Delille, Angela, et al., eds. *Perlon Zeit: Wie die Frauen ihr Wirtschaftswunder erlebten*. Berlin: Elefanten Press, 1985.

De Man, Paul. "Autobiography as De-facement." *Modern Language Notes* 95.5 (1979): 919–30.

Deussen, Christiane. *Erinnerung als Rechtfertigung: Autobiographien nach 1945, Gottfried Benn, Hans Carossa, Arnold Bronnen*. Tübingen: Stauffenburg, 1987.

Dietze, Gabriele, ed. *Die Überwindung der Sprachlosigkeit: Texte aus der neuen Frauenbewegung*. Darmstadt: Luchterhand, 1979.

Doane, Mary Ann. *The Desire to Desire: The Woman's Film of the 1940s*. Bloomington: Indiana University Press, 1987.

——. "The Voice Is the Cinema: The Articulation of the Body and Space." *Yale French Studies* 60 (1980): 33–50.

——, ed. *Re-Vision: Essays in Feminist Film Criticism*. Los Angeles: The American Film Institute, 1984.

Donato, Eugenio. "The Ruins of Memory: Archaeological Fragments and Textual Artifacts." *Modern Language Notes* 93 (1978): 575–96.

Durzak, Manfred, ed. *Deutsche Gegenwartsliteratur: Ausgangspositionen und aktuelle Entwicklungen*. Stuttgart: Reclam, 1981.

Eakin, Paul John. *Fictions in Autobiography: Studies in the Art of Self-Invention*. Princeton: Princeton University Press, 1985.

Ecker, Gisela, ed. *Feminist Aesthetics*. Translated by Harriet Anderson. Boston: Beacon Press, 1986.

Egan, Susanna. *Patterns of Experience in Autobiography*. Chapel Hill: University of North Carolina Press, 1984.

Eisenstein, Hester, and Alice Jardine, eds. *The Future of Difference*. New Brunswick, N.J.: Rutgers University Press, 1985.

Elbaz, Robert. *The Changing Nature of the Self: A Critical Study of the Auto-biographical Discourse*. Iowa City: University of Iowa Press, 1987.

Elsaesser, Thomas. *New German Cinema: A History*. New Brunswick, N.J.: Rutgers University Press, 1989.

Enzensberger, Hans Magnus. "Gemeinplätze, die neueste Literatur be-treffend." *Kursbuch* 15 (1968): 187–97.

Erikson, Erik. *Identity and the Life Cycle: Selected Papers*. New York: International Universities Press, 1959.

Ezergailis, Inta. *Women Writers: The Divided Self: Analysis of Novels by Christa Wolf, Ingeborg Bachmann, Doris Lessing and Others*. Bonn: Bouvier, 1982.

Fehervary, Helen, Claudia Lenssen, and Judith Mayne. "From Hitler to Hepburn: A Discussion of Women's Film Production and Reception." *New German Critique* 24–25 (1982): 172–85.

Felski, Rita. *Beyond Feminist Aesthetics: Feminist Literature and Social Change*. Cambridge: Harvard University Press, 1989.

Fischetti, Renate. *Das neue Kino: Acht Porträts von deutschen Regisseurinnen*. Dülmen-Hiddingsel: Tende, 1992.

Flax, Jane. "Re-membering the Selves: Is the Repressed Gendered?" *Michigan Quarterly Review* 26.1 (1987): 92–110.

Foucault, Michel. *The Order of Things*. New York: Vintage Books, 1973.

——. *Technologies of the Self: A Seminar with Michel Foucault*. Edited by Luther H. Martin et al. Amherst: Massachusetts University Press, 1988.

——. "What Is an Author?" In *Textual Strategies: Perspectives in Post-Structuralist Criticism*, edited by Josué V. Harari, 141–60. Ithaca: Cornell University Press, 1979.

Fout, John C. "The Woman's Role in the German Working-Class Family in the 1890s from the Perspective of Women's Autobiographies." In *German Women in the Nineteenth Century: A Social History*, edited by John C. Fout. New York: Holmes and Meier, 1984.

Franck, Barbara. *Ich schau in den Spiegel und sehe meine Mutter: Gesprächs-protokolle mit Töchtern*. Hamburg: Hoffmann und Campe, 1979.

Frauen Offensive: Aufständische Kultur 5 (1976).

Freud, Sigmund. "Melancholia and Mourning." In *General Psychological Theory*, 164–79. New York: Macmillan, 1963.

——. "Remembering, Repeating, and Working Through." In *The Complete Psychological Works*, vol. 12, translated and edited by James Strachey. London: Hogarth Press and the Institute of Psychoanalysis, 1966.

——. "Repression." In *General Psychological Theory*, 110–11. New York: Macmillan, 1963.

——. *Vorlesung zur Einführung in die Psychoanalyse*. Frankfurt am Main: Fischer, 1977.

——. *Zur Psychopathologie des Alltagslebens*. Frankfurt am Main: Fischer, 1954.

Freud, Sigmund, and Josef Breuer. *Studien über Hysterie*. Frankfurt am Main: Fischer, 1970.

Frieden, Sandra. " 'In eigener Sache': Christa Wolf's *Kindheitsmuster*." *German Quarterly* 54.4 (1981): 473–87.

——. *Self into Form: German Language Autobiographical Writings of the 1970s*. New York: Lang, 1983.

Frieden, Sandra, et al., eds. *Gender and German Cinema: Feminist Interventions*. Providence R.I.: Berg, 1993.

Friedman, Susan Stanford. "Women's Autobiographical Selves: Theory and Practice." In *The Private Self: Theory and Practice of Women's Autobiographical Writings*, edited by Shari Benstock, 34–62. Chapel Hill: University of North Carolina Press, 1988.

Frise, Maria. "War deine Mutter so wie du?" *Frankfurter Allgemeine*, 3 April 1985, p. 26.

Fröhlich, Roswitha. *Ich und meine Mutter: Mädchen erzählen*. Ravensburg: Maier, 1980.

Gallop, Jane. *The Daughter's Seduction: Feminism and Psychoanalysis*. Ithaca: Cornell University Press, 1982.

Gardiner, Judith Kegan. "On Female Identity and Writing by Women." In *Writing and Sexual Difference*, edited by Elizabeth Abel, 177–92. Chicago: University of Chicago Press, 1980.

——. "Self Psychology as Feminist Theory." *Signs: Journal of Women in Culture and Society* 12 (1987): 761–80.

Garner, Shirley Nelson, et al., eds. *The (M)other Tongue: Essays in Feminist Psychoanalytical Interpretation*. Ithaca: Cornell University Press, 1985.

Geertz, Clifford. *The Interpretation of Cultures: Selected Essays*. New York: Basic, 1973.

Geiger, Ruth, et al., eds. *Frauen, die pfeifen: Verständigungstexte*. Frankfurt am Main: Suhrkamp, 1978.

Gentile, Mary C. *Film Feminisms: Theory and Practice*. Westport, Conn.: Greenwood Press, 1985.

Gerhardt, Marlis. *Stimmen und Rhythmen: Weibliche Ästhetik und Avantgarde*. Darmstadt: Luchterhand, 1986.

——. "Wohin geht Nora? Auf der Suche nach der verlorenen Frau." *Kursbuch* 47 (1977): 77–89.

Gilbert, Sandra M., and Susan Gubar. *No Man's Land: The Place of the Woman Writer in the Twentieth Century*. New Haven: Yale University Press, 1988.

Gilligan, Carol. *In a Different Voice: Psychological Theory and Women's Development*. Cambridge: Harvard University Press, 1982.

Gnüg, Hiltrud, and Renate Möhrmann, eds. *Frauen, Literatur, Geschichte: Schreibende Frauen vom Mittelalter bis zur Gegenwart*. Stuttgart: Metzler, 1985.

Goodmann, Katherine. *Dis/Closures: Women's Autobiography in Germany between 1790 and 1914*. New York: Lang, 1986.

———. "Weibliche Autobiographien." In *Frauen, Literatur, Geschichte: Schreibende Frauen vom Mittelalter bis zur Gegenwart*, edited by Hiltrud Gnüg and Renate Möhrmann, 289–99. Stuttgart: Metzler, 1985.

Gordon, Linda. "What's New in Women's History." In *Feminist Studies/ Critical Studies*, edited by Teresa de Lauretis. Bloomington: Indiana University Press, 1986.

Greene, Gayle. "Feminist Fiction and the Uses of Memory." *Signs: Journal of Women in Culture and Society* 16.2 (1991): 290–321.

Greiner, Bernhard. " 'Mit der Erzählung gehe ich in den Tod': Kontinuität und Wandel des Erzählens im Schaffen von Christa Wolf." In *Erinnerte Zukunft*, edited by Wolfram Mauser. Würzburg: Königshausen and Neumann, 1985.

Greiner, Ulrich. "Söhne und ihre Väter: Über die Studentenbewegung als Konflikt der Generationen." *Die Zeit*, 6 May 1988, pp. 14–15.

Greve, Astrid, and Wolfgang Popp. *Die Neutralisierung der Ich oder: Wer spricht?* Essen: Die blaue Eule, 1987.

Grimm, Reinhold, and Jost Hermand, eds. *Vom Anderen und vom Selbst: Beiträge zu Fragen der Biographie und Autobiographie."* Königstein/Ts.: Athenäum Verlag, 1982.

Grosz, Elizabeth. "Philosophy, Subjectivity, and the Body: Kristeva and Irigaray." In *Feminist Challenges: Social and Political Theory*, edited by Carole Pateman and Elizabeth Grosz. Boston: Northeastern University Press, 1986.

Gunn, Janet Varner. *Autobiography: Toward a Poetics of Experience*. Philadelphia: University of Pennsylvania Press, 1982.

Gürtler, Christa. *Schreiben Frauen anders? Untersuchungen zu Ingeborg Bachmann und Barbara Frischmuth*. Stuttgart: Akademischer Verlag Hans-Dieter Heinz, 1983.

Gusdorf, Georges. "Conditions and Limits of Autobiography." In *Autobiography: Essays Theoretical and Critical*, edited by James Olney. Princeton: Princeton University Press, 1980.

Habermas, Jürgen, ed. *Stichworte zur "geistigen Situation der Zeit."* 2 vols. Frankfurt am Main: Suhrkamp, 1979.

Halbwachs, Maurice. *The Collective Memory*. Translated by Francis J. Ditter and Vida Yazdi Ditter. New York: Harper and Row, 1980.

Handke, Peter. "Gegen den tiefen Schlaf." *Die Zeit*, 8 October 1976.

———. *The Weight of the World*. Translated by Ralph Manheim. New York: Farrar, Straus and Giroux, 1984.

———. *Wunschloses Unglück: Erzählung [A Sorrow beyond Dreams]*. Frankfurt: Suhrkamp, 1972.

Hansen, Miriam. "Frauen und Film and Feminist Film Culture in West Germany." *Heresies* 16 (1983): 30–31.

Harari, Josué V., ed. *Textual Strategies: Perspectives in Post-Structuralist Criticism*. Ithaca: Cornell University Press, 1979.

Härtling, Peter. *Nachgetragene Liebe*. Frankfurt am Main: Büchergilde Gutenberg, 1980.

Hassauer, Friederike. "Der verRückte Diskurs der Sprachlosen: Gibt es eine weibliche Ästhetik?" *Notizbuch* 2 (1980) 48–65.

Haubl, Rolf, et al., eds. *Die Sprache des Vaters im Körper der Mutter*. Giessen: Anabas, 1984.

Heck, Alfons. *The Burden of Hitler's Legacy*. Frederick, Colo.: Renaissance, 1988.

Heckmann, Herbert, ed. *Literatur aus dem Leben: Autobiographische Tendenzen in der deutschsprachigen Gegenwartsdichtung*. Munich: Hanser, 1984.

Heidelberger-Leonard, Irene. "Brecht, Grimm, Sanders-Brahms—Drei Variationen zum selben Thema: *Deutschland, bleiche Mutter*." *Etudes Germaniques* 39 (1984): 51–55.

Heigert, Hans. "Die Zeit des Verdrängens." *Süddeutsche Zeitung*, 14–15 March 1987, p. 1.

Heilbrun, Carolyn G. *Writing a Woman's Life*. New York: W. W. Norton, 1988.

Helmecke, Monika. "*Kindheitsmuster*." *Sinn und Form* 29 (1977): 678–81.

Hewitt, Leah D. "Getting into the (Speech) Acts: Autobiography as Theory and Performance." *SubStance* 52.1 (1987): 32–44.

Hiller, Eva. "Mütter und Töchter: Zu 'Deutschland, bleiche Mutter' (Helma Sanders-Brahms), 'Hungerjahre' (Jutta Brückner), 'Daughter Rite' (Michelle Citron)." *Frauen und Film* 24 (1980): 29–33.

Hilzinger, Sonja. *Christa Wolf*. Stuttgart: Metzler, 1986.

Hirsch, Marianne. *The Mother/Daughter Plot: Narrative, Psychoanalysis, Feminism*. Bloomington: Indiana University Press, 1989.

——. "Mothers and Daughters." *Signs: Journal of Women in Culture and Society* 7.1 (1981): 200–222.

Hofer, Walter, ed. *Der Nationalsozialismus: Dokumente, 1933–1945*. Frankfurt am Main: Fischer, 1982.

Hoffmann, Leonore, and Margo Culley, eds. *Women's Personal Narratives: Essays in Criticism and Pedagogy*. New York: Modern Language Association, 1985.

Hohendahl, P. U., and Patricia Herminghouse, eds. *Literatur der DDR in den siebziger Jahren*. Frankfurt am Main: Suhrkamp, 1983.

Hörnigk, Therese. *Christa Wolf*. Göttingen: Steidl, 1989.

Hornung, Peter. "Von Räubern und Menschen: 'Deutschland, bleiche Mutter' von Helma Sanders-Brahms." *Saarbrücker Zeitung*, 7 November 1980.

Hutcheon. Linda. *A Poetics of Postmodernism: History, Theory, Fiction*. London: Routledge, 1988.

Hyams, Barbara. "Is the Apolitical Woman at Peace? A Reading of the Fairy Tale in *Germany, Pale Mother*." *Wide Angle* 10.3 (1988): 41–51.

Imgenberg, Klaus G., et al., eds. *Autobiographische Texte*. Stuttgart: Reclam, 1985.

Irigaray, Luce. *An Ethics of Sexual Difference*. Translated by Carolyn Burke and Gillian C. Gill. Ithaca: Cornell University Press, 1993.

——. *Speculum of the Other Woman*. Translated by Gillian C. Gill. Ithaca: Cornell University Press, 1985.

——. *This Sex Which Is Not One*. Translated by Catherine Porter with Carolyn Burke. Ithaca: Cornell University Press, 1985.

Jacobsen, Wolfgang, et al., eds. *Geschichte des deutschen Films*. Stuttgart: Metzler, 1993.

Jardine, Alice A. *Gynesis: Configurations of Woman and Modernity*. Ithaca: Cornell University Press, 1985.

Jay, Paul. *Being in the Text: Self-Representation from Wordsworth to Roland Barthes*. Ithaca: Cornell University Press, 1984.

Jelinek, Elfriede. "Begierde & Fahrerlaubnis." *Manuskripte* 26 (1986): 74–76

——. Interview. *Deutsche Bücher* 15. Edited by Ferdinand van Ingen. Amsterdam: Rodopi, 1985.

Jelinek, Estelle. *The Tradition of Women's Autobiography from Antiquity to the Present*. Boston: Twayne, 1986.

——, ed. *Women's Autobiography: Essays in Criticism*. Bloomington: Indiana University Press, 1980.

Johnston, Claire. "Toward a Feminist Film Practice: Some Theses." *Movies and Methods* II, edited by Bill Nichols, 315–27. Berkeley: University of California Press, 1985.

Jones, Ann Rosalind "Writing the Body: Toward an Understanding of l'Écriture Féminine." In *The New Feminist Criticism: Essays on Women, Literature, and Theory*, edited by Elaine Showalter. New York: Pantheon, 1985.

Kaes, Anton. *Deutschlandbilder: Die Wiederkehr der Geschichte als Film*. Munich: Edition Text + Kritik, 1987.

——. *From Hitler to Heimat: The Return of History as Film*. Cambridge: Harvard University Press, 1989.

Kane, B. M. "In Search of the Past: Christa Wolf's *Kindheitsmuster*." *Modern Language Notes* 59 (1978): 19–23.

Kaplan, E. Ann. *Motherhood and Representation: The Mother in Popular Culture and Melodrama*. New York: Routledge, 1992.

——. "The Search for the Mother/Land in Sanders-Brahms's *Germany, Pale Mother*." In *German Film and Literature*, edited by Eric Rentschler, 289–304. New York: Methuen, 1987.

——. *Women and Film: Both Sides of the Camera*. New York: Methuen, 1983.

Keitel, Evelyn. "Verständigungstexte: Form, Funktion, Wirkung." *German Quarterly* 56 (1983): 431–55.

Keller, Barbara. *Woman's Journey toward Self and Its Literary Exploration*. New York: Peter Lang, 1986.

King, Richard. "Memory and Phantasy." *Modern Language Notes* 98.5 (1983): 1197–1213.

Kluge, Alexander. "On Film and the Public Sphere." Translated by Thomas Levin and Miriam Hansen. *New German Critique* 24/25 (1981/82): 206–20.

——. *Die Patriotin* [*The Patriot*]. Kairos-Film, 1979.

——. "Das Politische als Intensität alltäglicher Gefühle." *Freibeuter* 1 (1979): 56–62.

Knight, Julia. *Women and New German Cinema*. New York: Verso, 1992.

Koch, Gertrud. "Blickwechsel: Aspekte feministischer Kinotheorie." *Neue Rundschau* 94 (1983): 121–35.

——. "Ex-Changing the Gaze: Re-visioning Feminist Film Theory." *New German Critique* 34 (1985): 139–53.

Kolkenbrock-Netz, Jutta, and Marianne Schuller. "Frau im Spiegel: Zum Verhältnis von autobiographischer Schreibweise und feministischer Praxis." *Argument* (1982): 154–74.

Koonz, Claudia. *Mothers in the Fatherland: Women, the Family, and Nazi Politics*. New York: St. Martin's Press, 1987.

Kraft, Helga, and Barbara Kosta. "Mother-Daughter Relationships: Problems of Self-Determination in Novak, Heinrich, and Wohmann." *German Quarterly* 46 (January 1983): 74–88.

Kramer, Karen Ruoff. "New Subjectivity: Third Thoughts on a Literary Discourse." Ph.D diss., Stanford University, 1983.

Krechel, Ursula. "Leben in Anführungszeichen: Das Authentische in der gegenwärtigen Literatur." *Literaturmagazin* 11 (1979): 80–107.

——. *Selbsterfahrung und Fremdbestimmung: Berichte aus der neuen Frauenbewegung*. Darmstadt: Luchterhand, 1975

Kreuzer, Helmut. "Neue Subjektivität: Zur Literatur der siebziger Jahre in der Bundesrepublik Deutschland." In *Deutsche Gegenwartsliteratur: Ausgangspositionen und aktuelle Entwicklungen*, edited by Manfred Durzak, 77–106. Stuttgart: Reclam, 1981.

Krininger, Doris, and Claudia Cippitelli. "Distanz, nicht Distanzierung." *Medium* 11 (1981): 45–46.

Kristeva, Julia. "Kein weibliches Schreiben: Fragen an Julia Kristeva." *Freibeuter* 2 (1979): 79–84.

——. *The Kristeva Reader*. Edited by Toril Moi. New York: Columbia University Press, 1986.

——. "Stabat Mater." In *The Julia Kristeva Reader*, edited by Toril Moi, 160–86. New York: Columbia University Press, 1986.

Kronsbein, Joachim. *Autobiographisches Erzählen: Die narrativen Strukturen der Autobiographie*. Munich: Minerva-Publikation, 1984.

Kuczynski, Jürgen. *Probleme der Autobiographie*. Berlin: Aufbau, 1983.

Kuhn, Anna K. *Christa Wolf's Utopian Vision: From Marxism to Feminism*. Cambridge: Cambridge University Press, 1988.

Kuhn, Annette. *Women's Pictures: Feminism and Cinema*. London: Routledge and Kegan Paul, 1982.

Kursbuch 15. "Tod der Literatur?" November 1968.

Langer, Ingrid. "Die Mohrinnen hatten ihre Schuldigkeit getan . . . Staatlich-moralische Aufrüstung der Familie." In *Die fünfziger Jahre*, edited by Dieter Bänsch, 108–30. Tübingen: Günter Narr, 1985.

Leigh, James. "The Figure of Autobiography." *Modern Language Notes: French Issue* 93.4 (1978): 733–49.

Lejeune, Philippe. "Autobiography in the Third Person." *New Literary History* 9 (1977): 27–50.

——. *On Autobiography*. Edited by Paul John Eakin. Translated by Katherine Leary. Minneapolis: University of Minnesota Press, 1989.

——. *Le Pacte autobiographique*. Paris: Editions du Seuil, 1975.

Lenk, Elisabeth. "Pariabewußtsein und Gesellschaftskritik bei einigen Schriftstellerinnen seit der Romantik." *Wespennest* 44 (1981): 23–36.

Lennox, Sara. "Trends in Literary Theory: The Female Aesthetic and German Women's Writing." *German Quarterly* 54 (1981): 63–75.

Lenssen, Claudia. "Women's Cinema in Germany." *Jump Cut* 29 (1984): 49–50.

Liebs, Elke, and Helga Kraft, eds. *Mütter-Töchter-Frauen: Weiblichkeitsbilder in der Literatur*. Stuttgart: Metzler, 1993.

Lindner, Burkhardt. "Das Interesse an der Kindheit." *Literaturmagazin* 14 (1979): 112–32.

——. "The *Passagen-Werk*, the *Berliner Kindheit*, and Archaeology of the 'Recent Past'." *New German Critique* 29 (1989): 25–28.

Lionnet, Françoise. *Autobiographical Voices: Race, Gender, Self-Portraiture*. Ithaca: Cornell University Press, 1989.

Loftus, Elizabeth F., et al. "Who Remembers What?: Gender Differences in Memory." *Michigan Quarterly Review* 26.1 (1987): 64–85.

Lourie, Margaret A., et al., eds. *Michigan Quarterly Review* 26.1 (1987).

Lüdke, Martin, ed. *Nach dem Protest: Literatur im Umbruch*. Frankfurt am Main: Suhrkamp, 1979.

Lukasz-Aden, Gudrun, and Christel Strobel. *Der Frauenfilm: Filme von und für Frauen*. Munich: Heyne, 1985.

Lützeler, Paul Michael, and Egon Schwarz, eds. *Deutsche Literatur in der Bundesrepublik seit 1965*. Königstein/Ts: Athenäum, 1980.

McCormick, Richard W. *Politics of the Self: Feminism and the Postmodern in West German Literature and Film*. Princeton: Princeton University Press, 1991.

Marks, Elaine, and Isabelle de Courtivron, eds. *New French Feminisms: An Anthology*. New York: Schocken Books, 1981.

Mason, Mary G. "The Other Voice: Autobiographies of Women Writers." In *Life/Lines: Theorizing Women's Autobiography*, edited by Bella Brodzki and Celeste Schenck, 19–44. Ithaca: Cornell University Press, 1988.

Mauser, Wolfram, ed. *Erinnerte Zukunft. 11 Studien zum Werk Christa Wolfs*. Würzburg: Königshausen and Neumann, 1985.

Mayne, Judith. "Visibility and Feminist Film Criticism." *Film Reader* 5 (1982): 120–24.

——. *The Woman at the Keyhole*. Bloomington: Indiana University Press, 1990.

——. "The Woman at the Keyhole: Women's Cinema and Feminist Criticism." *New German Critique* 23 (1981): 27–43.

Maynes, Mary Jo. "Feministische Ansätze in den Autobiographien von

Arbeiterinnen." In *Frauen in der Geschichte*, edited by Annette Kuhn et al. Düsseldorf: Schwann, 1985.

Meckel, Christoph. *Suchbild: Über meinen Vater*. Düsseldorf: Claassen, 1980.

Meerapfel, Jeanine. *Im Land meiner Eltern*. Westdeutscher Rundfunk, 1981.

——. *Malou*. Atlas Film, 1980.

Metz, Christian. *The Imaginary Signifier: Psychoanalysis and the Cinema*. Translated by Celia Britton et al. Bloomington: Indiana University Press, 1982.

——. "Story/Discourse: Notes on Two Kinds of Voyeurism." In *Movies and Methods* II, edited by Bill Nichols, 543–49. Berkeley: University of California Press, 1985.

Meyer, Eva. "Die Autobiographie der Schrift." *Eau de Cologne* 3 (1989).

——. "Vorspiel—Annäherung an eine andere Schreibweise." In *Weiblich-Männlich*, edited by Brigitte Wartmann, 62–76. Berlin: Ästhetik und Kommunikation, 1980.

——. *Zählen und Erzählen: Für eine Semiotik des Weiblichen*. Vienna: Medusa, 1983.

Meyer, Sibylle, and Eva Schulze. *Von Liebe sprach damals keiner: Familienalltag in der Nachkriegszeit*. Munich: Beck, 1986.

——. *"Wie wir das alles geschafft haben": Alleinstehende Frauen berichten über ihr Leben nach 1945*. Munich: Beck, 1984.

Miller, Alice. *Am Anfang war Erziehung*. Frankfurt am Main: Suhrkamp, 1980.

——. *For Your Own Good: Hidden Cruelty in Child-Rearing and the Roots of Violence*. Translated by Hildegard Hannum and Hunter Hannum. New York: Farrar, Straus and Giroux, 1983.

Miller, Nancy. "Changing the Subject: Authorship, Writing, and the Reader." In *Feminist Studies/Critical Studies*, edited by Teresa de Lauretis. Bloomington: Indiana University Press, 1986.

——. *Getting Personal: Feminist Occasions and Other Autobiographical Acts*. New York: Routledge, 1991.

——. "Writing Fictions: Women's Autobiography in France." In *Life/Lines: Theorizing Women's Autobiography*, edited by Bella Brodzki and Celeste Schenck, 45–61. Ithaca: Cornell University Press, 1988.

Misch, Georg. *A History of Autobiography in Antiquity*. Translated by E. W. Dickes. Cambridge: Harvard University Press, 1951.

Mitscherlich, Alexander, and Margarete Mitscherlich. *The Inability to Mourn: Principles of Collective Behavior*. Translated by Beverley R. Placzek. New York: Grove Press, 1975.

Mitscherlich, Margarete. "Die Frage der Selbstdarstellung." *Neue Rundschau* 91.2/3 (1980): 308–16

Modern Language Notes. "French Issue: Autobiography and the Problem of the Subject." Edited by Rodolphe Gasché. Vol. 93 (1978).

Modleski, Tania. *Loving with a Vengeance: Mass-produced Fantasies for Women*. New York: Methuen, 1982.

Möhrmann, Renate. "Feministische Trends in der deutschen Gegenwarts-literatur." In *Deutsche Gegenwartsliteratur: Ausgangspositionen und aktuelle Entwicklungen*, edited by Manfred Durzak, 336–58. Stuttgart: Reclam, 1981.

——. "Frauen erobern sich einen neuen Artikulationsort: den Film." In *Frauen, Literatur, Geschichte: Schreibende Frauen vom Mittelalter bis zur Gegenwart*, edited by Hiltrud Gnüg et al., 434–52. Stuttgart: Metzler, 1985.

——. *Die Frau mit der Kamera: Filmemacherinnen in der Bundesrepublik Deutschland. Situationen, Perspektiven: Zehn exemplarische Lebensläufe*. Munich: Hanser, 1980.

Monaco, Paul. *Ribbons in Time: Movies and Society since 1945*. Bloomington: Indiana University Press, 1988.

Müller, Klaus-Detlef. *Autobiographie und Roman: Studien zur literarischen Autobiographie der Goethezeit*. Tübingen: Niemeyer, 1976.

Mulvey, Laura. "Visual Pleasure and Narrative Cinema." In *Movies and Methods: An Anthology*, edited by Bill Nichols, 303–15. Berkeley: University of California Press, 1985.

Münzberg, Olav. "Schaudern vor der bleichen Mutter: Eine sozial-psychologische Analyse der Kritiken zum Film von Helma Sanders-Brahms." *Medium* 10.7 (1980): 34–37.

Murray, Bruce A., and Christopher J. Wickham, eds. *Framing the Past: The Historiography of German Cinema and Television*. Carbondale: Southern Illinois University Press, 1992.

Nägele, Rainer. "Geschichten und Geschichte. Reflexionen zum westdeutschen Roman seit 1965." In *Deutsche Gegenwartsliteratur: Ausgangspositionen und aktuelle Entwicklungen*, edited by Manfred Durzak, 234–51. Stuttgart: Reclam, 1981.

Narr, Wolf Dieter. "Der Stellenwert der Auseinandersetzung mit dem Nationalsozialismus in der gesellschaftlichen Diskussion heute." *Niemandsland* 1 (1987): 26–44.

Neubaur, Caroline. "Wenn Du noch eine Mutter hast." *Freibeuter* 4 (1980): 168–69.

Neumann, Bernd. " 'Als ob das Zeitgenössische leer wäre . . .': Über die Anwesenheit der 50er Jahre in der Gegenwartsliteratur." *Zeitschrift für Literaturwissenschaft und Linguistik* 9 (1979): 82–95.

——. *Identität und Rollenzwang: Zur Theorie der Autobiographie*. Frankfurt am Main: Athenäum, 1970.

——. "Die Wiedergeburt des Erzählens aus dem Geist der Autobiographie?" In *Basis Jahrbuch für deutsche Gegenwartsliteratur*, edited by R. Grimm and Jost Hermand, 91–120. Frankfurt am Main: Suhrkamp, 1979.

Nichols, Bill. *Ideology and the Image: Social Representation in the Cinema and Other Media*. Bloomington: Indiana University Press, 1981.

Niemandsland 1 (1987).

Niggl, Günther. *Geschichte der deutschen Autobiographie im 18. Jahrhundert: Theoretische Grundlegung und literarische Entfaltung*. Stuttgart: Metzler, 1977.

Nordhoff, Inge. "Frauen, die vor uns waren: Helma Sanders-Brahms und ihr autobiographischer Film 'Deutschland, bleiche Mutter'." *Stuttgarter Zeitung*, 29 June 1979.

Olivier, Christiane. *Jocasta's Children: The Imprint of the Mother.* New York: Routledge, 1989.

Olney, James, ed. *Autobiography: Essays Theoretical and Critical.* Princeton: Princeton University Press, 1980.

——. *Metaphors of the Self: The Meaning of Autobiography.* Princeton: Princeton University Press, 1972.

Owens, Craig. "The Discourse of Others: Feminism and Postmodernism." *The Anti-Aesthetic: Essays on Postmodern Culture*, edited by Hal Foster, 57–82. Port Townsend, Wash.: Bay Press, 1983.

Pascal, Roy. *Design and Truth in Autobiography.* Cambridge: Harvard University Press, 1960.

Penley, Constance. *Feminism and Film Theory.* New York: Routledge, 1988.

Pflaum, Hans Günther. *Germany on Film: Theme and Content in the Cinema of the Federal Republic of Germany.* Translated by Richard Helt and Roland Richter. Detroit: Wayne State University Press, 1990.

Pilling, John. *Autobiography and Imagination: Studies in Self-Scrutiny.* Boston: Routledge and Kegan Paul, 1981.

Plessen, Elisabeth. *Such Sad Tidings.* Translated by Ruth Hein. New York: Viking Press, 1979.

Presber, Gabriele, ed. *Die Kunst ist weiblich.* Munich: Knauer, 1988.

Quart, Barbara Koenig. *Women Directors: The Emergence of a New Cinema.* New York: Praeger, 1988.

Rabine, Leslie W. "Écriture Féminine as Metaphor." *Cultural Critique* 8 (1988): 19–44.

Rehmann, Ruth. "Die Väter bitten um eine neue Sicht: Folgen einer Rezeption." *Süddeutsche Zeitung* 85 (1982): 130.

Reinig, Christa. "Das weibliche Ich." *Frauen Offensive* 5 (1976): 50.

Rentschler, Eric. *West German Film in the Course of Time: Reflections on the Twenty Years since Oberhausen.* Bedford Hills: Redgrave, 1984.

——, ed. *German Film and Literature: Adaptations and Transformations.* New York: Methuen, 1986.

——, ed. *West German Filmmakers on Film: Visions and Voices.* New York: Holmes and Meier, 1988.

Renoldner, Klemens. "Im ungeistigen Raum unserer traurigen Länder." In *Der dunkle Schatten, dem ich schon seit Anfang folge. Ingeborg Bachmann Vorschläge zu einer neuen Lektüre des Werkes*, edited by Hans Höller, 185–97. Vienna: Löcker, 1982.

——. *Utopie und Geschichtsbewußtsein: Versuche zur Poetik Christa Wolfs.* Stuttgart: Akademischer Verlag, 1981.

Rich, Ruby. "The Crisis of Naming in Feminist Cinema." *Jump Cut* 19 (1979): 9–12.

——. "She Says, He Says: The Power of the Narrator in Modernist Film Politics." *Discourse* 6 (1983): 31–46.

Roberts, David. "Tendenzwenden: Die sechziger und siebziger Jahre in literaturhistorischer Perspektive." *Deutsche Vierteljahresschrift* 56 (1982): 290–313.

Roiphe, Anne. "This Butcher, Imagination: Beware of Your Life When a Writer's at Work." *New York Times Book Review*, 14 February 1988, p. 32.

Rosenbaum, Marianne. *Peppermint Frieden* [*Peppermint Peace*]. Basis-Film, 1982. U.S. distributor: West Glen Films, New York.

Rousseau, Jean-Jacques. *The Confessions*. Translated by J. M. Cohen. Middlesex, England: Penguin Books, 1953.

Runge, Erika. "Abschied von den Protokollen." *Frankfurter Allgemeine*, 17 July 1976.

———. "Überlegungen beim Abschied von der Dokumentarliteratur." *Kontexte* 1 (1976): 97–105.

Rutschky, Michael. *Erfahrungshunger: Ein Essay über die siebziger Jahre*. Frankfurt am Main: Fischer, 1982.

Ryan, Judith. *The Uncompleted Past: Postwar German Novels and the Third Reich*. Detroit: Wayne State University Press, 1983.

Sander, Helke. *Die allseitig reduzierte Persönlichkeit—REDUPERS* [*The All-Around Reduced Personality*]. Basis-Film, 1977.

———. *BeFreier und Befreite* [Liberator and liberated]. Basis-Film, 1992.

———. "Feminismus und Film." *Frauen und Film* 15 (1978): 5–10.

———. "Feminismus und Film: 'i like chaos, but i don't know whether chaos likes me'." *Frauen und Film* 15 (1978): 10.

———. "Krankheit als Sprache." *Frauen und Film* 23 (1980): 25.

———. "Speech by the Action Council for Women's Liberation." In *German Feminism: Readings in Politics and Literature*, translated and edited by Edith Hoshino Altbach. Albany: State University of New York Press, 1985.

———. *Der subjektive Faktor* [*The Subjective Factor*]. Basis-Film, 1980.

Sanders-Brahms, Helma. *Das Dunkle zwischen den Bildern: Essays, Porträts, Kritiken*. Edited by Norbert Grob. Frankfurt am Main: Verlag der Autoren, 1992.

Sandford, John. *The New German Cinema*. New York: Da Capo Press, 1980.

Santner, Eric L. *Stranded Objects: Mourning, Memory, and Film in Postwar Germany*. Ithaca: Cornell University Press, 1990.

Sauer, Klaus, ed. *Christa Wolf: Materialienbuch*. Darmstadt: Luchterhand, 1979.

Saunders, Barbara. *Contemporary German Autobiography: Literary Approaches to the Problem of Identity*. Leeds, England: W. S. Maney & Sons, 1986.

Scherpe, Klaus R., and Hans-Ulrich Treichel. "Vom Überdruß leben: Sensibilität und Intellektualität als Ereignis bei Handke, Born, und Strauss." *Monatshefte* 3 (1981): 187–206.

Schlüpmann, Heide. "Deutsche Liebespaare." *Frauen und Film* 35 (1983): 12–23.

———. " 'Wir Wunderkinder': Tradition und Regression im bundesdeutschen Film der fünfziger Jahre." *Frauen und Film* 35 (1983): 4–13.

Schmidt, Delf. "Gegen die Placebo-Literatur." *Literaturmagazin* 11 (1979): 11–18.

Schmidt, Ricarda. *Westdeutsche Frauenliteratur in den 70er Jahren.* Frankfurt: R. J. Fischer, 1982.

Schneider, Manfred. *Die erkaltete Herzensschrift: Der autobiographische Text im 20. Jahrhundert.* Munich: Hanser, 1986.

Schneider, Michael. "Fathers and Sons Retrospectively: The Damaged Relationship between Two Generations." Translated by Jamie Owen Daniel. *New German Critique* 31 (1984): 3–51.

——. *Den Kopf verkehrt aufgesetzt, oder, die melancholische Linke: Aspekte des Kulturzerfalls in den siebziger Jahren.* Darmstadt: Luchterhand, 1981.

Schneider, Peter. *Lenz: Eine Erzählung.* West Berlin: Rotbuch, 1973.

Schülein, Johann August. "Von der Studentenrevolte zur Tendenzwende oder der Rückzug ins Private." *Kursbuch* 48 (1977): 101–17.

Schütte, Wolfram. "Brief an den Vater." *Frankfurter Rundschau,* 27 November 1976.

——. "Mütter, Töchter, Krieg und Terror: Filme von Recha Jungmann, Jutta Brückner, Helma Sanders, und Luc Bondy." *Frankfurter Rundschau,* 25 February 1980.

Schutting, Jutta. *Der Vater.* Hamburg: Rowohlt, 1983.

Schwab, Sylvia. *Autobiographie und Lebenserfahrung: Versuch einer Typologie deutschsprachiger autobiographischer Schriften zwischen 1968 und 1975.* Würzburg: Königshausen und Neumann, 1981.

Schwaiger, Brigitte. *Lange Abwesenheit.* Hamburg: Rowohlt, 1980.

——. *Wie kommt das Salz ins Meer?* [*Why Is There Salt in the Sea?*]. Hamburg: Rowohlt, 1977.

Schwarzer, Alice, ed. *So fing es an!* Cologne: Emma, 1981.

Seeba, Hinrich. "Persönliches Engagement: Zur Autorenpoetik der siebziger Jahre." *Monatshefte* 73.2 (1981): 140–54.

Seiter, Ellen E. "Women's History, Women's Melodrama: *Deutschland, bleiche Mutter.*" *German Quarterly* 59.4 (1986): 569–81.

Sichrovsky, Peter. *Born Guilty: Children of Nazi Families.* Translated by Jean Steinberg. New York: Basic Books, 1988

Sichtermann, Barbara. "Das Phantom 'weibliche Sexualität'." *Freibeuter* 17 (1983): 43–51.

——. "Die Schwierigkeiten über Sexualität zu sprechen. *Freibeuter* 16 (1985): 38–45.

——. "Schwule Musen?" *Die Zeit,* 3 October 1986, p. 49.

Silberman, Marc. "Ciné-Feminists in West Berlin." *Quarterly Review of Film Studies* 5 (1980): 217–32.

——. "From the Outside Moving In." Introduction to Special Section "Film and Feminism in Germany Today." *Jump Cut* 27 (1982): 41–42.

——. "Writing What—for Whom? Vergangenheitsbewältigung in GDR Literature." *German Studies Review* 10.3 (1987): 527–38.

Silverman, Kaja. *The Acoustic Mirror: The Female Voice in Psychoanalysis and Cinema.* Bloomington: Indiana University Press, 1988.

——. "Dis-Embodying the Female Voice." *Re-Vision: Essays in Feminist Film Criticism* 3 (1984): 131–49.

——. "Helke Sander and the Will to Change." *Discourse* 6 (1983): 10–30.

Sloterdijk, Peter. *Literatur und Organisation von Lebenserfahrung: Autobiographien der zwanziger Jahre*. Munich: Hanser, 1978.

Smith, Paul. *Discerning the Subject*. Minneapolis: University of Minnesota Press, 1988.

Smith, Sidonie. *A Poetics of Women's Autobiography: Marginality and the Fictions of Self-Representation*. Bloomington: Indiana University Press, 1987.

———. "Who's Talking/Who's Talking Back? The Subject of Personal Narrative." *Signs: Journal of Women in Culture and Society* 18.2 (1993): 392–407.

Smith, Sidonie, and Julia Watson, eds. *De/Colonizing the Subject: The Politics of Gender in Women's Autobiography*. Minneapolis: University of Minnesota Press, 1992.

Spacks, Patricia Meyer. "Selves in Hiding." In *Women's Autobiography: Essays in Criticism*, edited by Estelle Jelinek, 112–32. Bloomington: Indiana University Press, 1980.

———. "Women's Stories, Women's Selves." *Hudson Review* 30 (1977): 26–46.

Spengemann, William C. *The Forms of Autobiography: Episodes in the History of a Literary Genre*. New Haven: Yale University Press, 1980.

Sperr, Monika, ed. *Liebe Mutter, Liebe Tochter: Frauenbriefe von heute*. Munich: Rogner and Bernhard, 1981.

Sprinker, Michael. "Fictions of the Self: The End of Autobiography." In *Autobiography: Essays Theoretical and Critical*, edited by James Olney, 321–42. Princeton: Princeton University Press, 1980.

Stanton, Domna C., ed. *The Female Autograph: Theory and Practice of Autobiography from the Tenth to the Twentieth Century*. Chicago: University of Chicago Press, 1987.

Starobinski, Jean. "The Style of Autobiography." In *Autobiography: Essays Theoretical and Critical*, edited by James Olney, 73–83. Princeton: Princeton University Press, 1972.

———. "The Style of Autobiography." In *Literary Style*, edited by Seymour Chatman. New York: Oxford University Press, 1971.

Stefan, Inge, et al., eds. *Frauenliteratur ohne Tradition?* Frankfurt am Main: Fischer, 1987.

Stefan, Verena. *Häutungen [Shedding]*. Munich: Frauenoffensive, 1975.

Stephan, Alexander. *Christa Wolf*. Amsterdam: Rodopi, 1980.

Stephan, Cora. "Nun muß sich alles, alles wenden." *Kursbuch* 71 (1983): 10–25.

Stephens, Anthony. "Vom Nutzen der zeitgenössischen Metafiktion: Christa Wolfs *Kindheitsmuster*." In *Erzählung und Erzählforschung im 20. Jahrhundert*, edited by Rolf Kloepfer and Gisela Janetzke-Dillner. Stuttgart: Kohlhammer, 1981.

Strauss, Botho. *Devotion*. Translated by Sophie Wilkins. New York: Farrar, Straus and Giroux, 1979.

Strobl, Ingrid, ed. *Das kleine Mädchen, das ich war: Schriftstellerinnen erzählen ihre Kindheit*. Munich: Deutsches Taschenbuch Verlag, 1984.

Stumm, Reinhardt. "Vater-Lieber Vater." *Die Zeit*, 22 February 1980, p. 17.

Suleiman, Susan Rubin. "Feminism and Postmodernism." In *Zeitgeist in Babel: The Postmodernist Controversy*, edited by Ingeborg Hoesterey. Bloomington: Indiana University Press, 1991.

——, ed. *The Female Body in Western Culture: Contemporary Perspectives*. Cambridge: Harvard University Press, 1985.

Tarot, Rolf. "Die Autobiographie." In *Prosakunst ohne Erzählen*, edited by Klaus Weissenberger. Tübingen: Niemeyer, 1985.

Tatar, Maria. *The Hard Facts of the Grimms' Fairy Tales*. Princeton: Princeton University Press, 1987.

Vesper, Bernhard. *Die Reise: Romanessay*. Frankfurt am Main: März Verlag, 1977.

Vogt, Guntram. "Kindheit und Jugend im Faschismus: Zur literarischen Verarbeitung eines Wirklichkeitsverlusts." *Diskussion Deutsch* (June 1986): 271–89.

Vogt, Marianne. *Autobiographie bürgerlicher Frauen*. Würzburg: Königshausen and Neumann, 1981.

Wagener, Hans, ed. *Gegenwartsliteratur und Drittes Reich: Deutsche Autoren in der Auseinandersetzung mit der Vergangenheit*. Stuttgart: Reclam, 1977.

Walker, Cheryl. "Feminist Literary Criticism and the Author." *Critical Inquiry* 16 (1990): 551–71.

Weber, Heinz-Dieter. *Über Christa Wolfs Schreibart*. Konstanz: Universitätsverlag Konstanz, 1984.

Weedon, Chris. *Feminist Practice and Poststructuralist Theory*. Oxford: Basil Blackwell, 1987.

Weigel, Sigrid. "Contemporary German Women's Literature." *New German Critique* 31 (1984): 53–94.

——. "Double Focus: On the History of Women's Writing." In *Feminist Aesthetics*, edited by Gisela Ecker, 59–80. Boston: Beacon Press, 1986.

——. "Frau und 'Weiblichkeit' Theoretische Überlegungen zur feministischen Literaturkritik." *Argument-Sonderband* (1984): 103–13.

——. "Overcoming Absence: Contemporary German Women's Literature." *New German Critique* 32 (1984): 3–22.

——. *Die Stimme der Medusa: Schreibweisen in der Gegenwartsliteratur von Frauen*. Dülmen-Hiddingsel: Tende, 1987.

Weinberger, Gabriele. *Nazi Germany and Its Aftermath in Women Directors' Autobiographical Films of the Late 1970s*. San Francisco: Mellen Research University Press, 1992.

Weintraub, Karl J. *The Value of the Individual: Self and Circumstance in Autobiography*. Chicago: University of Chicago Press, 1978.

Westerhagen, Dörte von. "Die Kinder der Täter." *Die Zeit*, 28 March 1986, p. 17–20.

Wittstock, Uwe. *Über die Fähigkeit zu trauern*. Frankfurt am Main: Athenäum, 1987.

Wolf, Christa. *Ansprachen*. Darmstadt: Luchterhand, 1988.

———. *Cassandra: A Novel and Four Essays*. Translated by Jan van Heurck. New York: Farrar, Straus and Giroux, 1984.

———. "Culture Is What You Experience—An Interview with Christa Wolf." *New German Critique* 27 (1982): 89–100.

———. *Die Dimension des Autors* I and II. Berlin: Aufbau, 1986.

———. "Dokumentation Christa Wolf." *German Quarterly* (1984): 91–115.

———. *Im Dialog*. Darmstadt: Luchterhand, 1990.

———. *Lesen und Schreiben: Neue Sammlung*. Darmstadt: Luchterhand, 1980.

Wolf, Christa, ed. *Karoline von Günderrode: Der Schatten eines Traumes Gedichte, Prosa, Briefe, Zeugnisse von Zeitgenossen*. Darmstadt: Luchterhand, 1981.

Zahlmann, Christel. *Christa Wolfs Reise "ins Tertiär": Eine literaturpsychologische Studie zu "Kindheitsmuster."* Würzburg: Königshausen and Neumann, 1986.

Index

Reading Women Writing

A SERIES EDITED BY

Shari Benstock and Celeste Schenck